Domovoi™

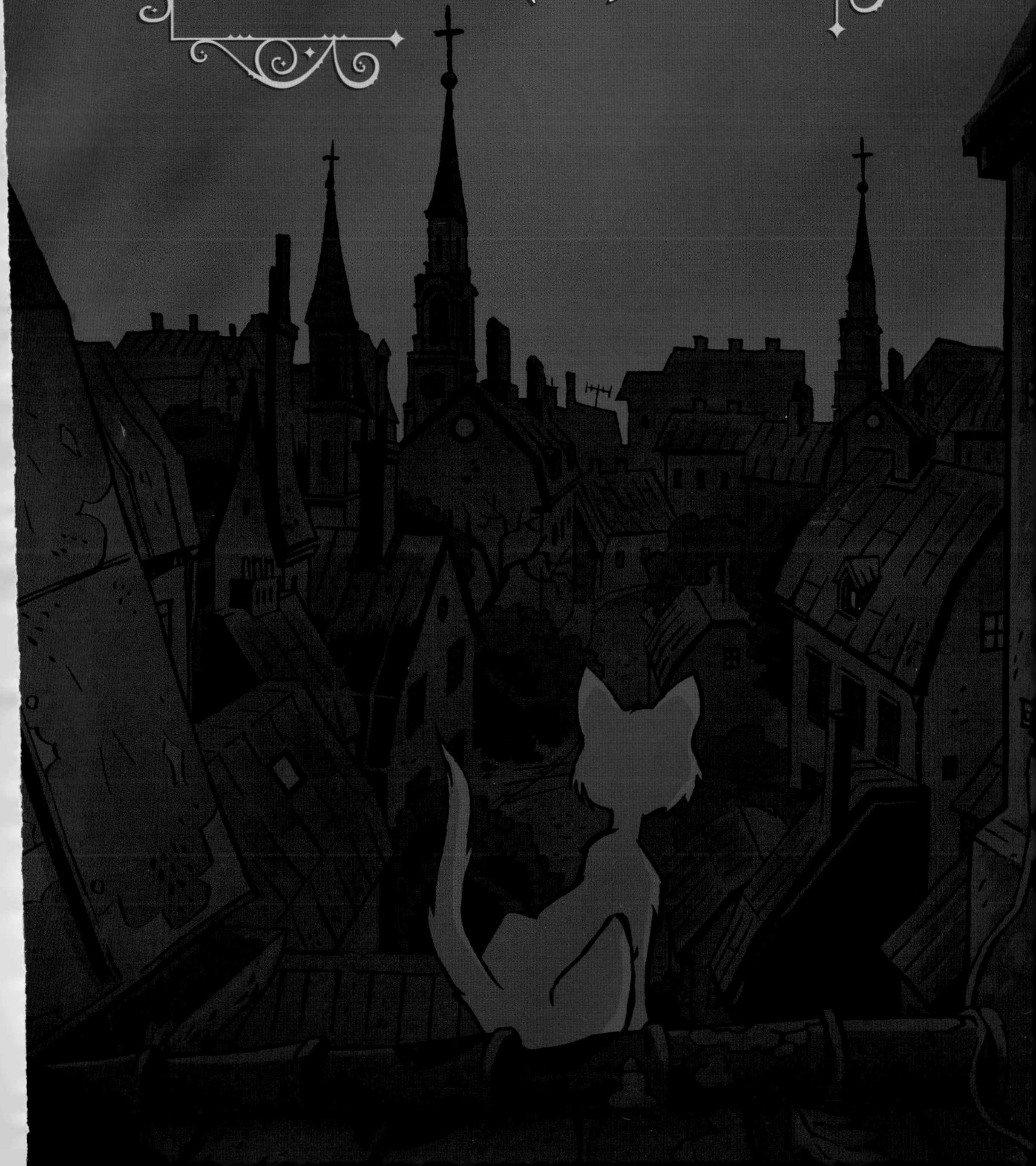

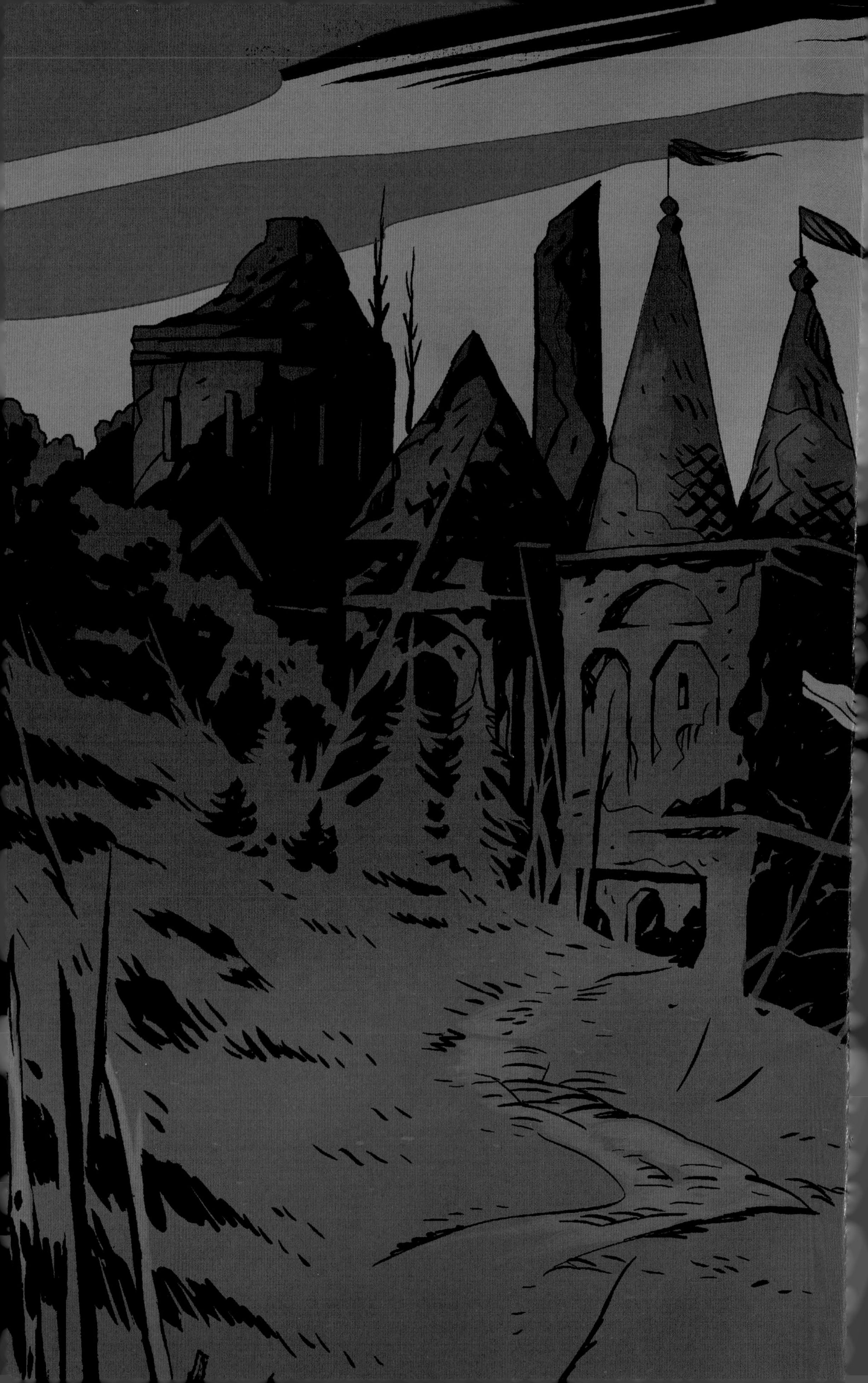

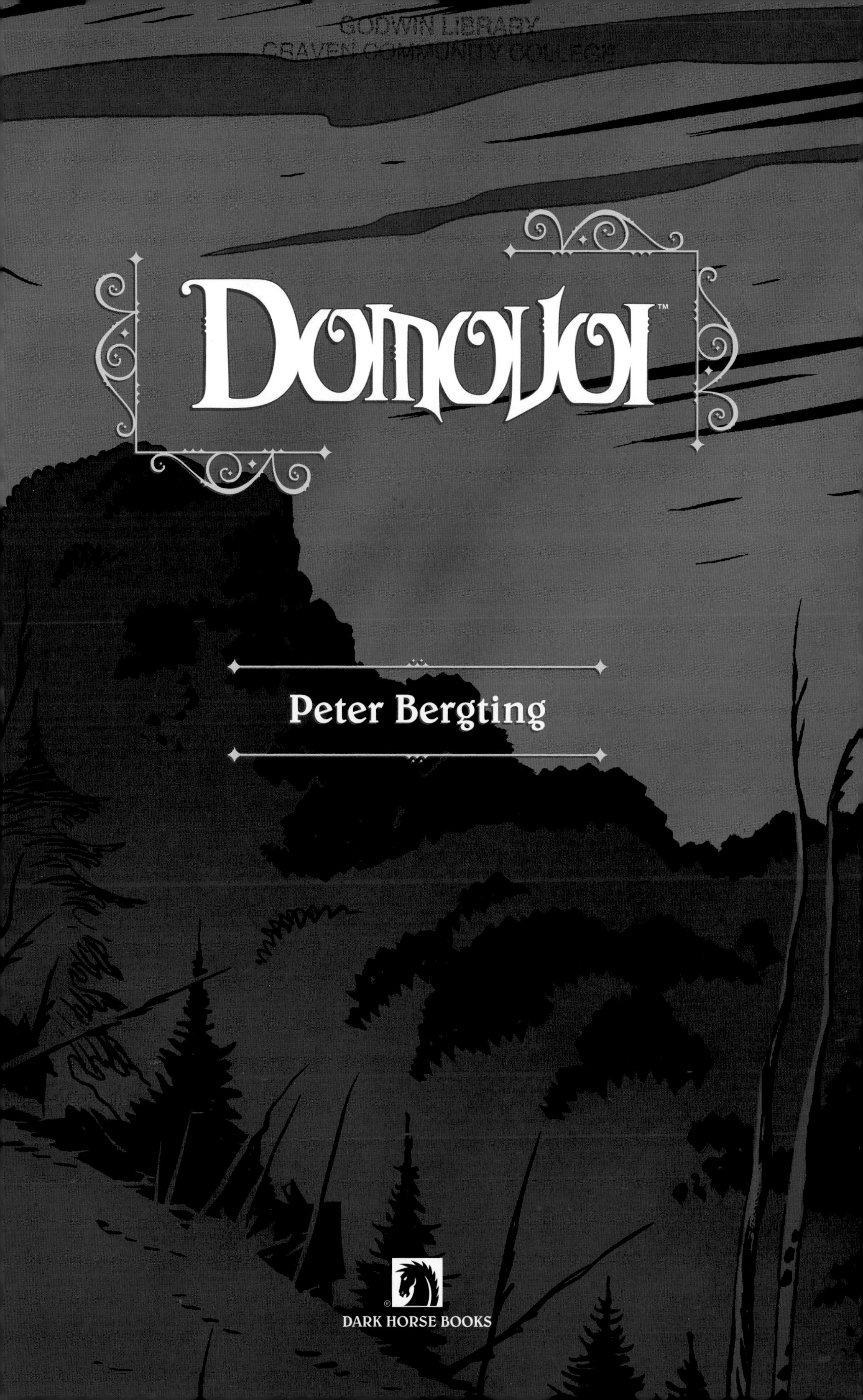

Domovoi™

Peter Bergting

DARK HORSE BOOKS®

Publisher **MIKE RICHARDSON**
Editor **RACHEL EDIDIN**
Assistant Editor **JEMIAH JEFFERSON**
Designer **KAT LARSON**

Special thanks to
John Arcudi, Mike Mignola, Scott Allie,
and Jan-Erik Saarinen.

Sofia, Tilde, and Amelíe,
this one is for you.

Published by Dark Horse Books,
a division of Dark Horse Comics, Inc.
10956 SE Main Street
Milwaukie, OR 97222

DarkHorse.com | Bergting.com

International Licensing: (503) 905-2377
To find a comics shop in your area,
call the Comic Shop Locator Service
toll-free at 1-888-266-4226

First edition: June 2013
ISBN 978-1-61655-090-5

1 3 5 7 9 10 8 6 4 2
Printed in China

INTRODUCTION

When I first saw the work of Swedish-born Peter Bergting, I felt like I was learning something new about comics storytelling—and I have to tell you, that's a nice, refreshing feeling. Instantly, I wanted to see more stories by him, *and* I wanted to be able to read them. I guess that's how Dark Horse felt too, and so we have this wonderful graphic novel. Not a translation or a reprint, but newly produced exclusively for Dark Horse, and like all his other work it's pretty special. For *Domovoi*, Peter has created a strange, moody, ethereal aesthetic which matches the oddly charming qualities of the story itself. Hilarious yet spooky, simultaneously familiar and arcane, this is the perfect marriage of art and script that usually can only be found in the works of the lone cartoonist.

Trying to describe Peter's work is a challenge. You've seen it by now, maybe even read a little of it, so you know what I mean. It's unusual and as such difficult to compare to anything else—and when I do start comparing it, that seems reductive. Sure, it's the easiest thing in the world for me to say that *Domovoi* feels like one part *Tintin* adventure, one part *Girl with the Dragon Tattoo*, and one part Theodor Kittelsen–limned fairy tale. It all happens to be true, but whatever influences may be at sway here, the work really is 100 percent Peter Bergting. Nowhere is that more evident than in his unique storytelling choices, some of them obvious, and some—the really important ones—not so obvious.

When comics artists want to show the reader a fast-moving car in a story, for instance, most often they'll draw a full frontal shot of the car zooming right at you. Not Peter. He shows us the side of the car skidding away from the reader, or the tail end of the car speeding out of panel with a chaotic cloud of dust, debris, loose leaves, and a flying shoe (!) partially obscuring an expertly drawn alleyway, or (and this is my favorite) he gives us a view of the bottom of the car as it flies overhead! And every one of these innovative shots works perfectly! You gotta love that, but great as these all are, as

potent and effective as they may be, what about those "less obvious" choices I mentioned? Well, you honestly don't have to go any further than the very first page. Yes, beautifully illustrated, those little Old World houses in the background, a cat calmly sitting on a copper and ceramic sheathed roof littered with a few autumn leaves in the foreground, and the dark, ominous clouds that hang in between over an otherwise rosy dawn. But there's more going on here than just a pretty picture, and I'm not talking about the foreshadowing the lugubrious sky portends, or the time of year that the leaves suggest. Everything you see in that single splash panel was carefully chosen, and that goes beyond the art. Right off, we have a talking cat. The stage is set, and the reader is fully informed that supernatural shenanigans may ensue, so when a couple of thuggish spirits show up driving an old coupe, we're prepared. Still, that's a bit obvious, but consider the layered nuance here. There's one major component of the art on that first page I didn't mention: the TV antenna. That background may suggest to you the seventeenth century, but the antenna? That's all twentieth century. *Twentieth*—and most decidedly *not* twenty-first. Now think about that for a second. It's familiar ground for most of us, but not exactly up to date, not precisely the world we currently inhabit. It adds a small dimension of distance between the reader and the setting without making it wholly bizarre. It semisecretly amplifies the fantasy.

Or to put it another way, Peter has wasted absolutely no time in letting you know you've just entered a world where speaking animals are more common than cable television. Likely you don't even think about it when you see it, but trust me, it's things like that—these tiny, little, virtually invisible details—that make *Domovoi* a journey worth taking and Peter Bergting a creator worth watching.

John Arcudi
January 2013

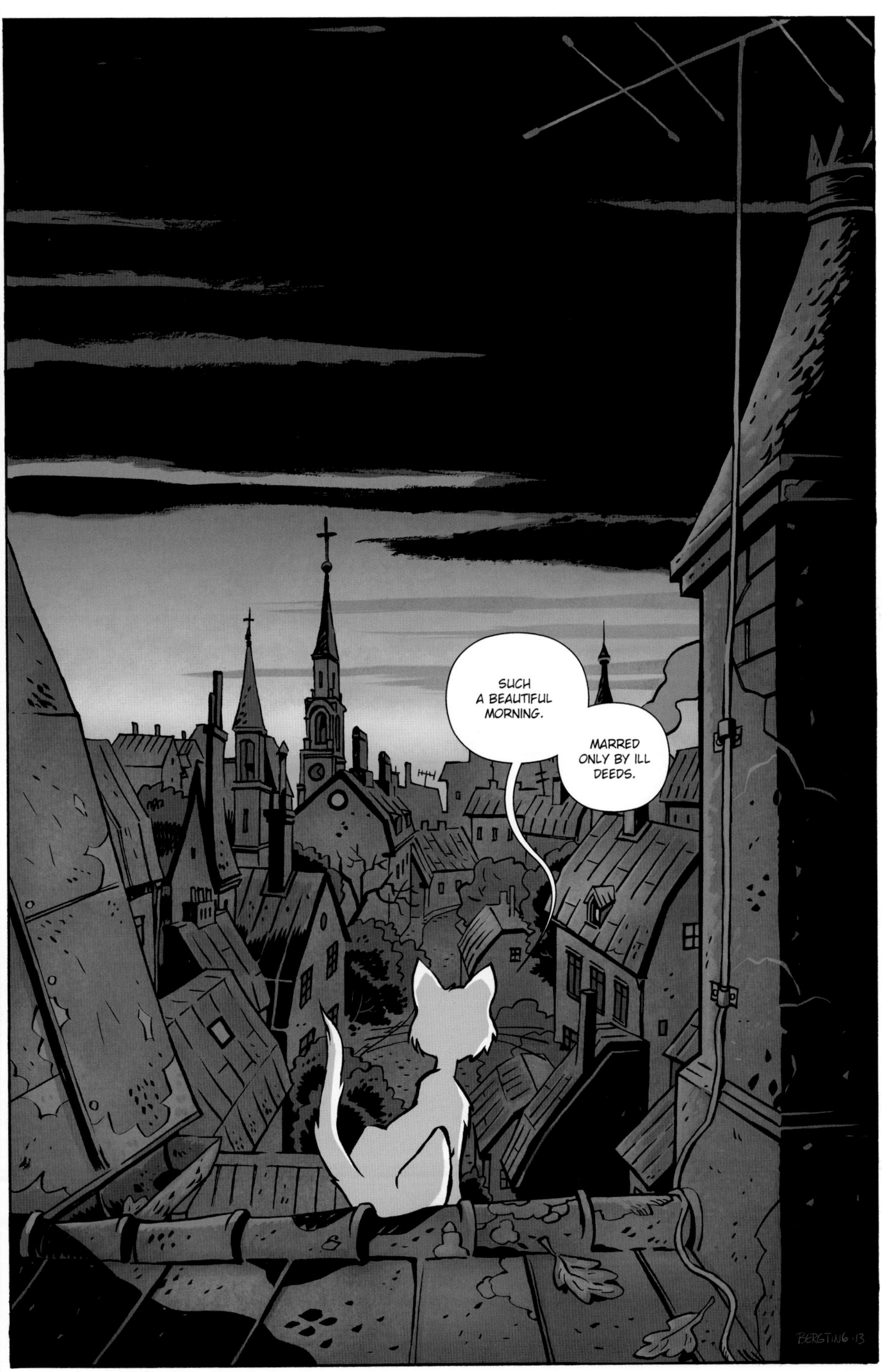
SUCH A BEAUTIFUL MORNING.
MARRED ONLY BY ILL DEEDS.
BERGTING·13

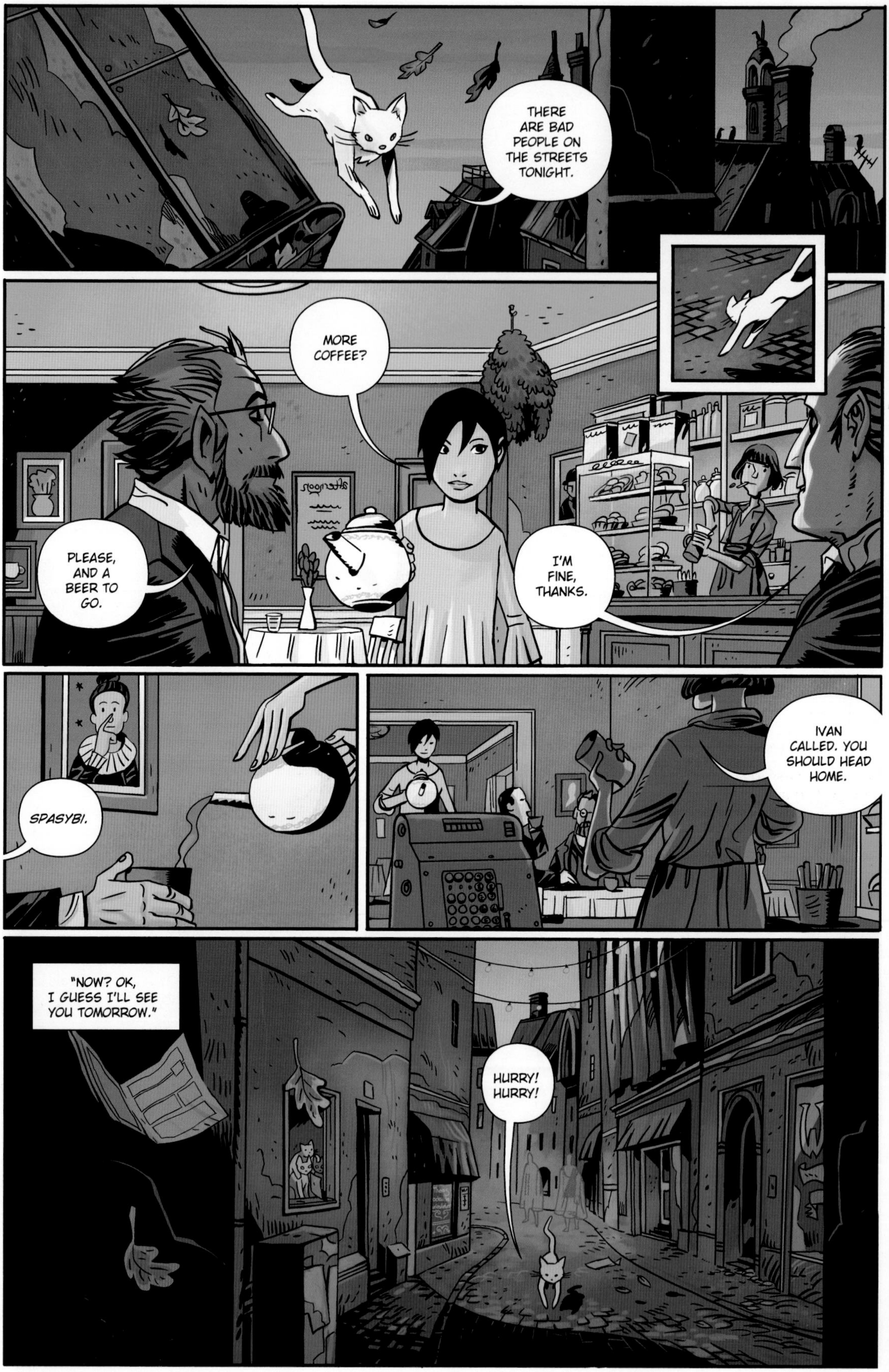

THERE ARE BAD PEOPLE ON THE STREETS TONIGHT.
MORE COFFEE?
PLEASE, AND A BEER TO GO.
I'M FINE, THANKS.
SPASYBI.
IVAN CALLED. YOU SHOULD HEAD HOME.
"NOW? OK, I GUESS I'LL SEE YOU TOMORROW."
HURRY! HURRY!

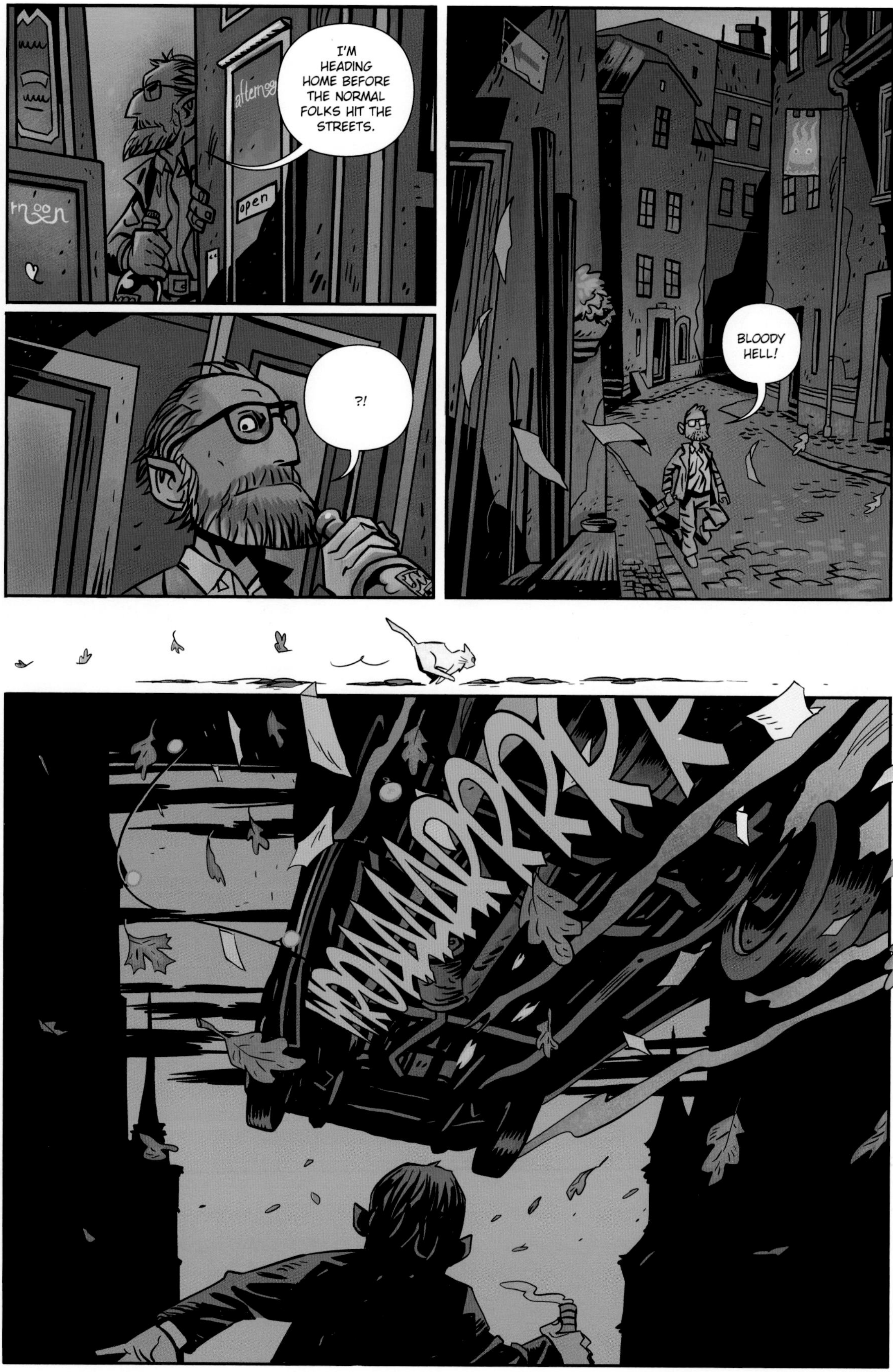
I'M HEADING HOME BEFORE THE NORMAL FOLKS HIT THE STREETS.
afternoon
open
moon
?!
BLOODY HELL!
VROOAARRRRRK

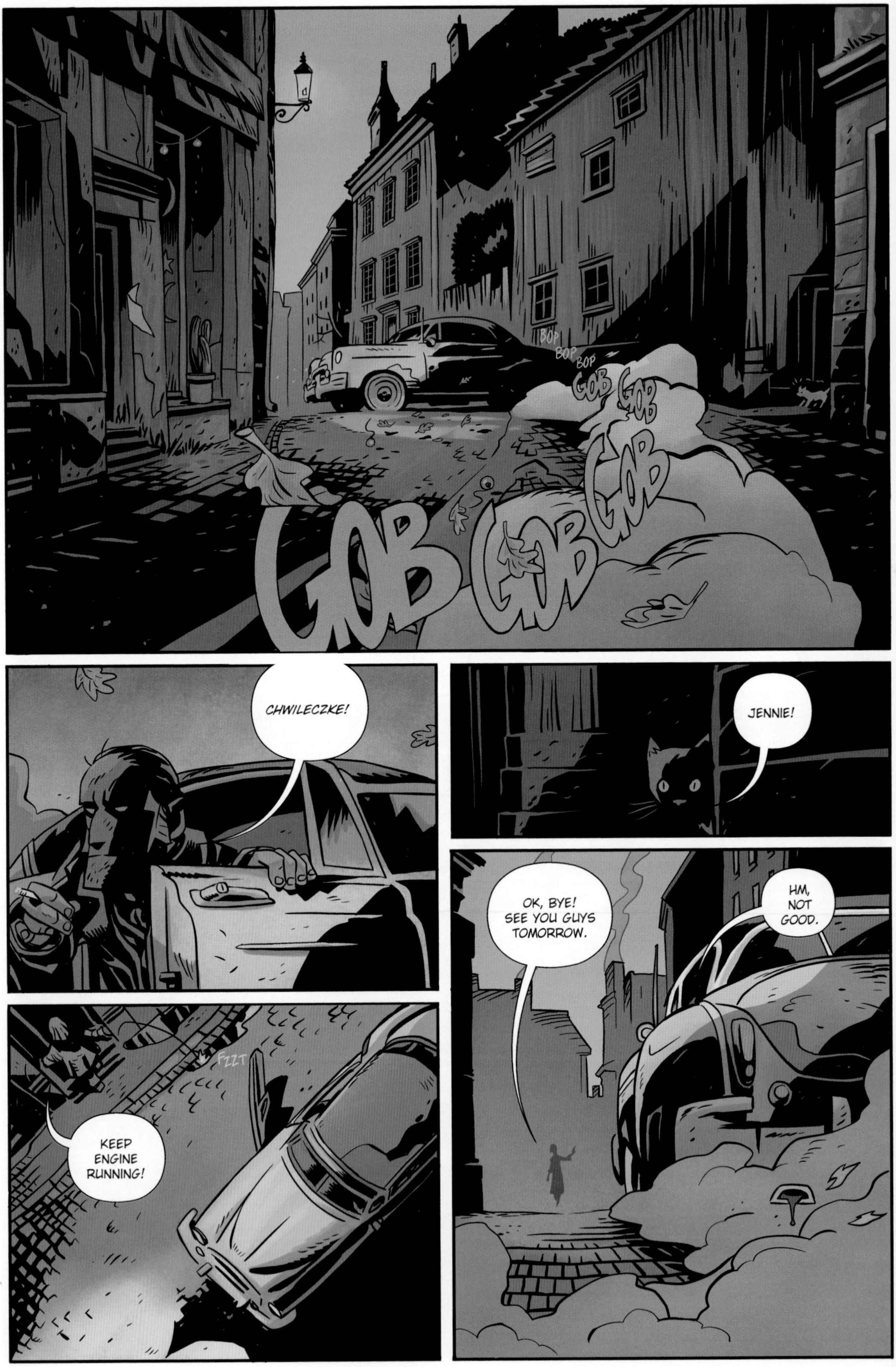
BOP
BOP
BOP
GOB GOB
GOB GOB
GOB GOB GOB
CHWILECZKE!
JENNIE!
OK, BYE! SEE YOU GUYS TOMORROW.
HM, NOT GOOD.
FZZT
KEEP ENGINE RUNNING!

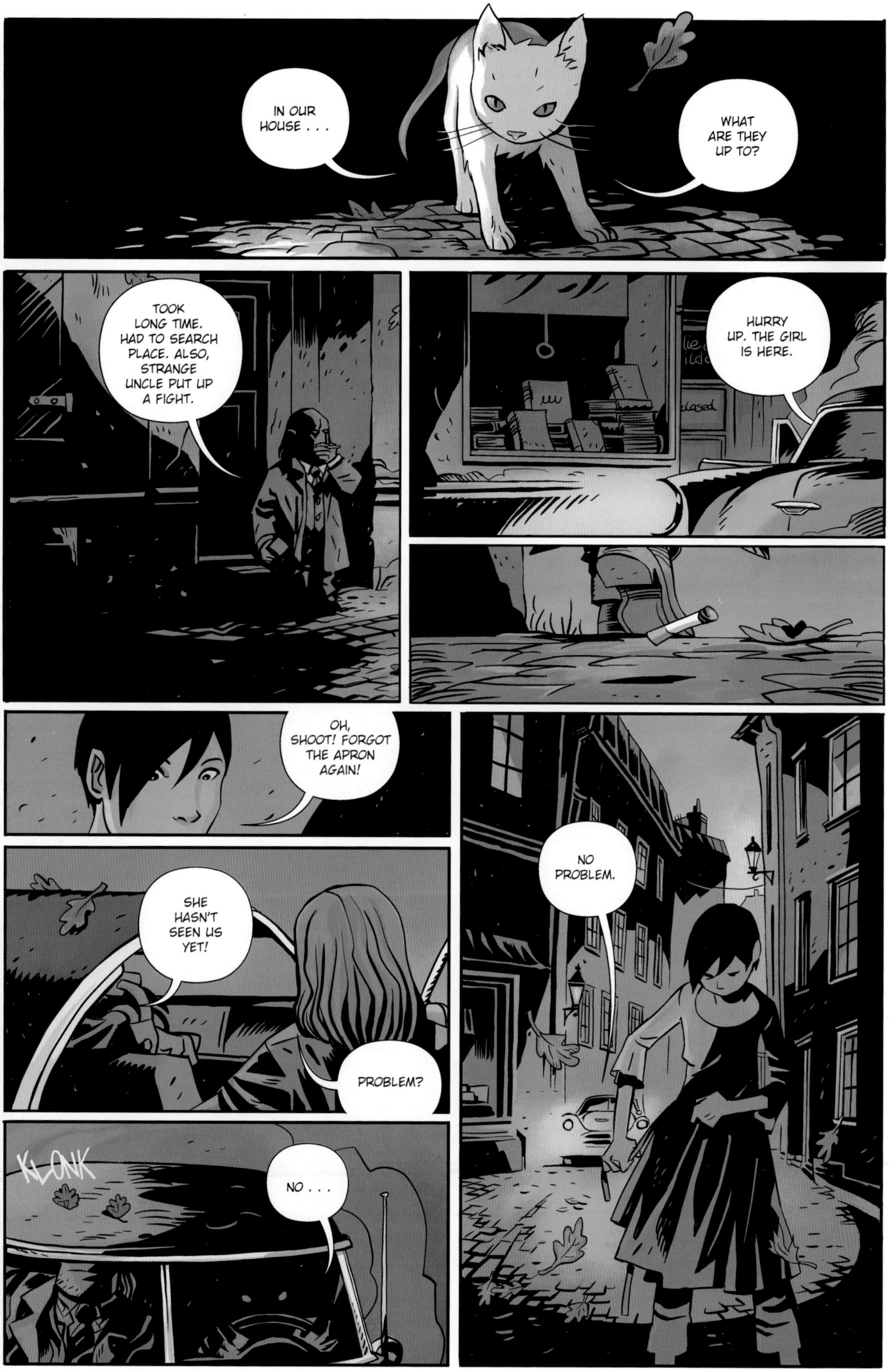

IN OUR HOUSE . . .
WHAT ARE THEY UP TO?
TOOK LONG TIME. HAD TO SEARCH PLACE. ALSO, STRANGE UNCLE PUT UP A FIGHT.
HURRY UP. THE GIRL IS HERE.
closed
OH, SHOOT! FORGOT THE APRON AGAIN!
SHE HASN'T SEEN US YET!
PROBLEM?
NO PROBLEM.
KLONK
NO . . .

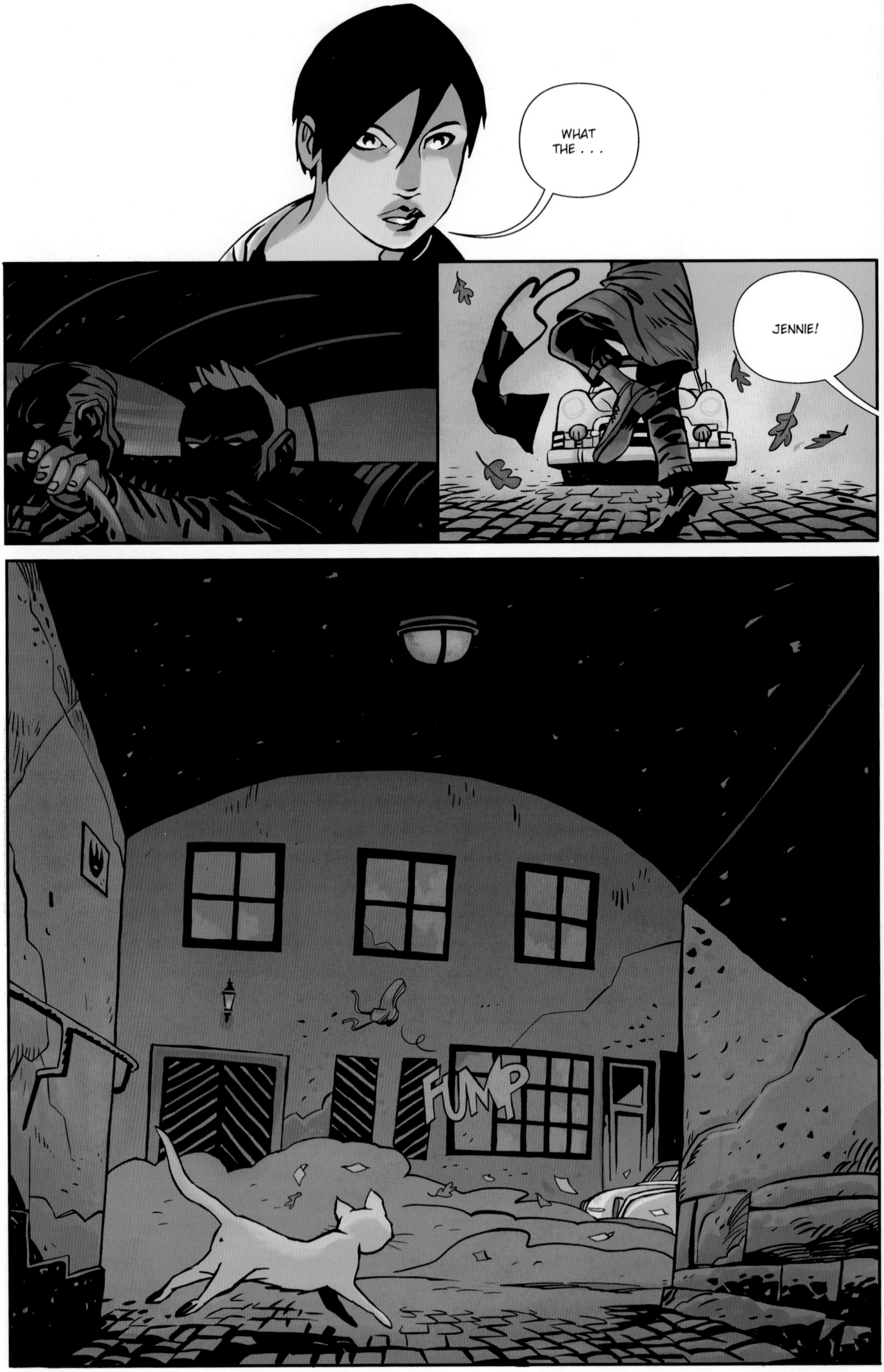
WHAT THE . . .
JENNIE!
FUMP

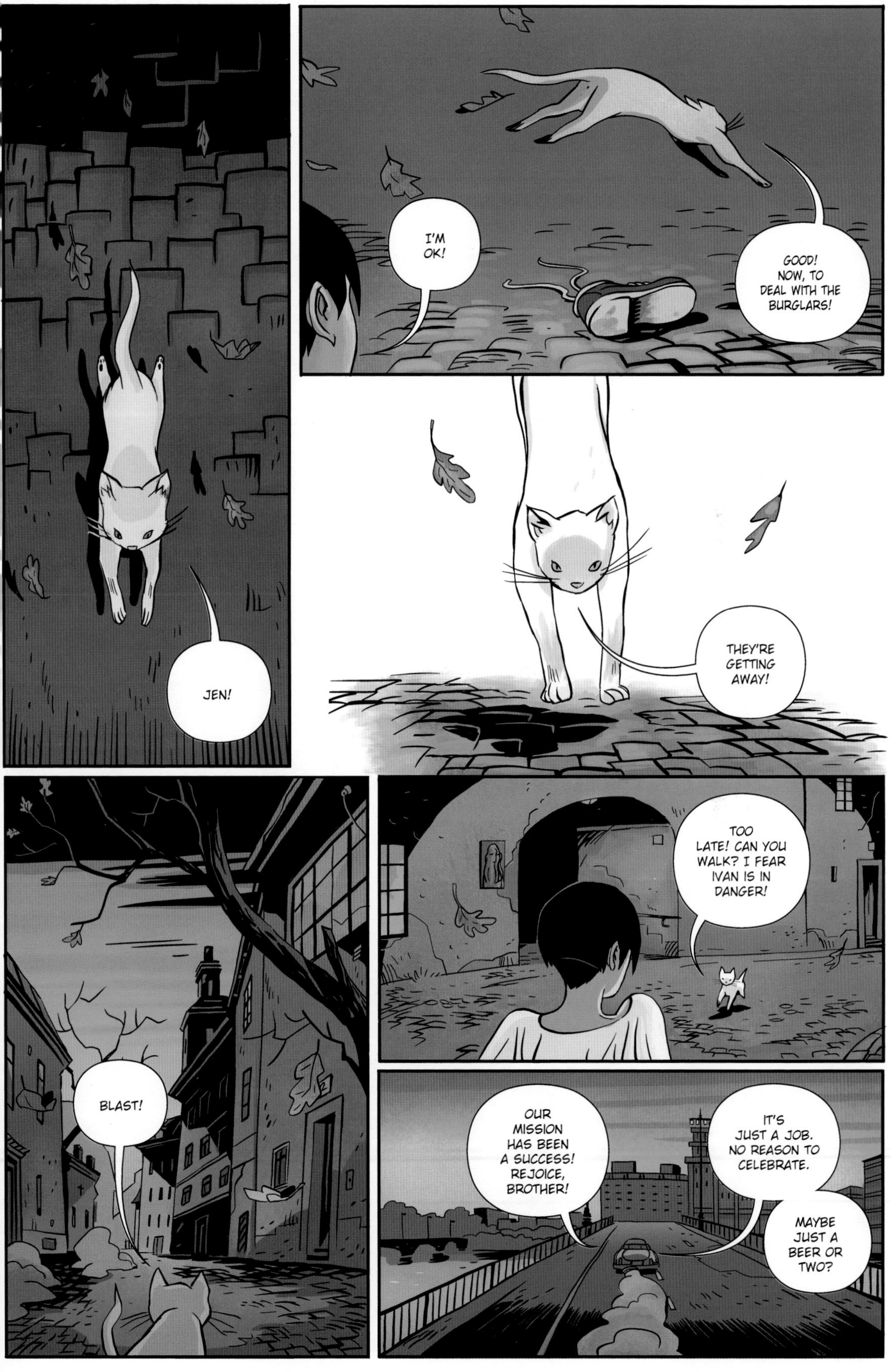
JEN!
I'M OK!
GOOD! NOW, TO DEAL WITH THE BURGLARS!
THEY'RE GETTING AWAY!
BLAST!
TOO LATE! CAN YOU WALK? I FEAR IVAN IS IN DANGER!
OUR MISSION HAS BEEN A SUCCESS! REJOICE, BROTHER!
IT'S JUST A JOB. NO REASON TO CELEBRATE.
MAYBE JUST A BEER OR TWO?

YEAH, I CAN WALK!

GOOD! LET'S GET OUT OF HERE!

THEY WERE IN OUR HOUSE!

WHAT WAS THAT? FIELD SPIRITS? AND AT THIS HOUR?

WELL, TAKES MORE THAN TWO *POLEVIKI* TO SHAKE UP IVAN. YOU SHOULD KNOW THAT.

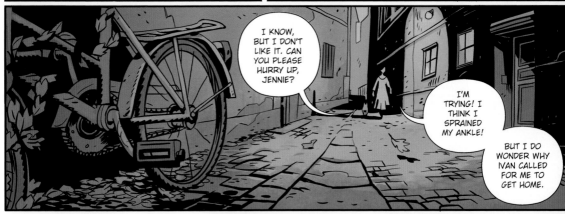

I KNOW, BUT I DON'T LIKE IT. CAN YOU PLEASE HURRY UP, JENNIE?

I'M TRYING! I THINK I SPRAINED MY ANKLE!

BUT I DO WONDER WHY IVAN CALLED FOR ME TO GET HOME.

HE DID? OK, NOW I'M WORRIED!

BULKA, WAIT UP!

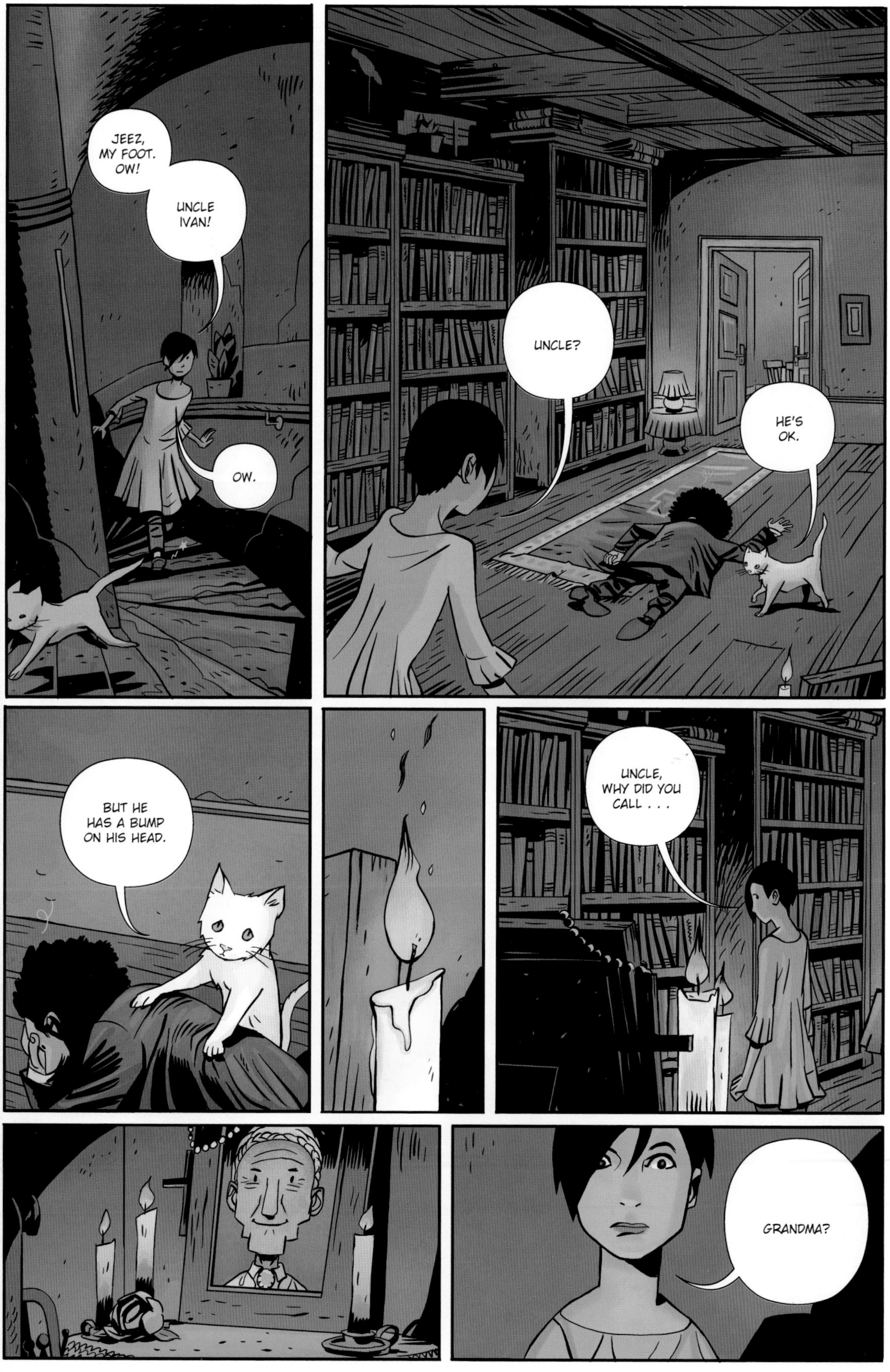
JEEZ, MY FOOT. OW!
UNCLE IVAN!
OW.
UNCLE?
HE'S OK.
BUT HE HAS A BUMP ON HIS HEAD.
UNCLE, WHY DID YOU CALL . . .
GRANDMA?

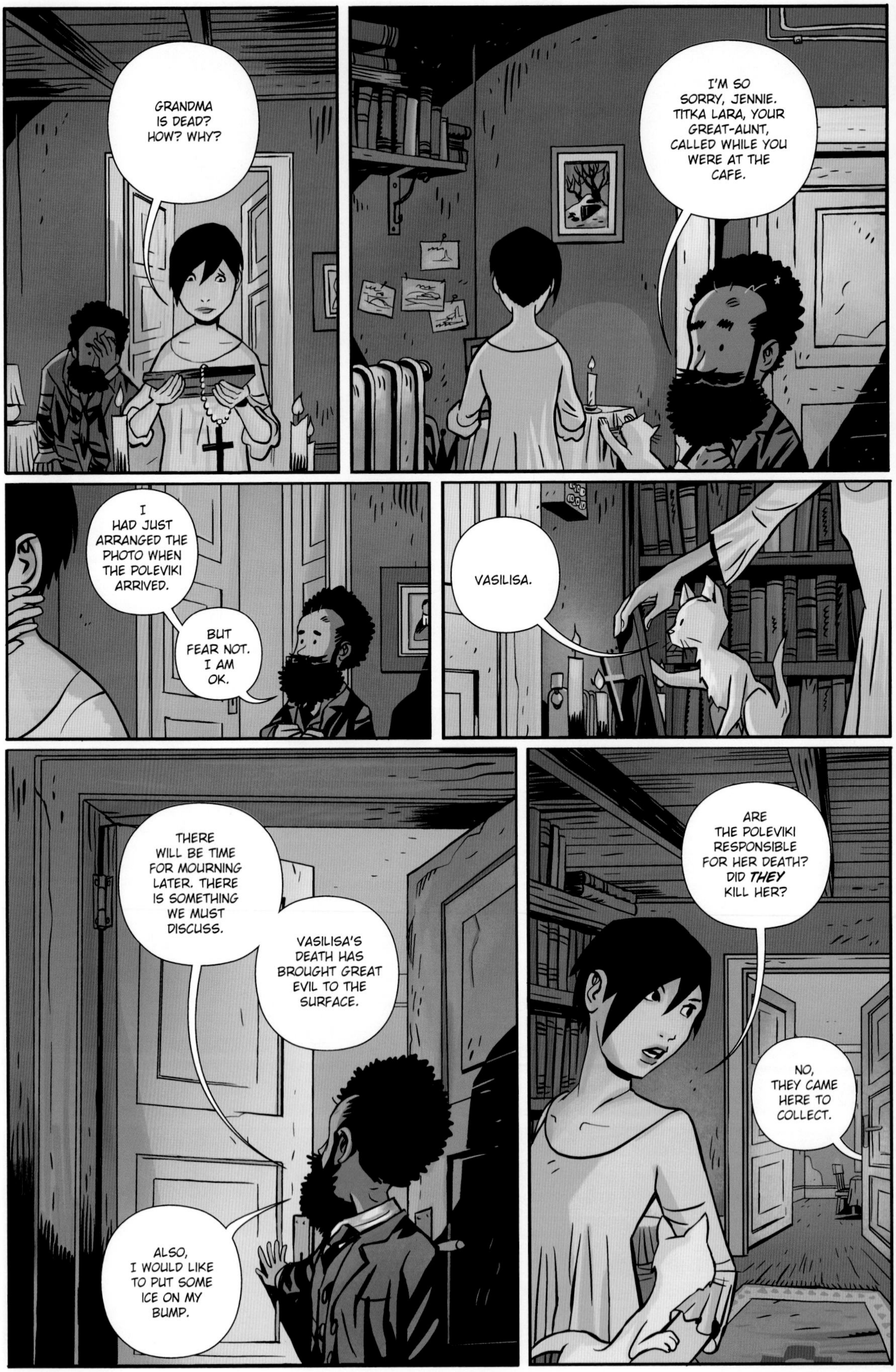
GRANDMA IS DEAD? HOW? WHY?
I'M SO SORRY, JENNIE. TITKA LARA, YOUR GREAT-AUNT, CALLED WHILE YOU WERE AT THE CAFE.
I HAD JUST ARRANGED THE PHOTO WHEN THE POLEVIKI ARRIVED.
BUT FEAR NOT. I AM OK.
VASILISA.
THERE WILL BE TIME FOR MOURNING LATER. THERE IS SOMETHING WE MUST DISCUSS.
VASILISA'S DEATH HAS BROUGHT GREAT EVIL TO THE SURFACE.
ALSO, I WOULD LIKE TO PUT SOME ICE ON MY BUMP.
ARE THE POLEVIKI RESPONSIBLE FOR HER DEATH? DID *THEY* KILL HER?
NO, THEY CAME HERE TO COLLECT.

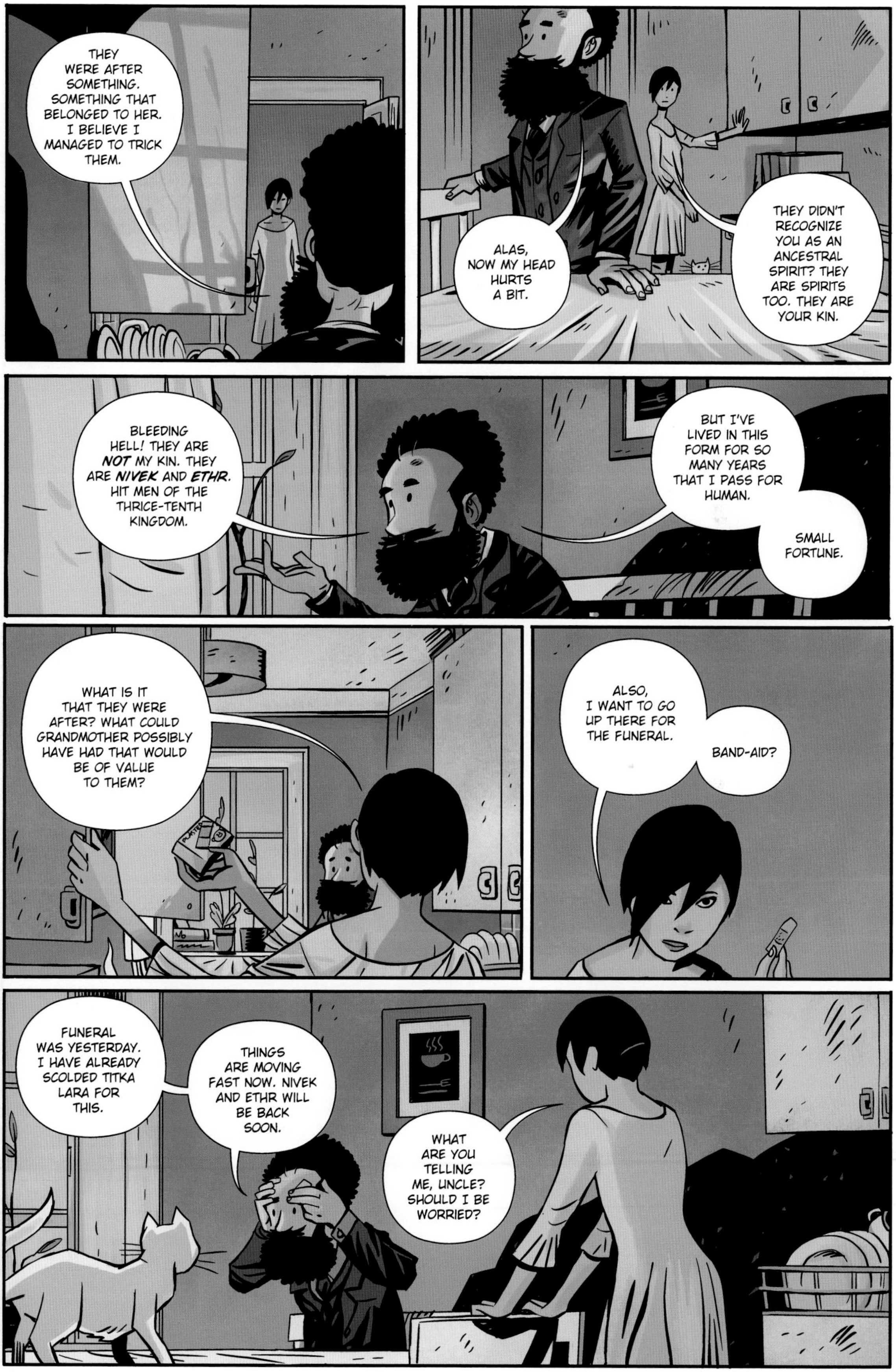
THEY WERE AFTER SOMETHING. SOMETHING THAT BELONGED TO HER. I BELIEVE I MANAGED TO TRICK THEM.
ALAS, NOW MY HEAD HURTS A BIT.
THEY DIDN'T RECOGNIZE YOU AS AN ANCESTRAL SPIRIT? THEY ARE SPIRITS TOO. THEY ARE YOUR KIN.
BLEEDING HELL! THEY ARE *NOT* MY KIN. THEY ARE *NIVEK* AND *ETHR*. HIT MEN OF THE THRICE-TENTH KINGDOM.
BUT I'VE LIVED IN THIS FORM FOR SO MANY YEARS THAT I PASS FOR HUMAN.
SMALL FORTUNE.
WHAT IS IT THAT THEY WERE AFTER? WHAT COULD GRANDMOTHER POSSIBLY HAVE HAD THAT WOULD BE OF VALUE TO THEM?
ALSO, I WANT TO GO UP THERE FOR THE FUNERAL.
BAND-AID?
FUNERAL WAS YESTERDAY. I HAVE ALREADY SCOLDED TITKA LARA FOR THIS.
THINGS ARE MOVING FAST NOW. NIVEK AND ETHR WILL BE BACK SOON.
WHAT ARE YOU TELLING ME, UNCLE? SHOULD I BE WORRIED?

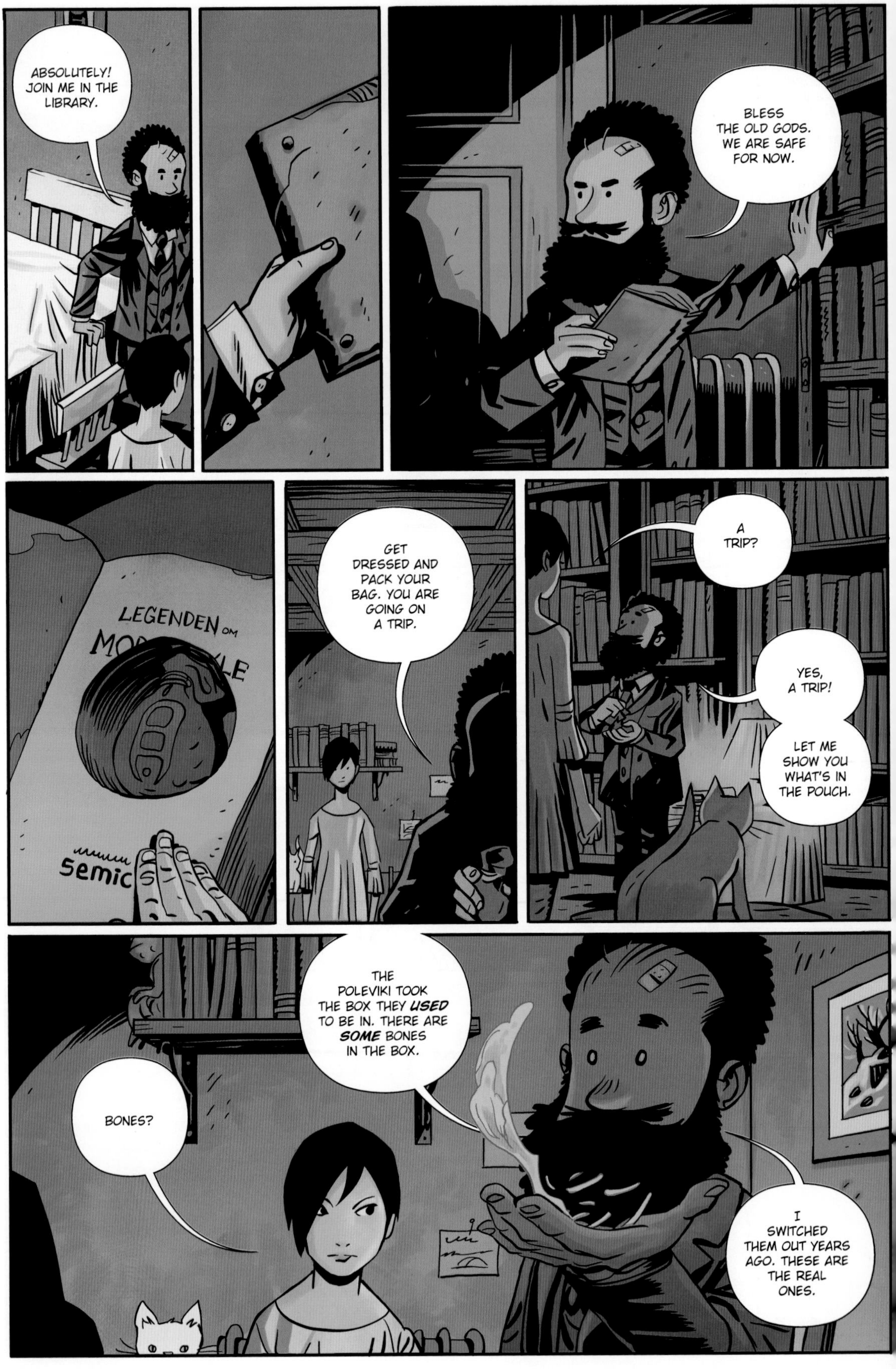
ABSOLUTELY! JOIN ME IN THE LIBRARY.
BLESS THE OLD GODS. WE ARE SAFE FOR NOW.
LEGENDEN OM
semic
GET DRESSED AND PACK YOUR BAG. YOU ARE GOING ON A TRIP.
A TRIP?
YES, A TRIP!
LET ME SHOW YOU WHAT'S IN THE POUCH.
THE POLEVIKI TOOK THE BOX THEY *USED* TO BE IN. THERE ARE *SOME* BONES IN THE BOX.
BONES?
I SWITCHED THEM OUT YEARS AGO. THESE ARE THE REAL ONES.

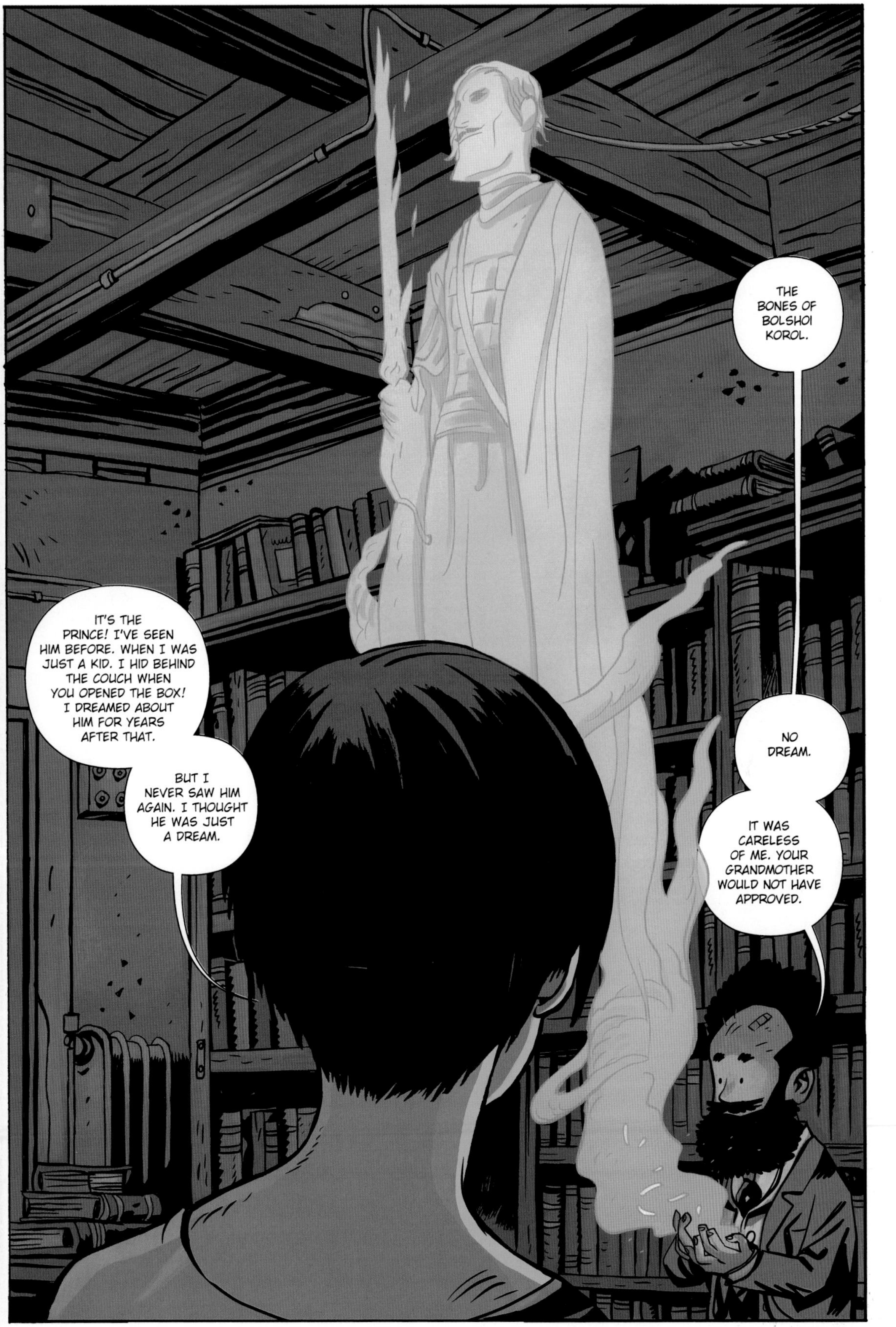
THE BONES OF BOLSHOI KOROL.
IT'S THE PRINCE! I'VE SEEN HIM BEFORE. WHEN I WAS JUST A KID. I HID BEHIND THE COUCH WHEN YOU OPENED THE BOX! I DREAMED ABOUT HIM FOR YEARS AFTER THAT.
BUT I NEVER SAW HIM AGAIN. I THOUGHT HE WAS JUST A DREAM.
NO DREAM.
IT WAS CARELESS OF ME. YOUR GRANDMOTHER WOULD NOT HAVE APPROVED.

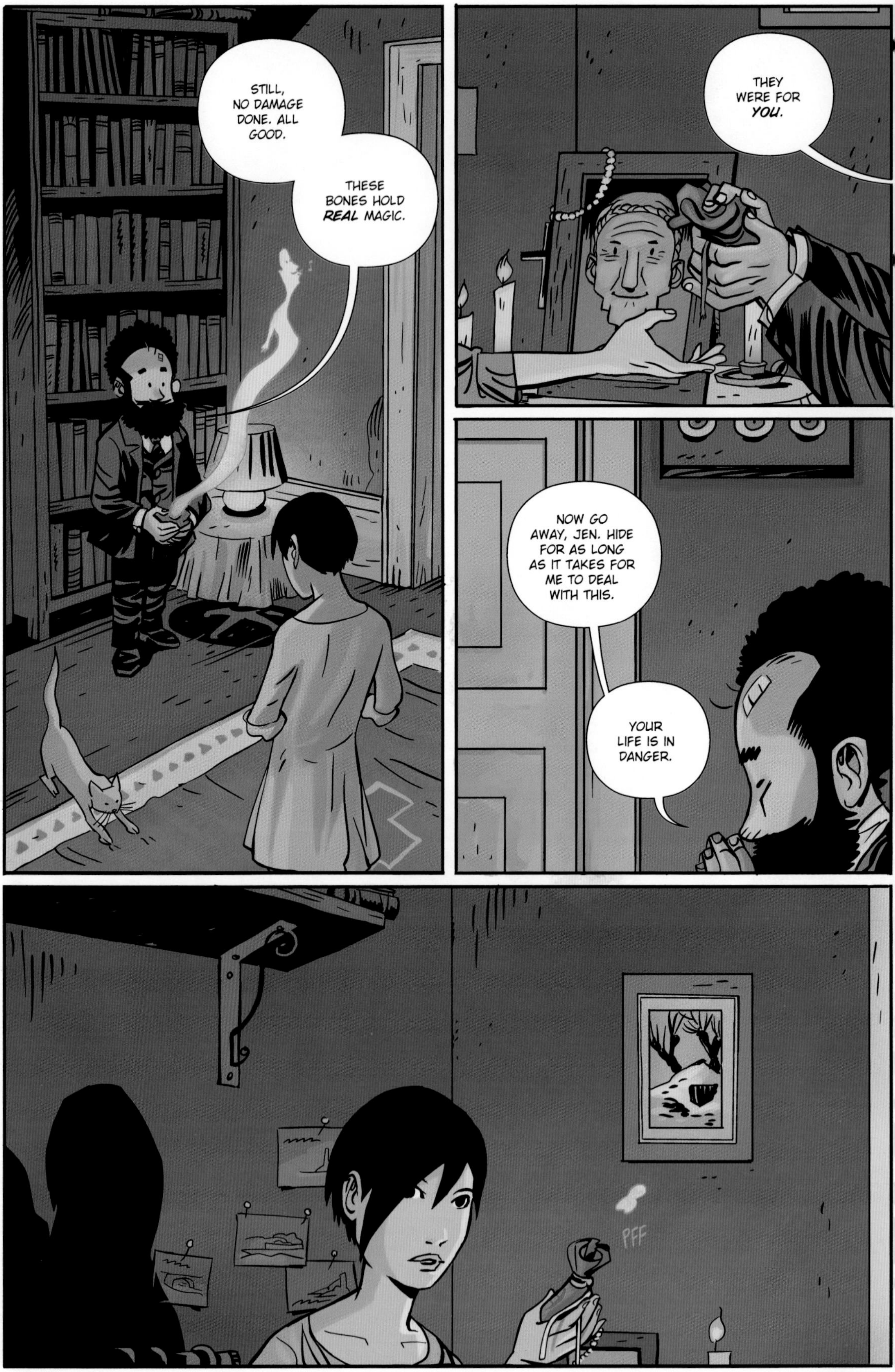
STILL, NO DAMAGE DONE. ALL GOOD.
THESE BONES HOLD REAL MAGIC.
THEY WERE FOR YOU.
NOW GO AWAY, JEN. HIDE FOR AS LONG AS IT TAKES FOR ME TO DEAL WITH THIS.
YOUR LIFE IS IN DANGER.
PFF

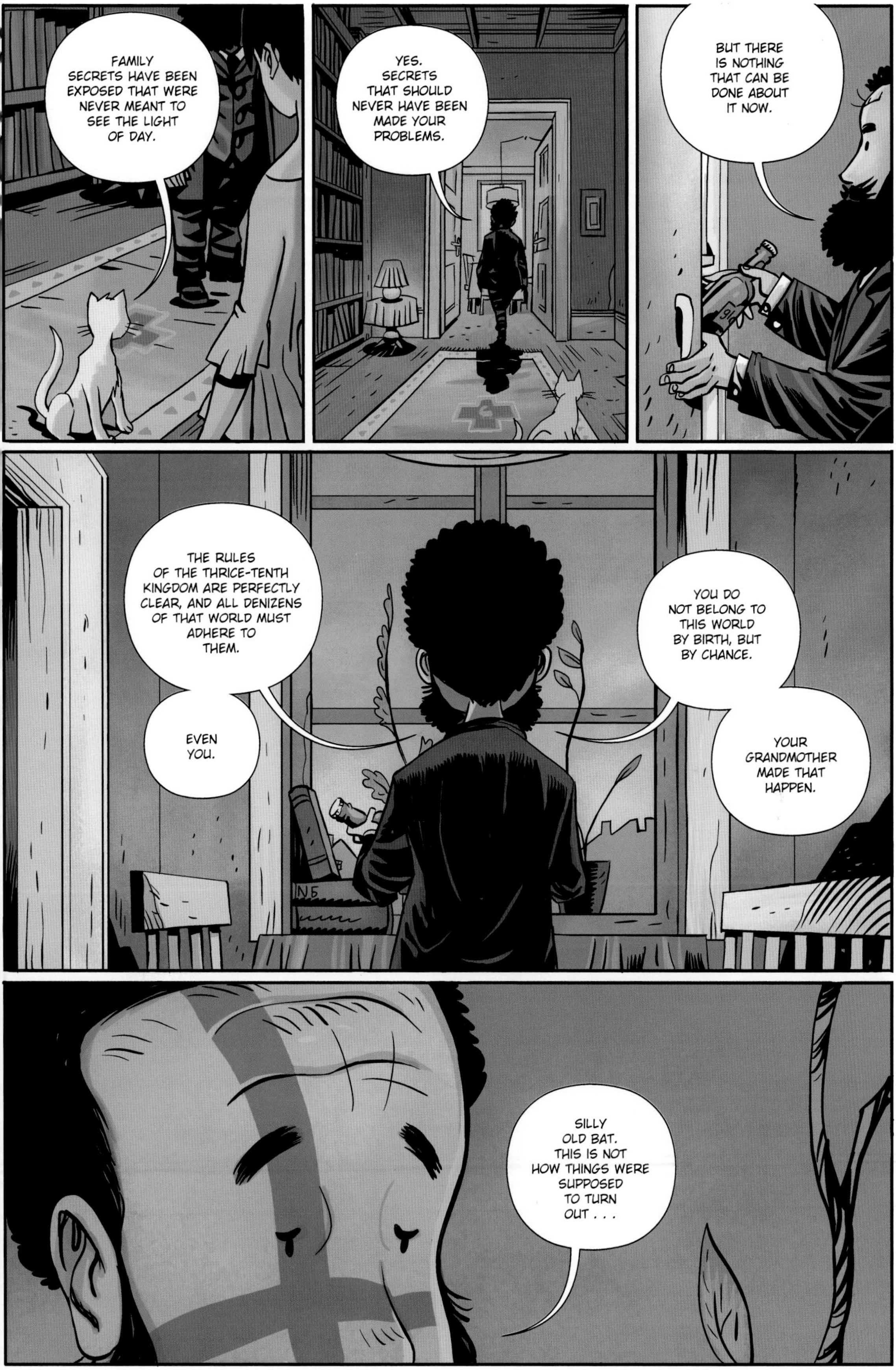
FAMILY SECRETS HAVE BEEN EXPOSED THAT WERE NEVER MEANT TO SEE THE LIGHT OF DAY.
YES. SECRETS THAT SHOULD NEVER HAVE BEEN MADE YOUR PROBLEMS.
BUT THERE IS NOTHING THAT CAN BE DONE ABOUT IT NOW.
THE RULES OF THE THRICE-TENTH KINGDOM ARE PERFECTLY CLEAR, AND ALL DENIZENS OF THAT WORLD MUST ADHERE TO THEM.
EVEN YOU.
YOU DO NOT BELONG TO THIS WORLD BY BIRTH, BUT BY CHANCE.
YOUR GRANDMOTHER MADE THAT HAPPEN.
SILLY OLD BAT. THIS IS NOT HOW THINGS WERE SUPPOSED TO TURN OUT . . .

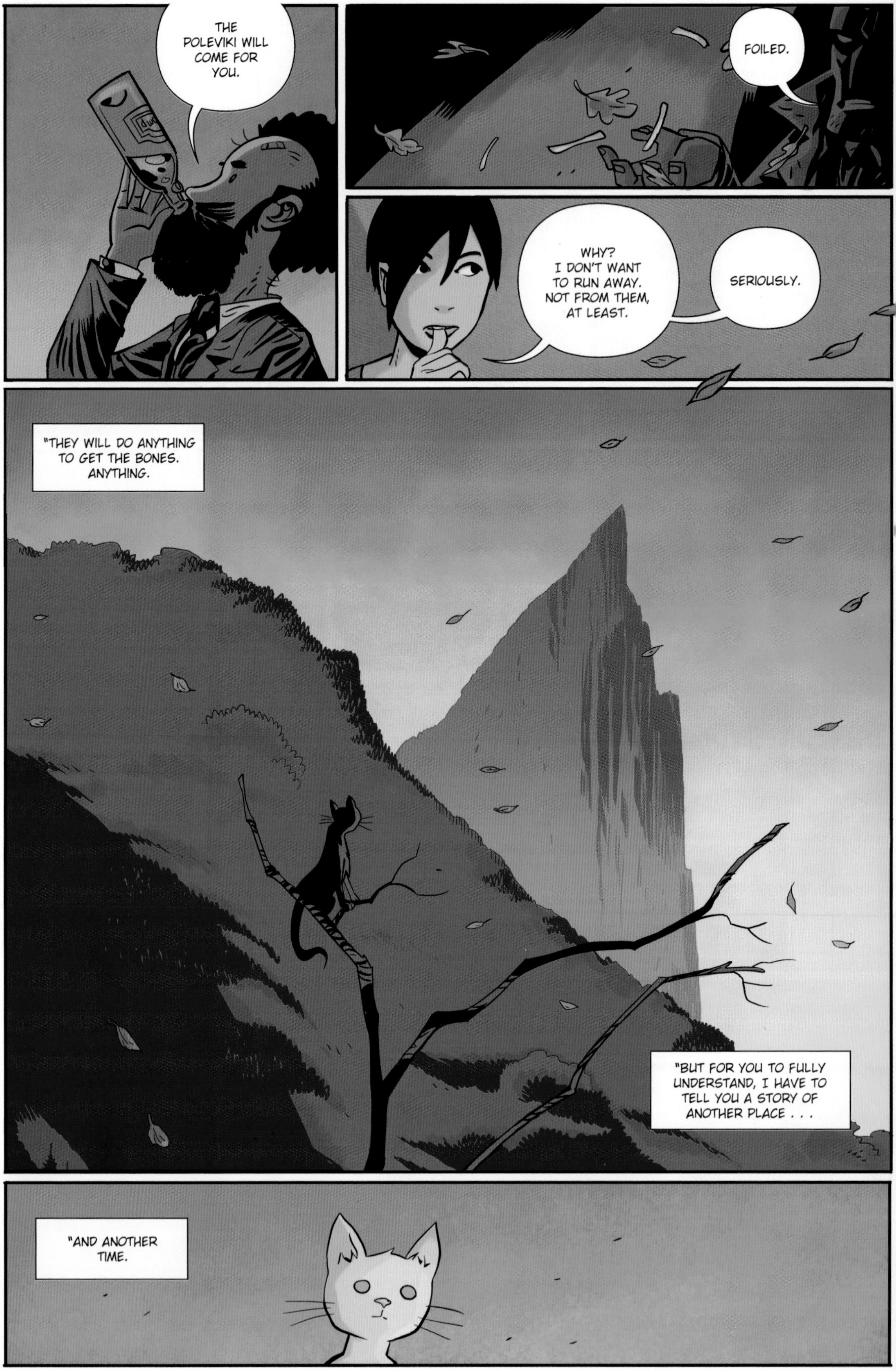
THE POLEVIKI WILL COME FOR YOU.
FOILED.
WHY? I DON'T WANT TO RUN AWAY. NOT FROM THEM, AT LEAST.
SERIOUSLY.
"THEY WILL DO ANYTHING TO GET THE BONES. ANYTHING.
"BUT FOR YOU TO FULLY UNDERSTAND, I HAVE TO TELL YOU A STORY OF ANOTHER PLACE . . .
"AND ANOTHER TIME.

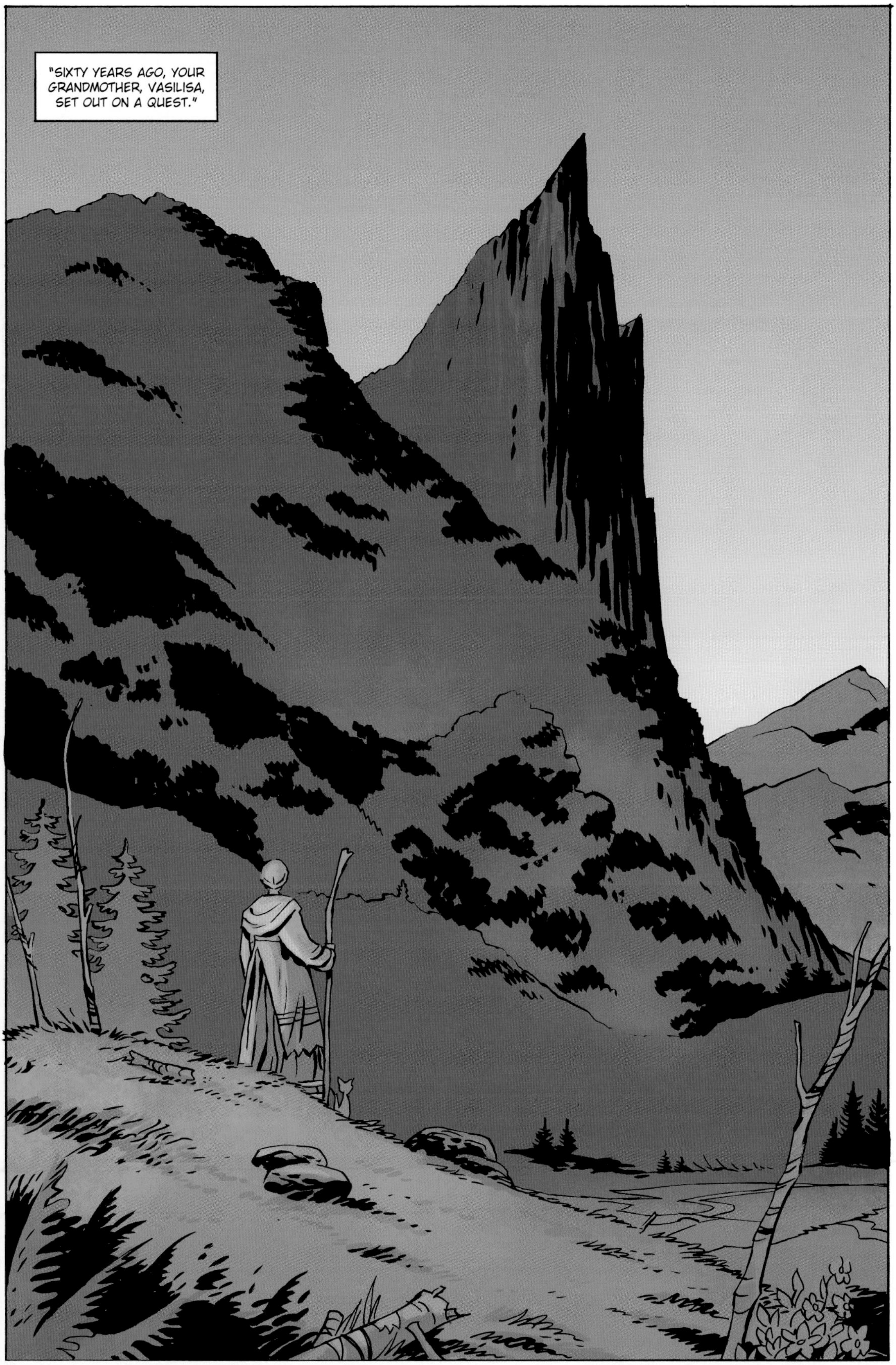
"SIXTY YEARS AGO, YOUR GRANDMOTHER, VASILISA, SET OUT ON A QUEST."

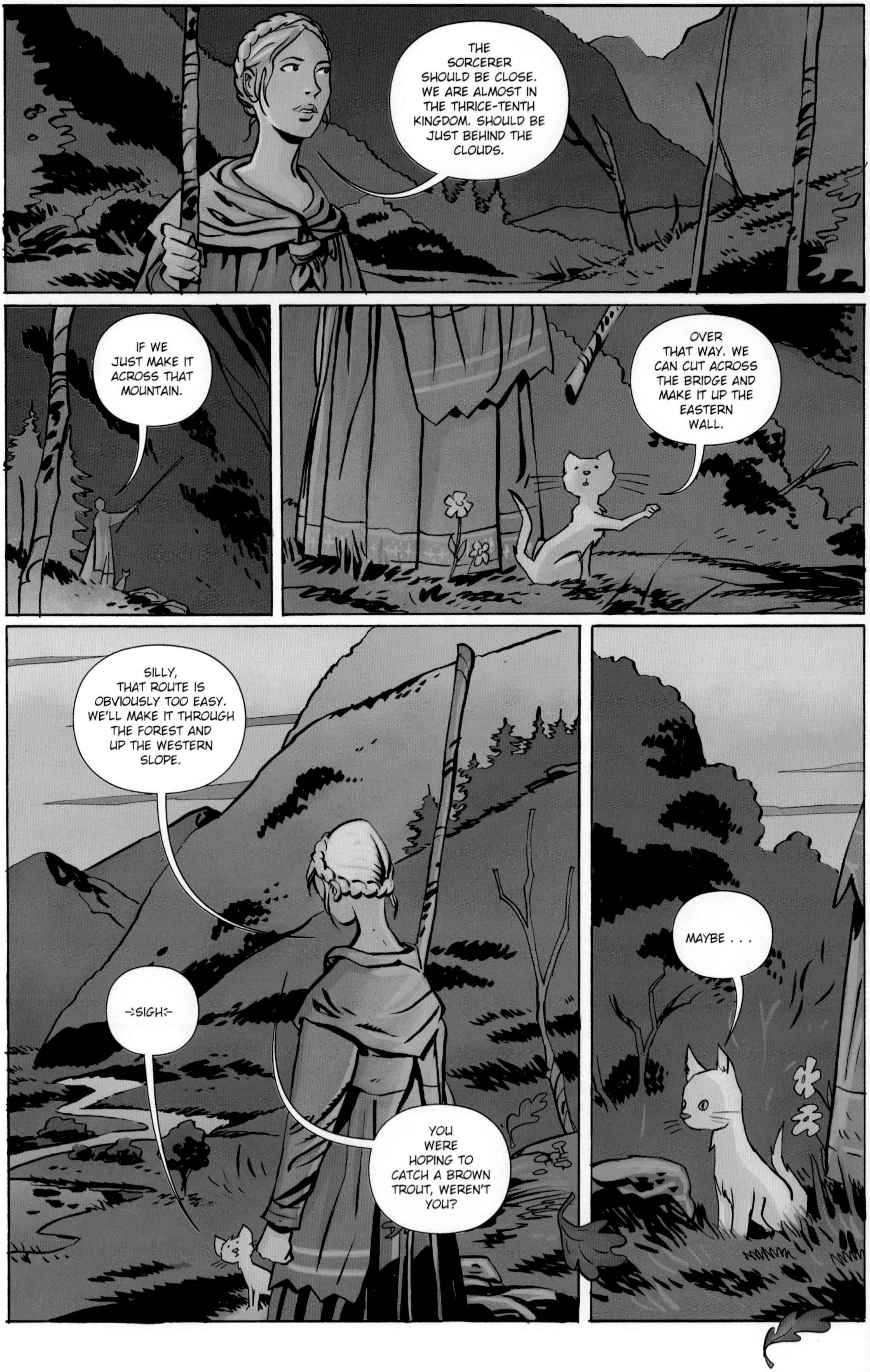
THE SORCERER SHOULD BE CLOSE. WE ARE ALMOST IN THE THRICE-TENTH KINGDOM. SHOULD BE JUST BEHIND THE CLOUDS.
IF WE JUST MAKE IT ACROSS THAT MOUNTAIN.
OVER THAT WAY. WE CAN CUT ACROSS THE BRIDGE AND MAKE IT UP THE EASTERN WALL.
SILLY, THAT ROUTE IS OBVIOUSLY TOO EASY. WE'LL MAKE IT THROUGH THE FOREST AND UP THE WESTERN SLOPE.
-SIGH-
YOU WERE HOPING TO CATCH A BROWN TROUT, WEREN'T YOU?
MAYBE . . .

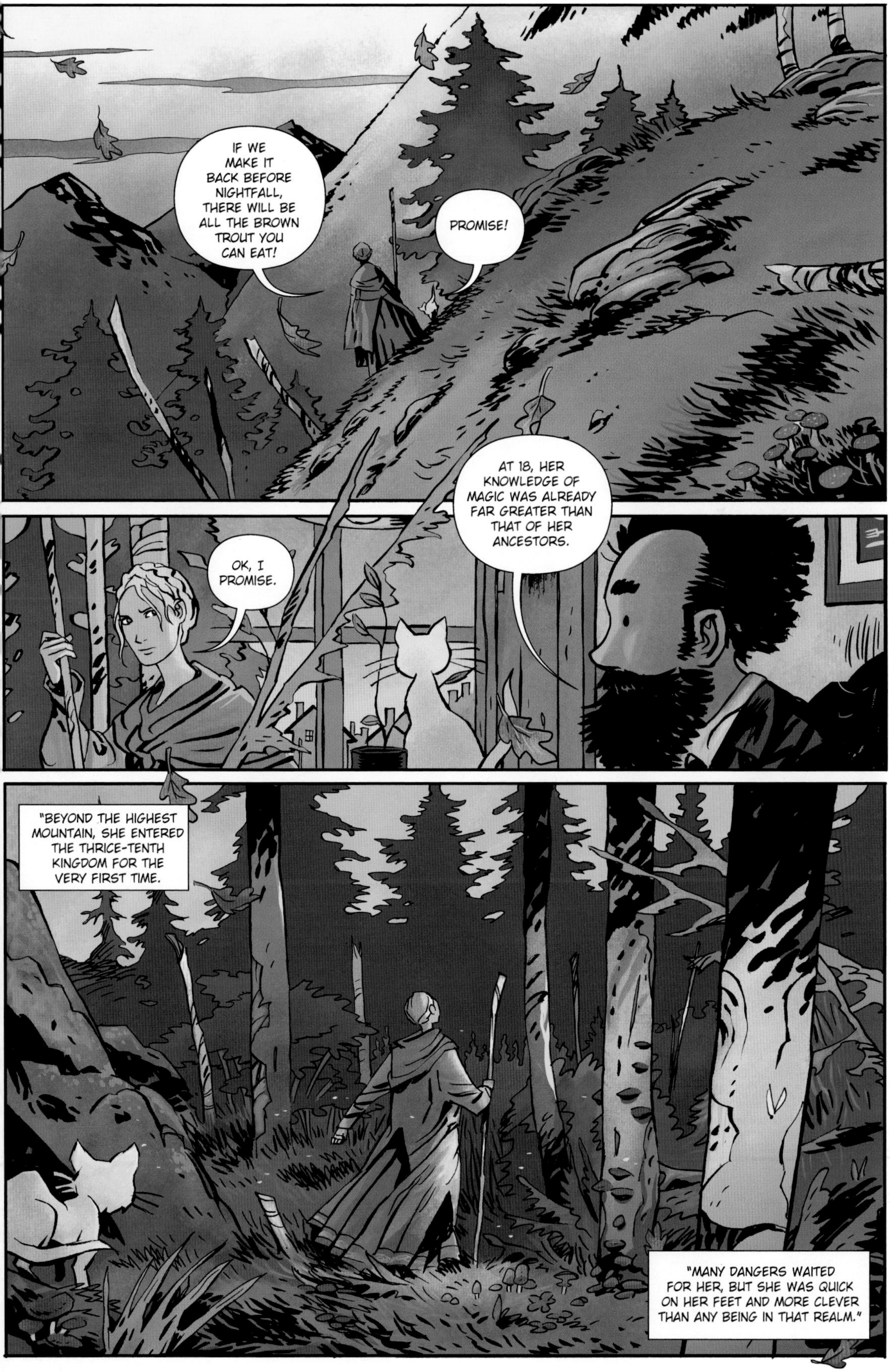
IF WE MAKE IT BACK BEFORE NIGHTFALL, THERE WILL BE ALL THE BROWN TROUT YOU CAN EAT!
PROMISE!
OK, I PROMISE.
AT 18, HER KNOWLEDGE OF MAGIC WAS ALREADY FAR GREATER THAN THAT OF HER ANCESTORS.
"BEYOND THE HIGHEST MOUNTAIN, SHE ENTERED THE THRICE-TENTH KINGDOM FOR THE VERY FIRST TIME.
"MANY DANGERS WAITED FOR HER, BUT SHE WAS QUICK ON HER FEET AND MORE CLEVER THAN ANY BEING IN THAT REALM."

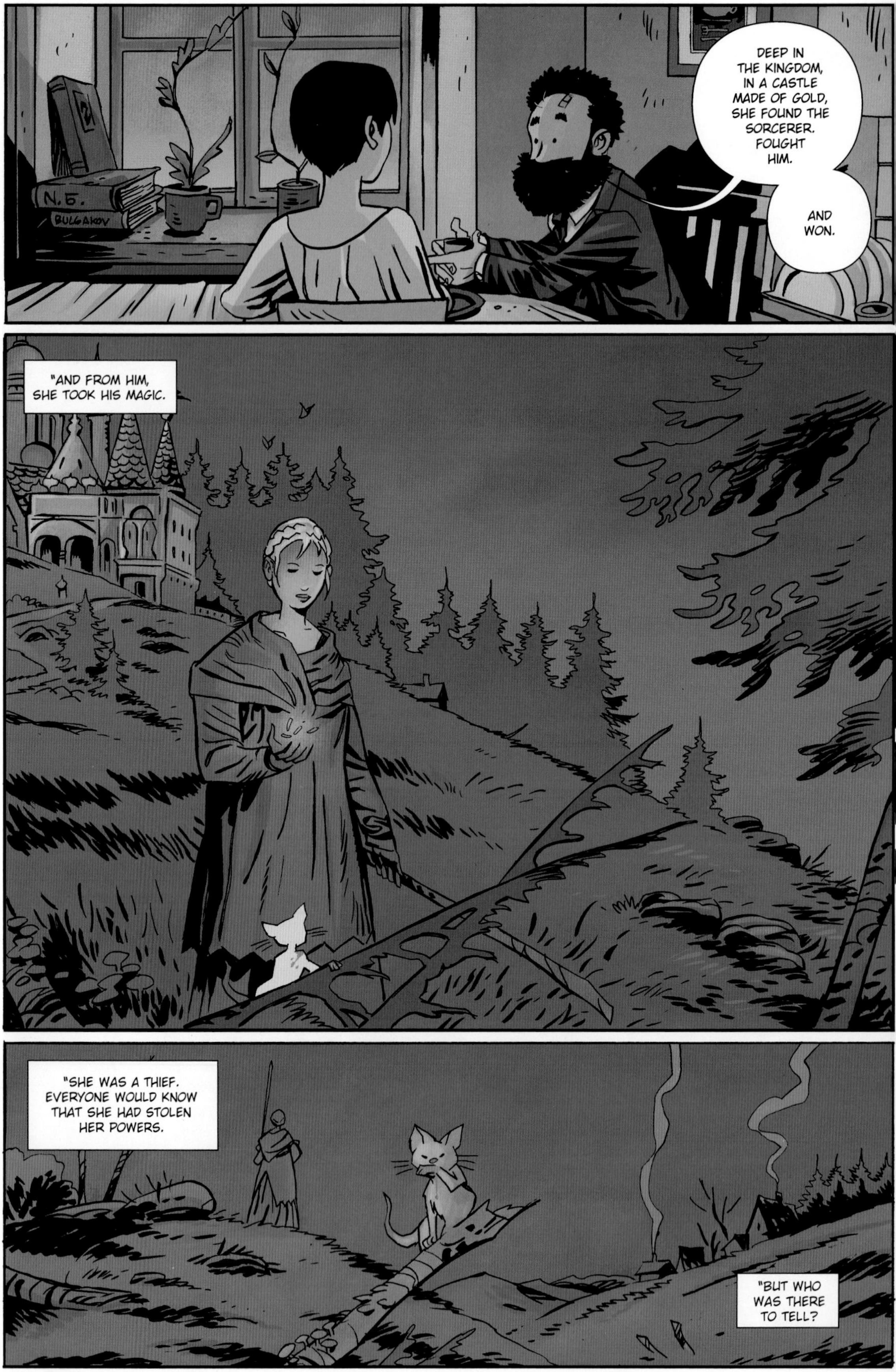
BULGAKOV
DEEP IN THE KINGDOM, IN A CASTLE MADE OF GOLD, SHE FOUND THE SORCERER. FOUGHT HIM.
AND WON.
"AND FROM HIM, SHE TOOK HIS MAGIC.
"SHE WAS A THIEF. EVERYONE WOULD KNOW THAT SHE HAD STOLEN HER POWERS.
"BUT WHO WAS THERE TO TELL?

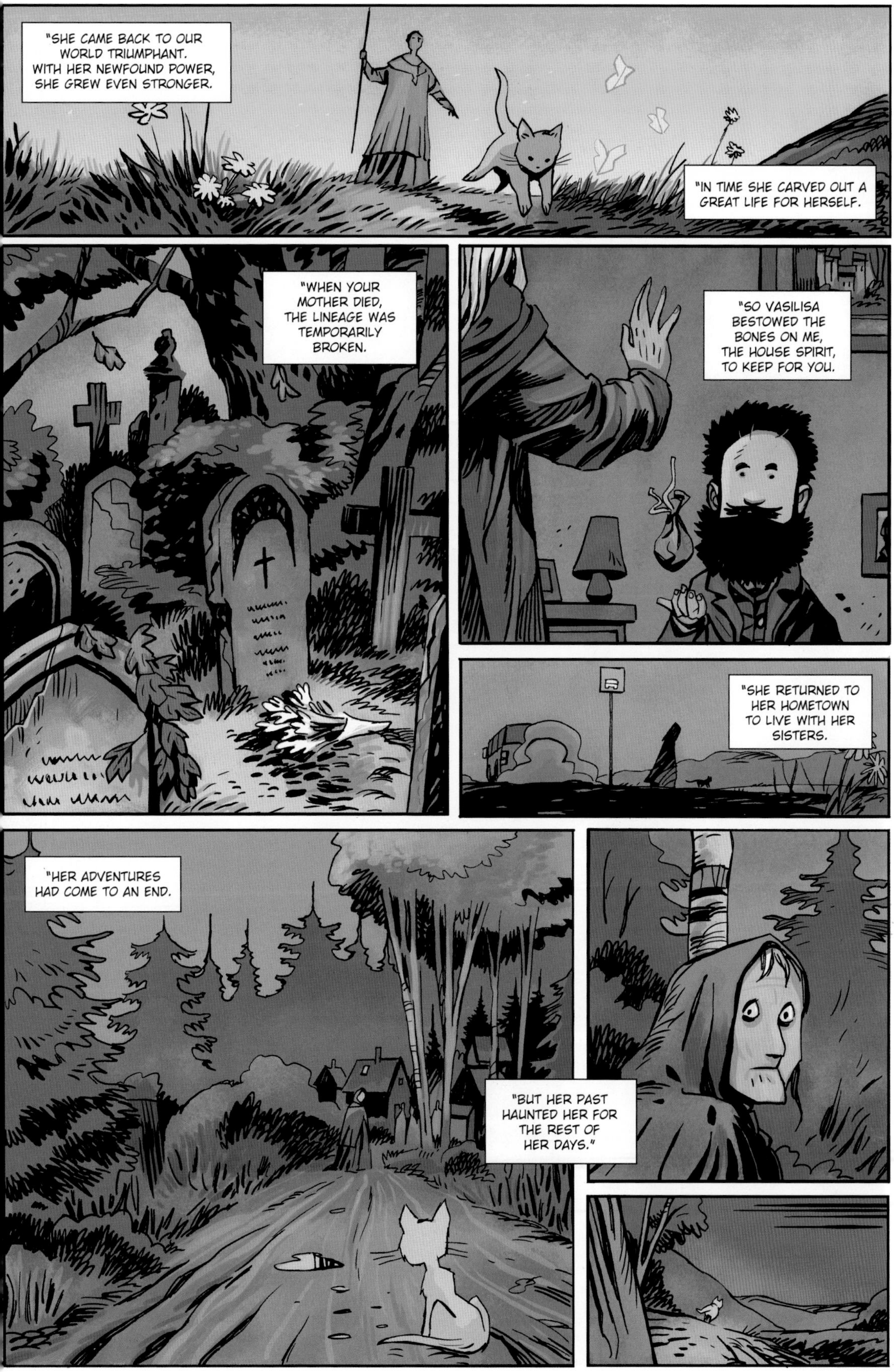
"SHE CAME BACK TO OUR WORLD TRIUMPHANT. WITH HER NEWFOUND POWER, SHE GREW EVEN STRONGER.
"IN TIME SHE CARVED OUT A GREAT LIFE FOR HERSELF.
"WHEN YOUR MOTHER DIED, THE LINEAGE WAS TEMPORARILY BROKEN.
"SO VASILISA BESTOWED THE BONES ON ME, THE HOUSE SPIRIT, TO KEEP FOR YOU.
"SHE RETURNED TO HER HOMETOWN TO LIVE WITH HER SISTERS.
"HER ADVENTURES HAD COME TO AN END.
"BUT HER PAST HAUNTED HER FOR THE REST OF HER DAYS."

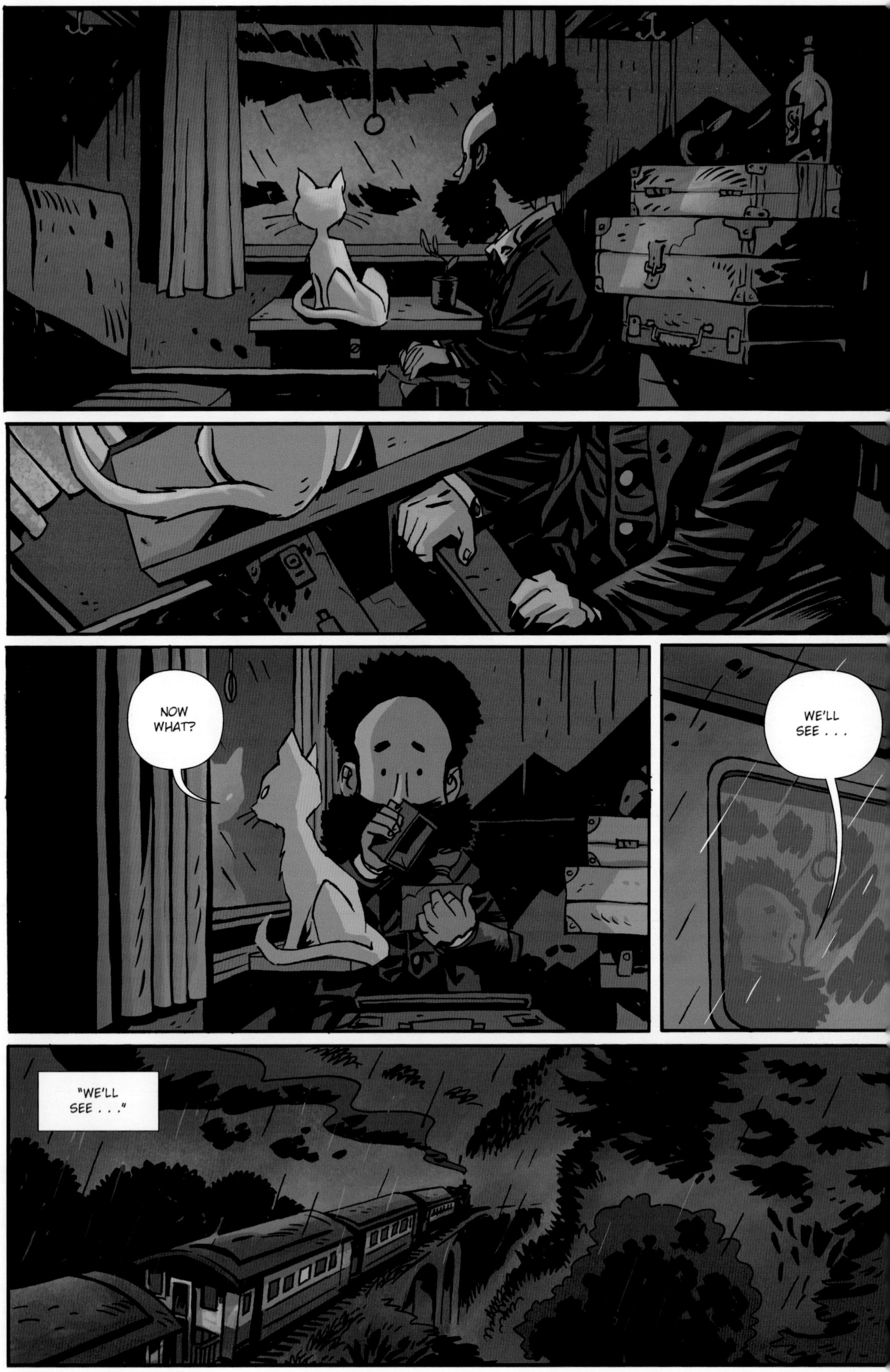
NOW WHAT?
WE'LL SEE . . .
"WE'LL SEE . . ."

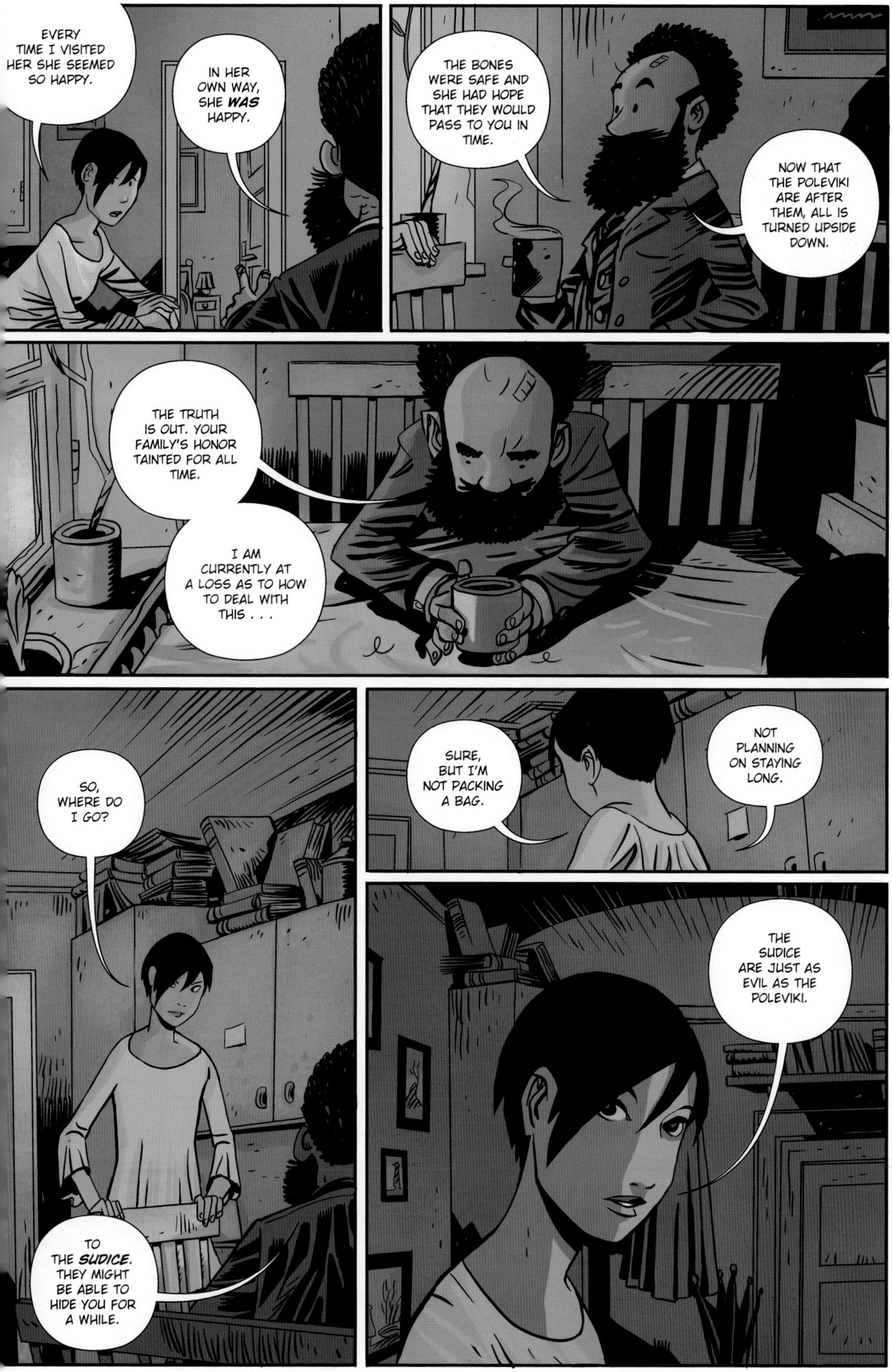
EVERY TIME I VISITED HER SHE SEEMED SO HAPPY.
IN HER OWN WAY, SHE *WAS* HAPPY.
THE BONES WERE SAFE AND SHE HAD HOPE THAT THEY WOULD PASS TO YOU IN TIME.
NOW THAT THE POLEVIKI ARE AFTER THEM, ALL IS TURNED UPSIDE DOWN.
THE TRUTH IS OUT. YOUR FAMILY'S HONOR TAINTED FOR ALL TIME.
I AM CURRENTLY AT A LOSS AS TO HOW TO DEAL WITH THIS . . .
SO, WHERE DO I GO?
TO THE *SUDICE*. THEY MIGHT BE ABLE TO HIDE YOU FOR A WHILE.
SURE, BUT I'M NOT PACKING A BAG.
NOT PLANNING ON STAYING LONG.
THE SUDICE ARE JUST AS EVIL AS THE POLEVIKI.

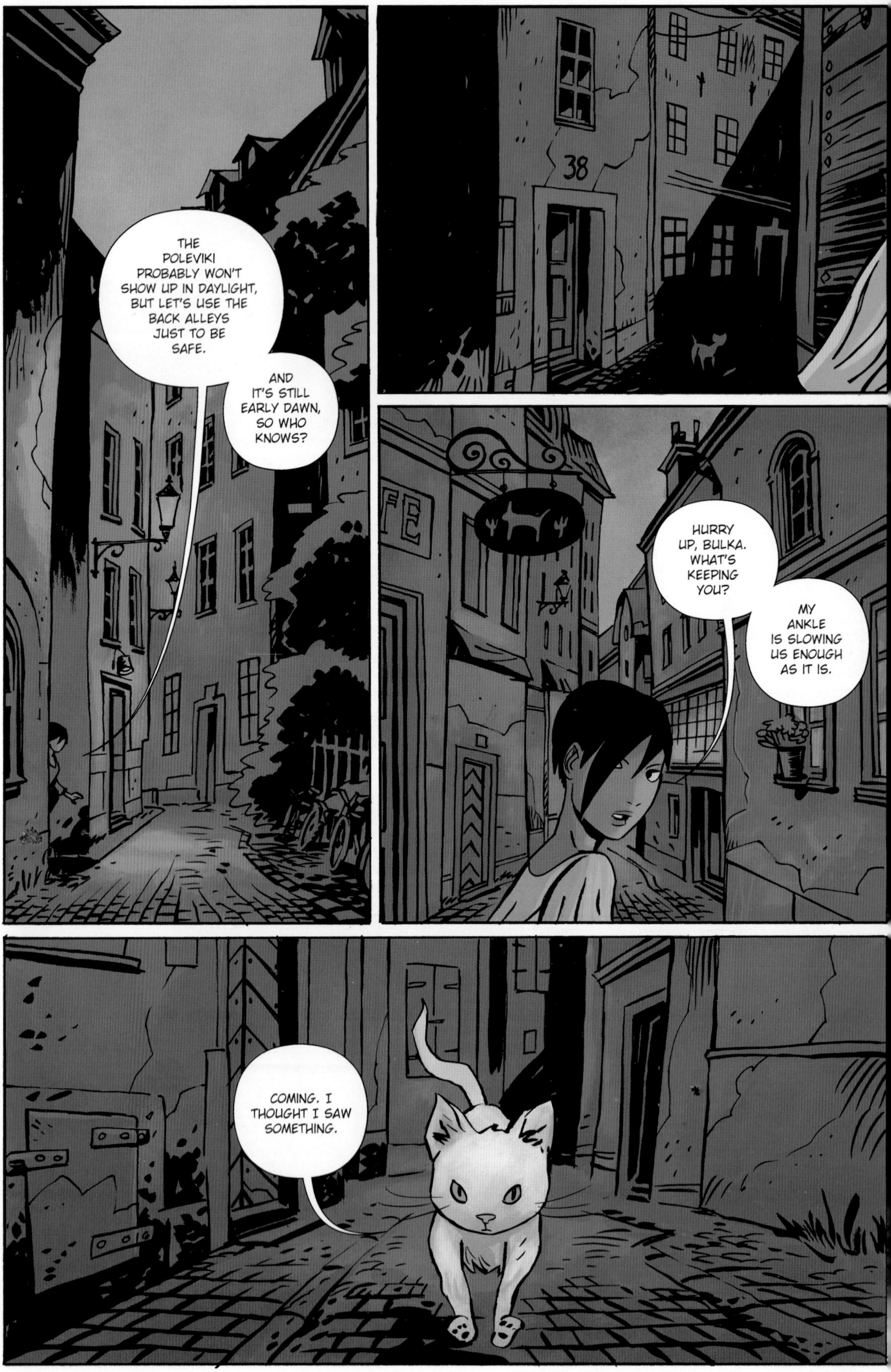
THE POLEVIKI PROBABLY WON'T SHOW UP IN DAYLIGHT, BUT LET'S USE THE BACK ALLEYS JUST TO BE SAFE.
AND IT'S STILL EARLY DAWN, SO WHO KNOWS?
38
HURRY UP, BULKA. WHAT'S KEEPING YOU?
MY ANKLE IS SLOWING US ENOUGH AS IT IS.
COMING. I THOUGHT I SAW SOMETHING.

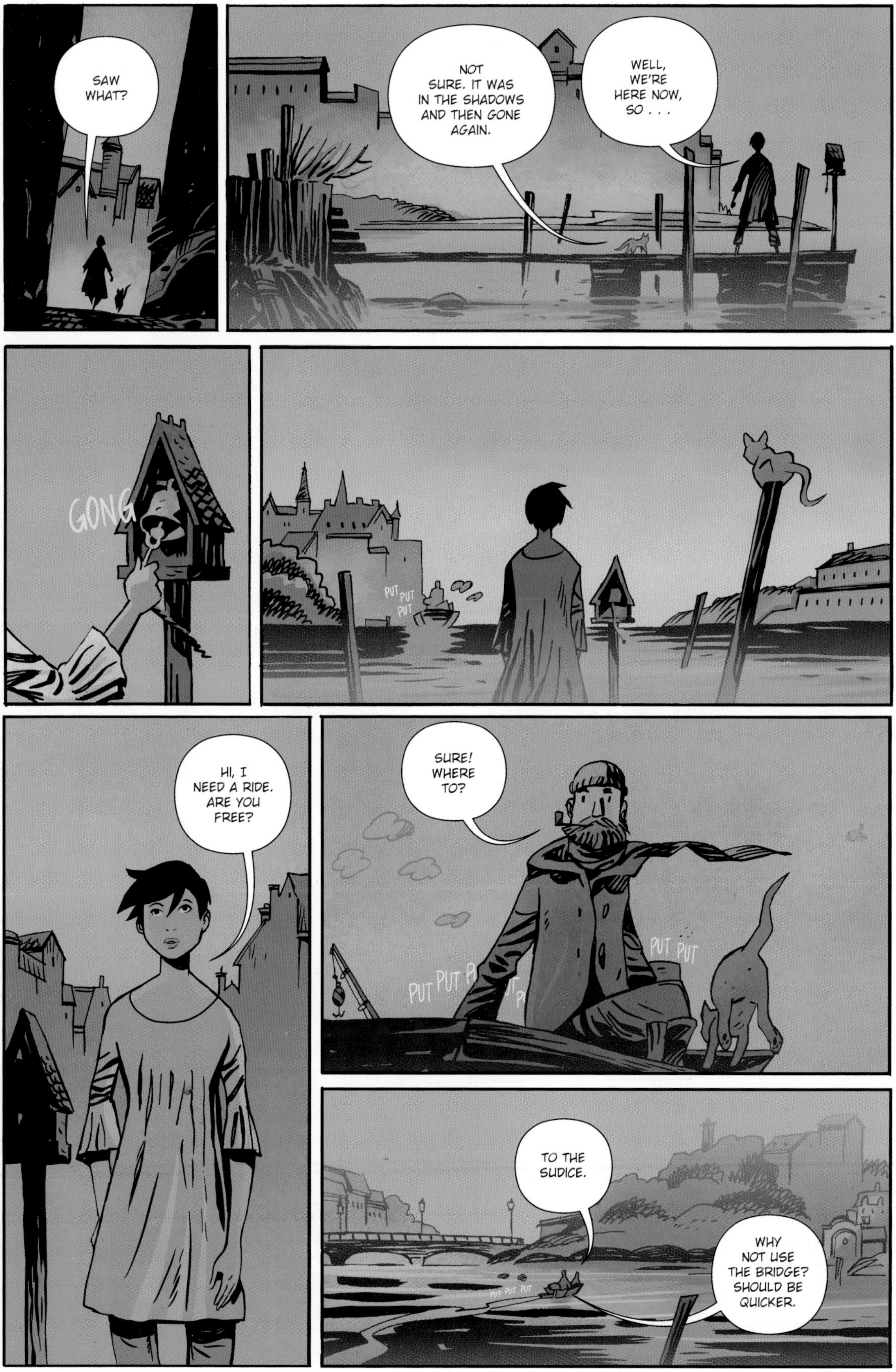
SAW WHAT?
NOT SURE. IT WAS IN THE SHADOWS AND THEN GONE AGAIN.
WELL, WE'RE HERE NOW, SO . . .
GONG
PUT PUT PUT
HI, I NEED A RIDE. ARE YOU FREE?
SURE! WHERE TO?
PUT PUT
PUT PUT
TO THE SUDICE.
PUT PUT PUT
WHY NOT USE THE BRIDGE? SHOULD BE QUICKER.

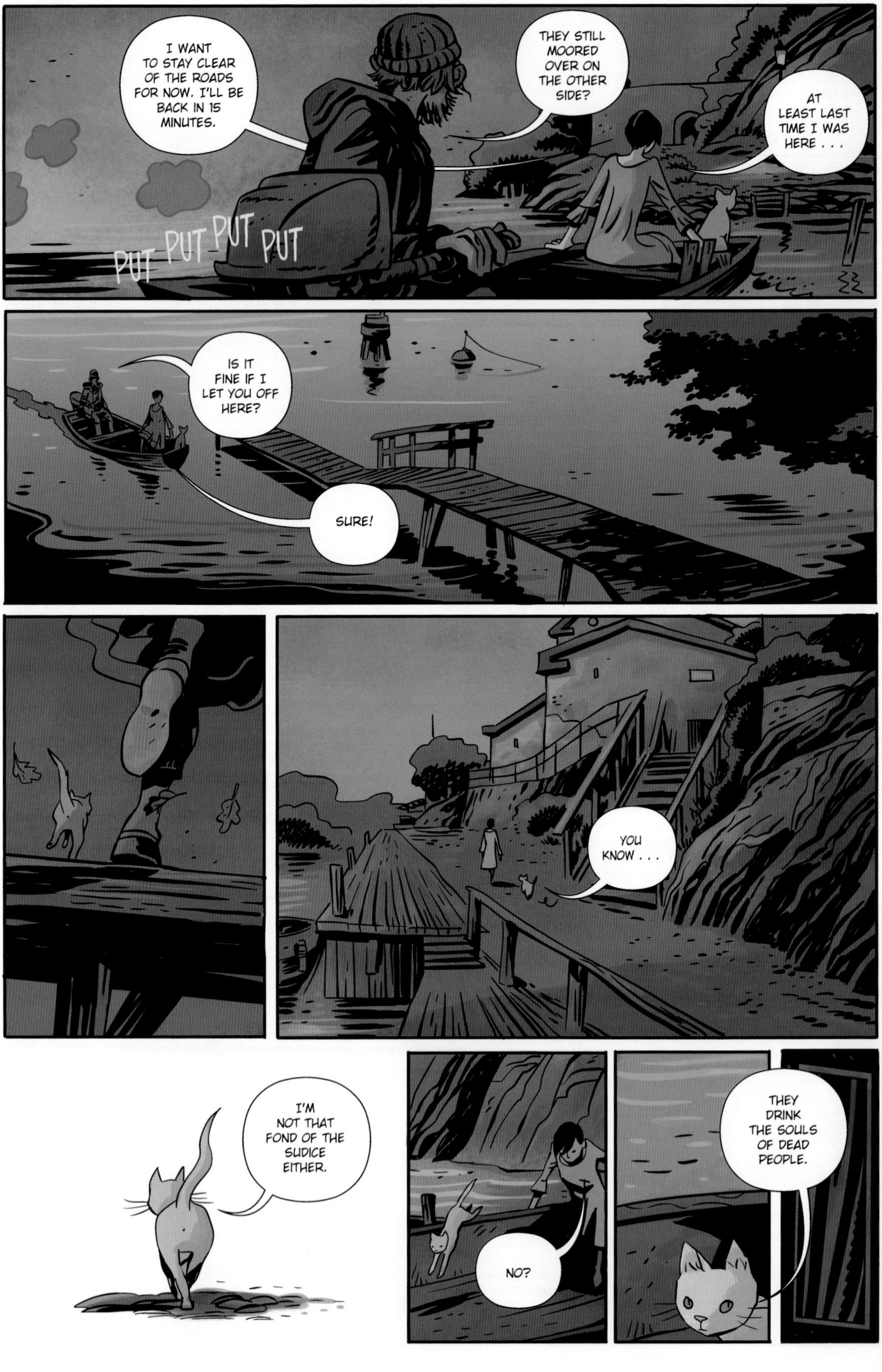
I WANT TO STAY CLEAR OF THE ROADS FOR NOW. I'LL BE BACK IN 15 MINUTES.
PUT PUT PUT PUT
THEY STILL MOORED OVER ON THE OTHER SIDE?
AT LEAST LAST TIME I WAS HERE . . .
IS IT FINE IF I LET YOU OFF HERE?
SURE!
YOU KNOW . . .
I'M NOT THAT FOND OF THE SUDICE EITHER.
NO?
THEY DRINK THE SOULS OF DEAD PEOPLE.

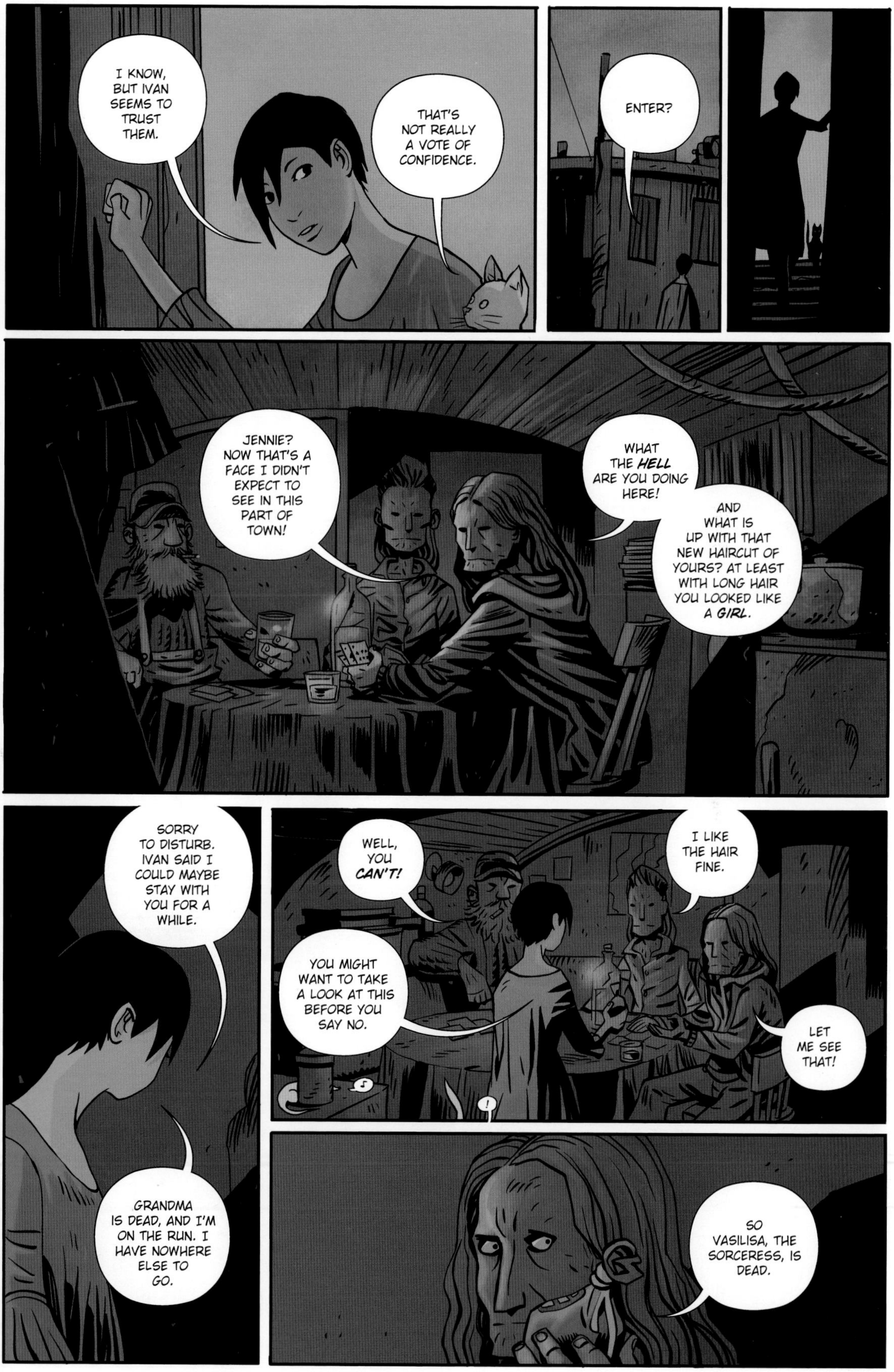
I KNOW, BUT IVAN SEEMS TO TRUST THEM.
THAT'S NOT REALLY A VOTE OF CONFIDENCE.
ENTER?
JENNIE? NOW THAT'S A FACE I DIDN'T EXPECT TO SEE IN THIS PART OF TOWN!
WHAT THE **HELL** ARE YOU DOING HERE!
AND WHAT IS UP WITH THAT NEW HAIRCUT OF YOURS? AT LEAST WITH LONG HAIR YOU LOOKED LIKE A **GIRL**.
SORRY TO DISTURB. IVAN SAID I COULD MAYBE STAY WITH YOU FOR A WHILE.
GRANDMA IS DEAD, AND I'M ON THE RUN. I HAVE NOWHERE ELSE TO GO.
WELL, YOU **CAN'T!**
I LIKE THE HAIR FINE.
YOU MIGHT WANT TO TAKE A LOOK AT THIS BEFORE YOU SAY NO.
LET ME SEE THAT!
!
SO VASILISA, THE SORCERESS, IS DEAD.

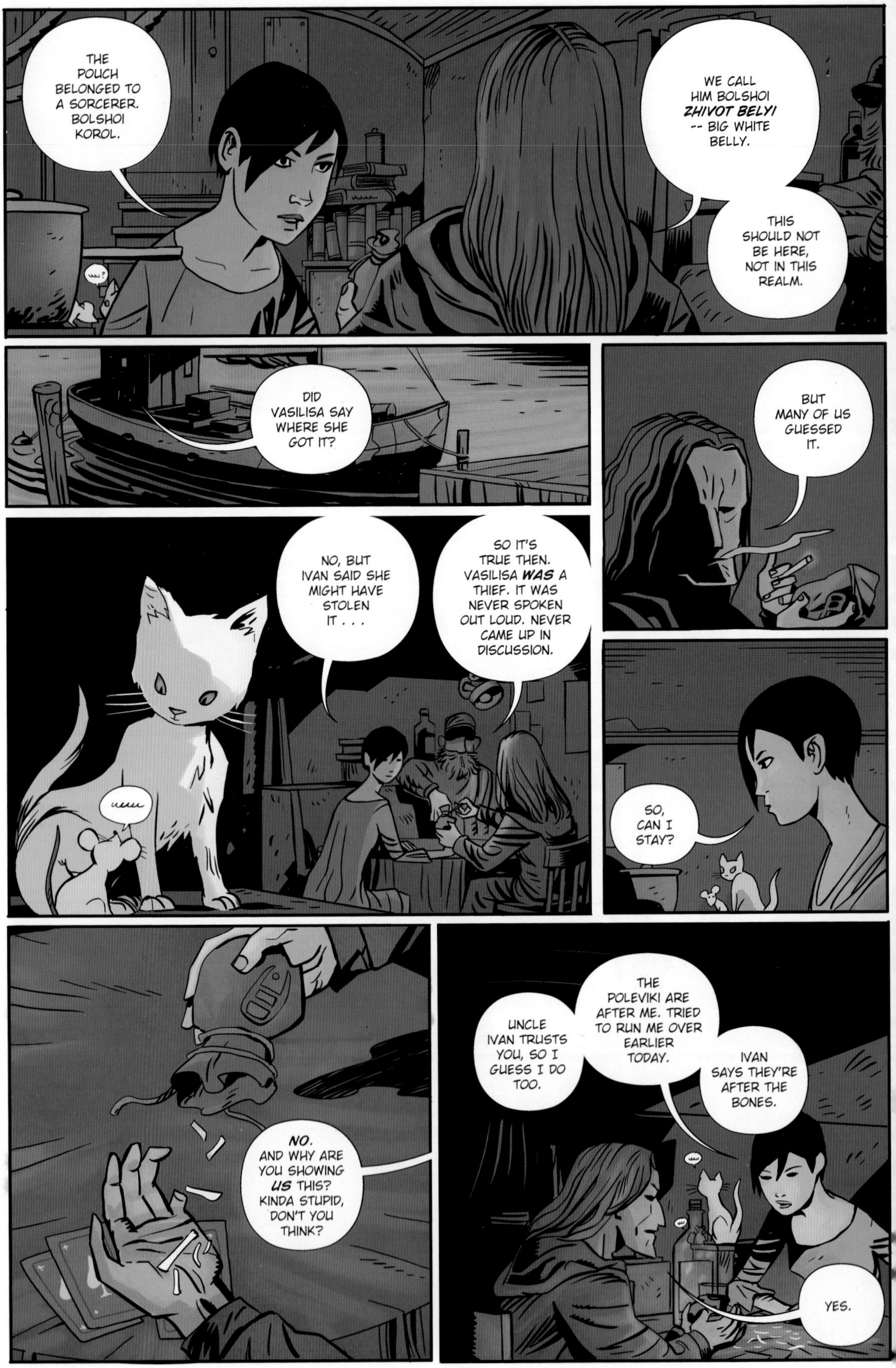

THE POUCH BELONGED TO A SORCERER. BOLSHOI KOROL.
WE CALL HIM BOLSHOI *ZHIVOT BELYI* -- BIG WHITE BELLY.
THIS SHOULD NOT BE HERE, NOT IN THIS REALM.
DID VASILISA SAY WHERE SHE GOT IT?
BUT MANY OF US GUESSED IT.
NO, BUT IVAN SAID SHE MIGHT HAVE STOLEN IT . . .
SO IT'S TRUE THEN. VASILISA ***WAS*** A THIEF. IT WAS NEVER SPOKEN OUT LOUD. NEVER CAME UP IN DISCUSSION.
SO, CAN I STAY?
NO. AND WHY ARE YOU SHOWING ***US*** THIS? KINDA STUPID, DON'T YOU THINK?
UNCLE IVAN TRUSTS YOU, SO I GUESS I DO TOO.
THE POLEVIKI ARE AFTER ME. TRIED TO RUN ME OVER EARLIER TODAY.
IVAN SAYS THEY'RE AFTER THE BONES.
YES.

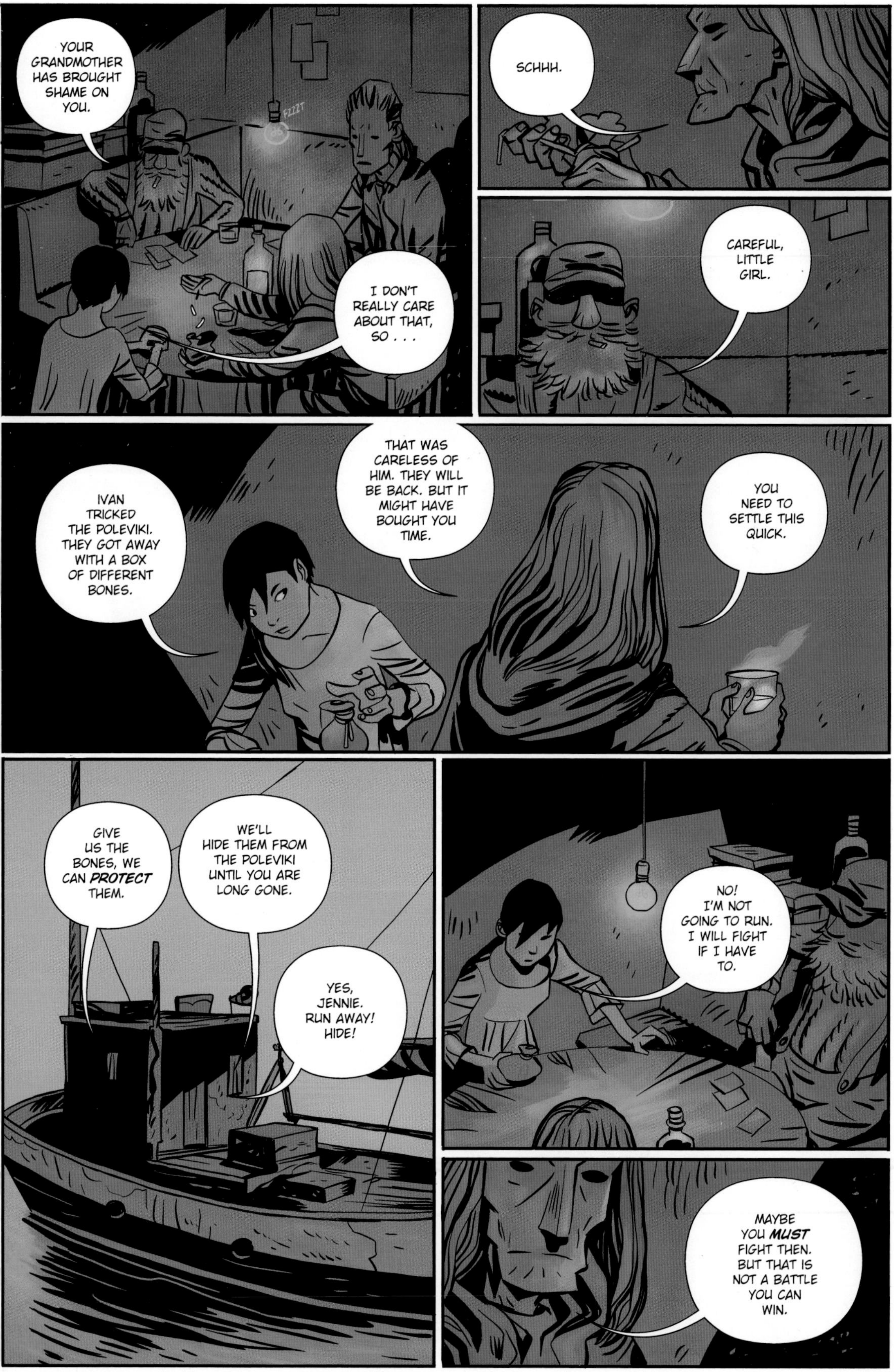
YOUR GRANDMOTHER HAS BROUGHT SHAME ON YOU.
FZZZT
I DON'T REALLY CARE ABOUT THAT, SO . . .
SCHHH.
CAREFUL, LITTLE GIRL.
IVAN TRICKED THE POLEVIKI. THEY GOT AWAY WITH A BOX OF DIFFERENT BONES.
THAT WAS CARELESS OF HIM. THEY WILL BE BACK. BUT IT MIGHT HAVE BOUGHT YOU TIME.
YOU NEED TO SETTLE THIS QUICK.
GIVE US THE BONES, WE CAN PROTECT THEM.
WE'LL HIDE THEM FROM THE POLEVIKI UNTIL YOU ARE LONG GONE.
YES, JENNIE. RUN AWAY! HIDE!
NO! I'M NOT GOING TO RUN. I WILL FIGHT IF I HAVE TO.
MAYBE YOU MUST FIGHT THEN. BUT THAT IS NOT A BATTLE YOU CAN WIN.

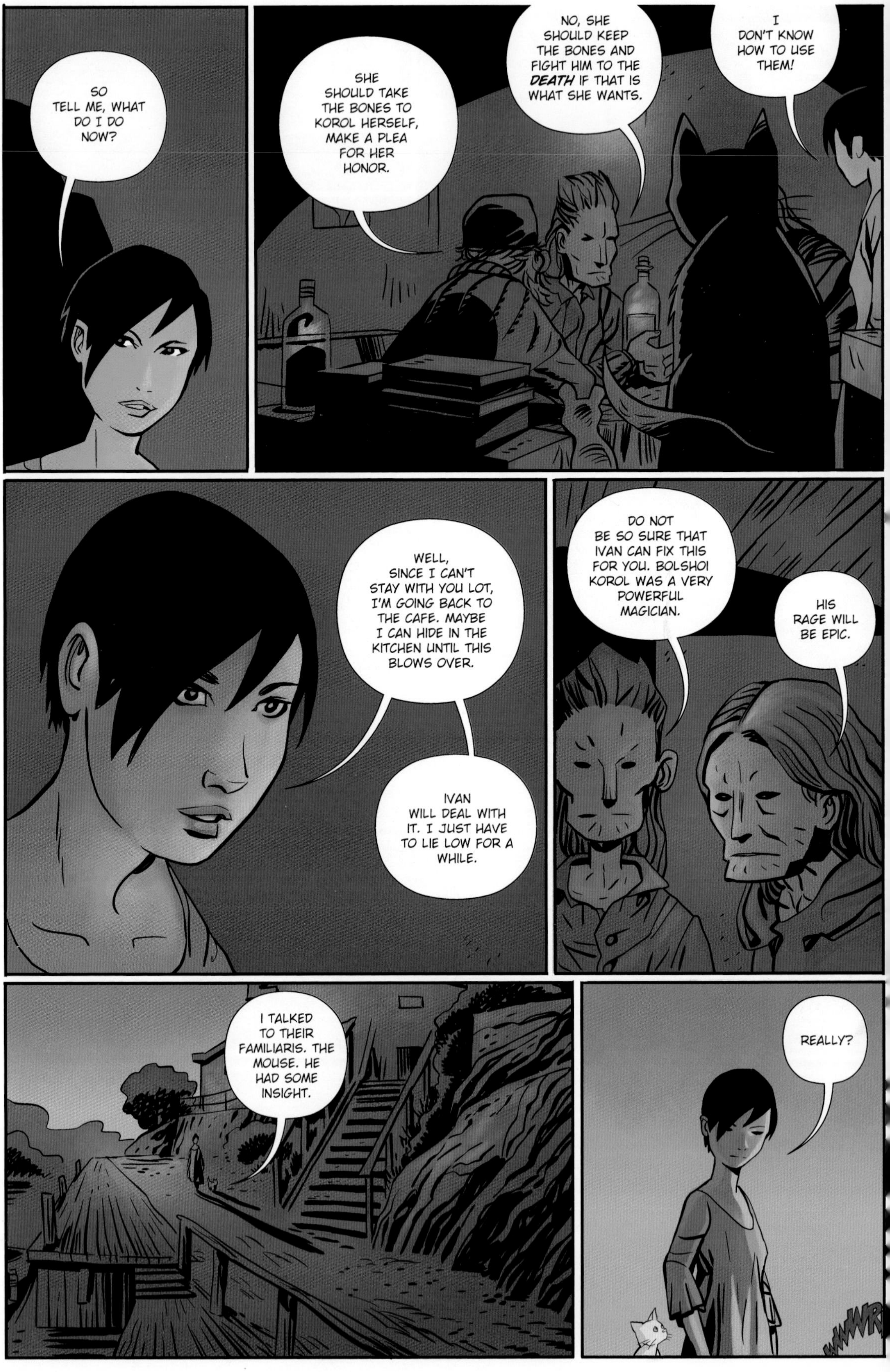
SO TELL ME, WHAT DO I DO NOW?
SHE SHOULD TAKE THE BONES TO KOROL HERSELF, MAKE A PLEA FOR HER HONOR.
NO, SHE SHOULD KEEP THE BONES AND FIGHT HIM TO THE *DEATH* IF THAT IS WHAT SHE WANTS.
I DON'T KNOW HOW TO USE THEM!
WELL, SINCE I CAN'T STAY WITH YOU LOT, I'M GOING BACK TO THE CAFE. MAYBE I CAN HIDE IN THE KITCHEN UNTIL THIS BLOWS OVER.
IVAN WILL DEAL WITH IT. I JUST HAVE TO LIE LOW FOR A WHILE.
DO NOT BE SO SURE THAT IVAN CAN FIX THIS FOR YOU. BOLSHOI KOROL WAS A VERY POWERFUL MAGICIAN.
HIS RAGE WILL BE EPIC.
I TALKED TO THEIR FAMILIARIS. THE MOUSE. HE HAD SOME INSIGHT.
REALLY?

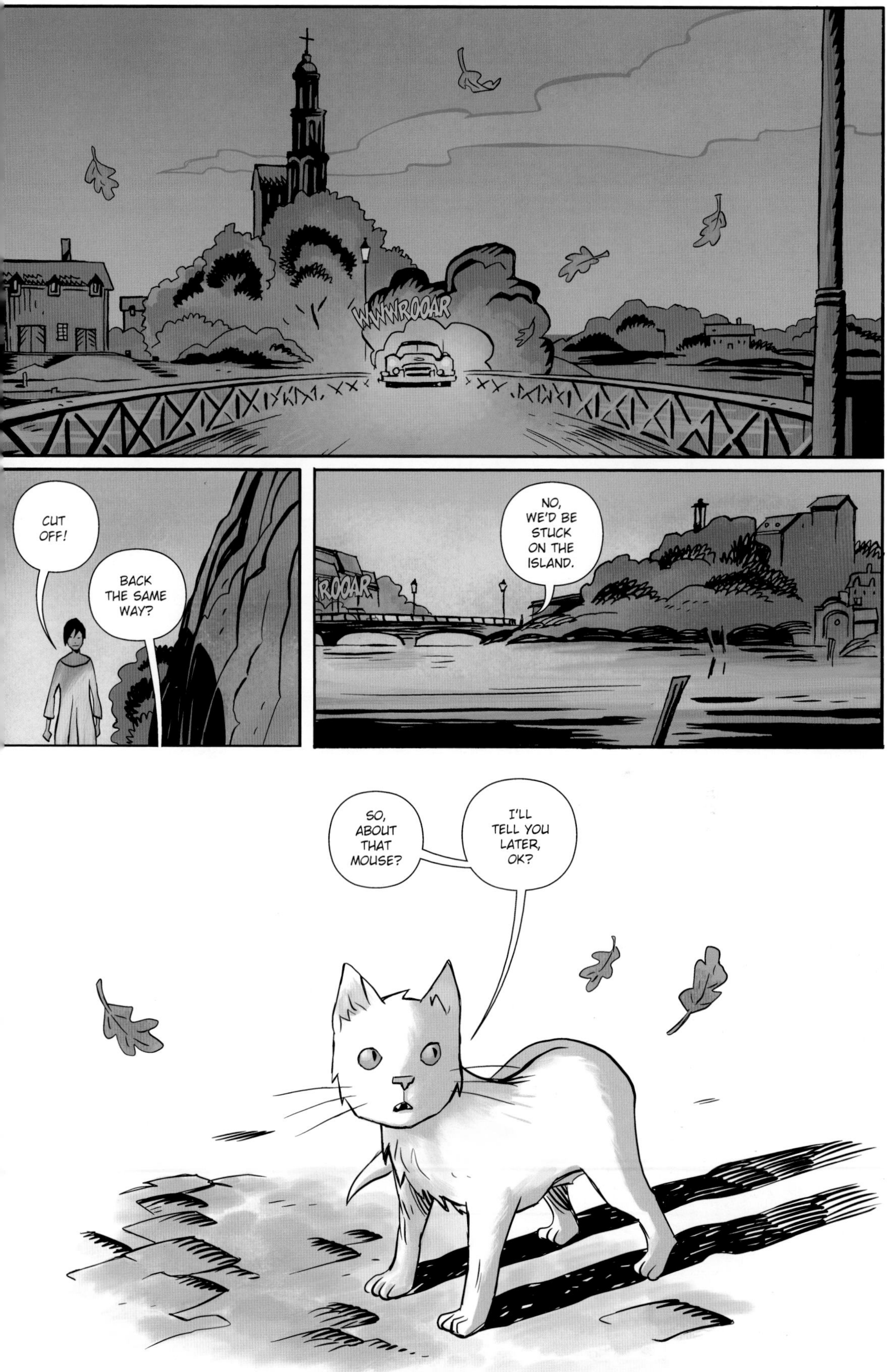
WWWWROOAR
CUT OFF!
BACK THE SAME WAY?
NO, WE'D BE STUCK ON THE ISLAND.
ROOAR
SO, ABOUT THAT MOUSE?
I'LL TELL YOU LATER, OK?

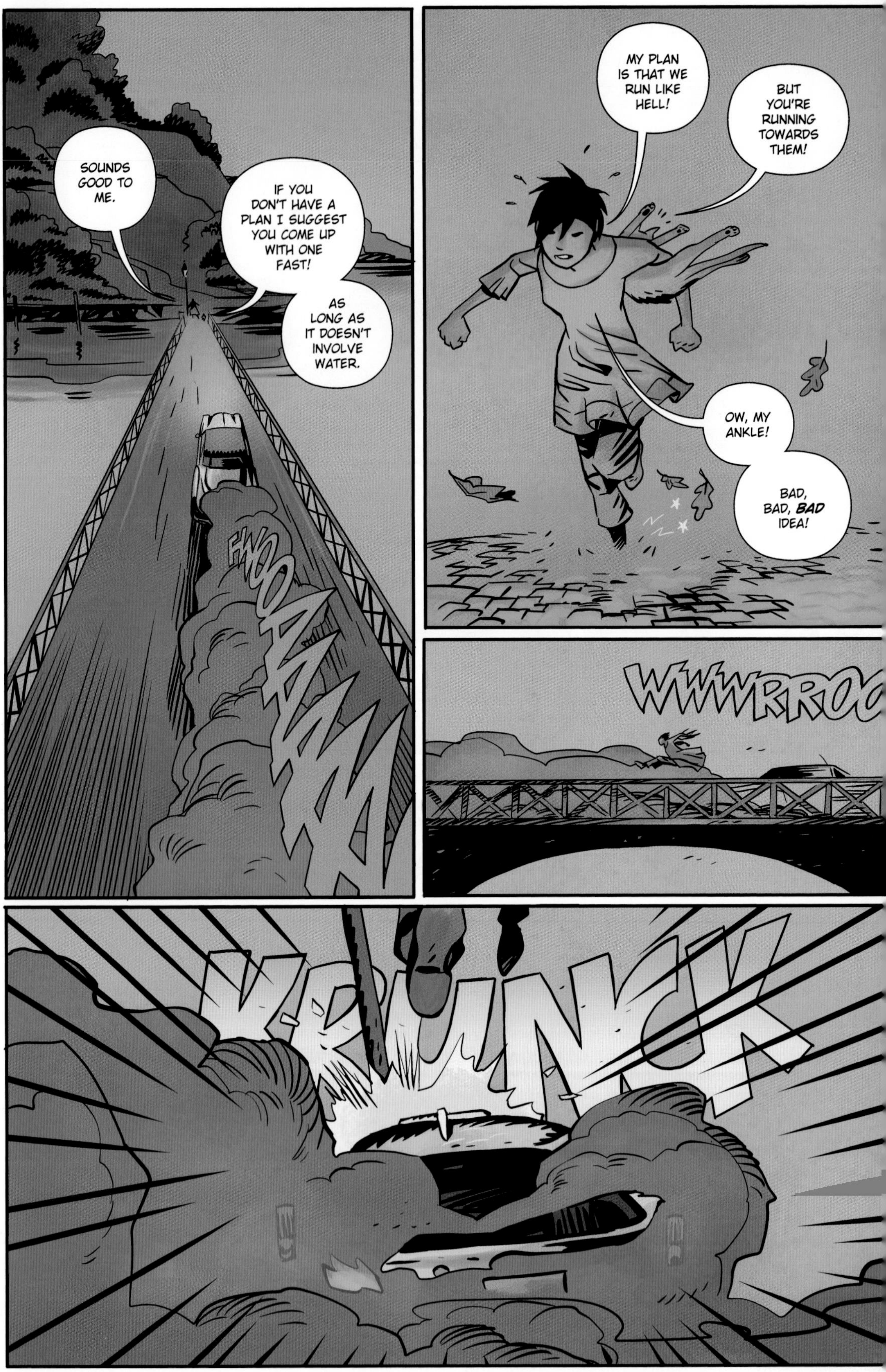
SOUNDS GOOD TO ME.
IF YOU DON'T HAVE A PLAN I SUGGEST YOU COME UP WITH ONE FAST!
AS LONG AS IT DOESN'T INVOLVE WATER.
MY PLAN IS THAT WE RUN LIKE HELL!
BUT YOU'RE RUNNING TOWARDS THEM!
OW, MY ANKLE!
BAD, BAD, ***BAD*** IDEA!

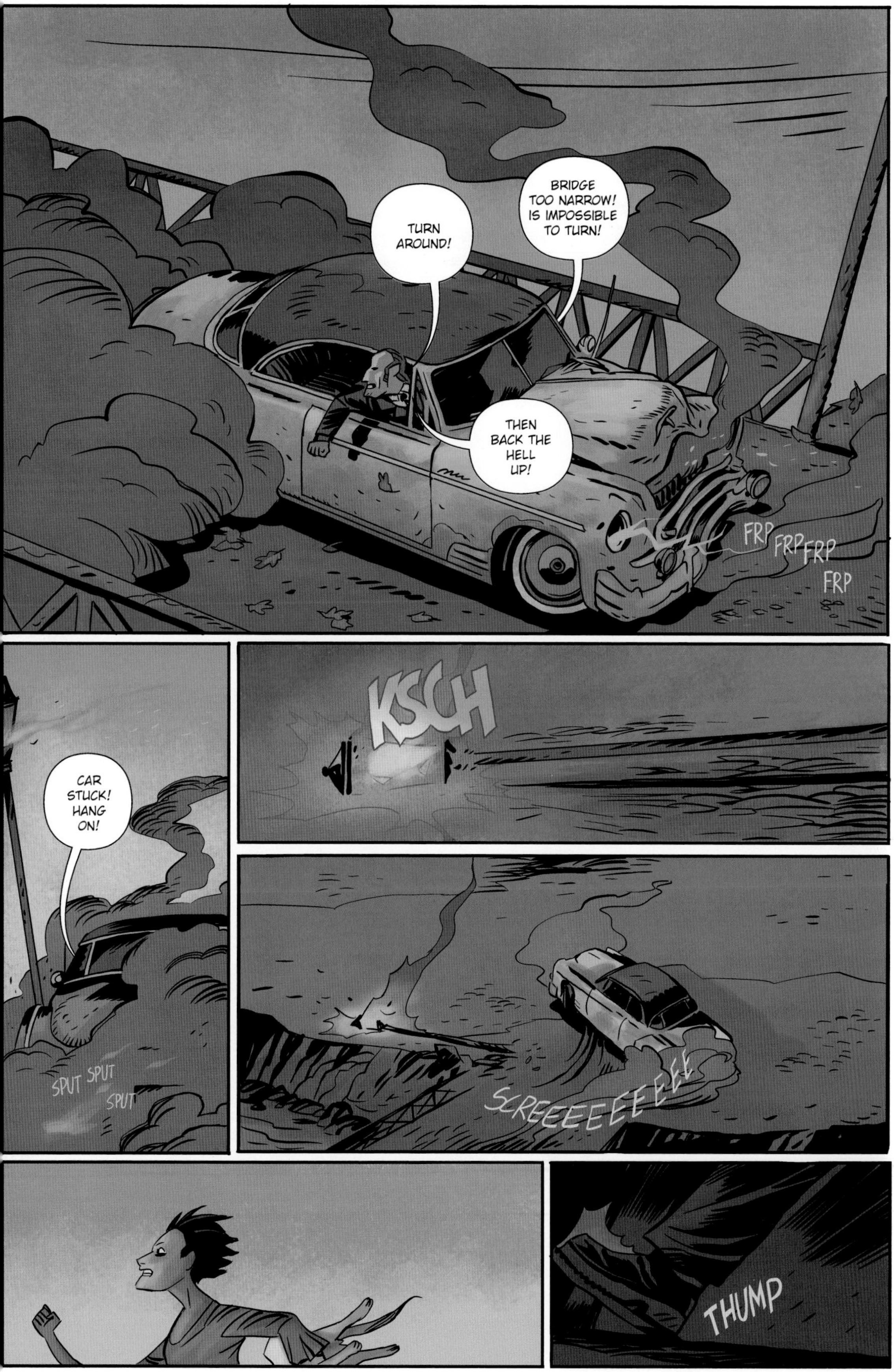
TURN AROUND!
BRIDGE TOO NARROW! IS IMPOSSIBLE TO TURN!
THEN BACK THE HELL UP!
FRP FRP FRP FRP
CAR STUCK! HANG ON!
SPUT SPUT SPUT
KSCH
SCREEEEEEEEEE
THUMP

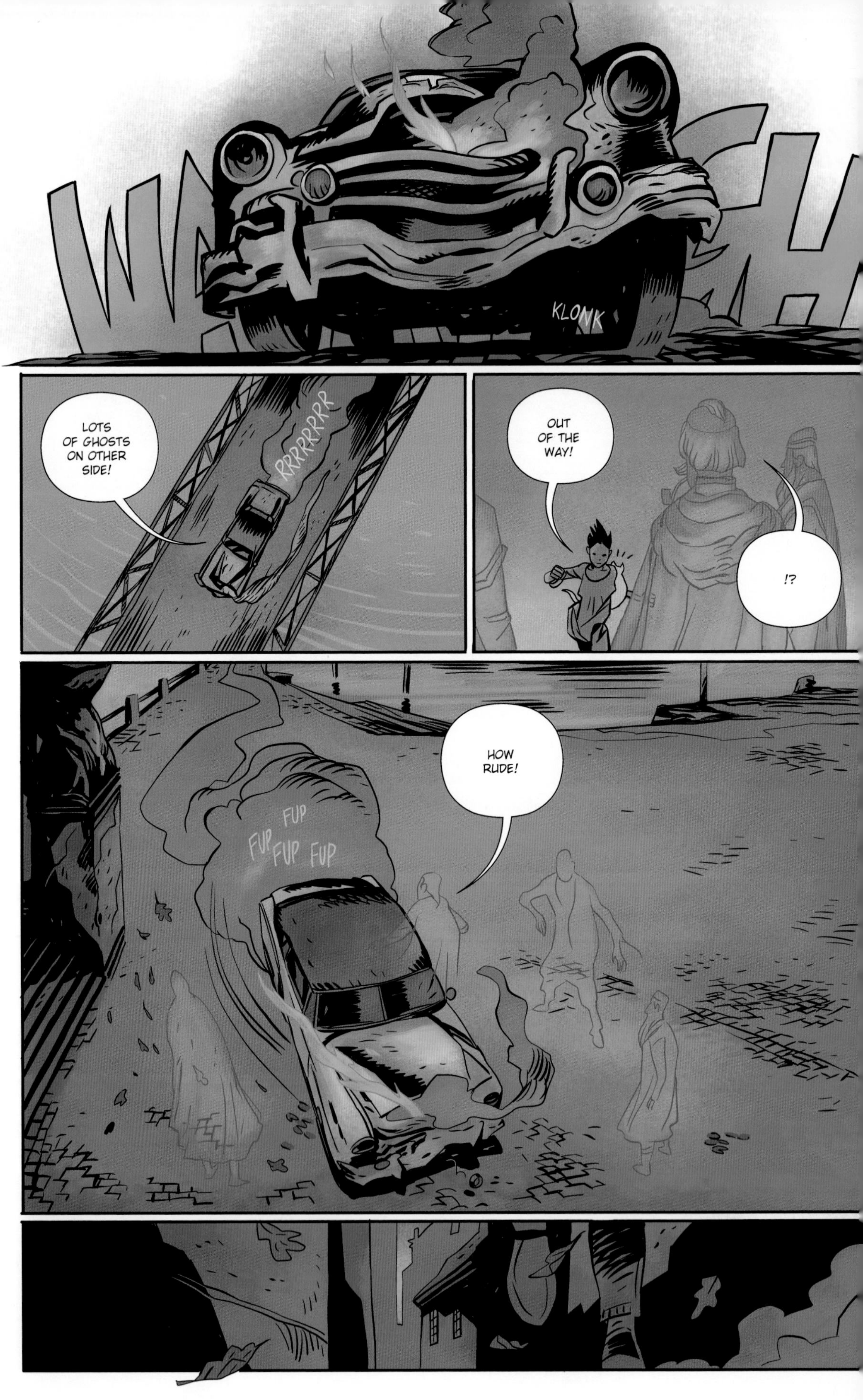

KLONK
LOTS OF GHOSTS ON OTHER SIDE!
RRRRRRRR
OUT OF THE WAY!
!?
HOW RUDE!
FUP FUP FUP FUP

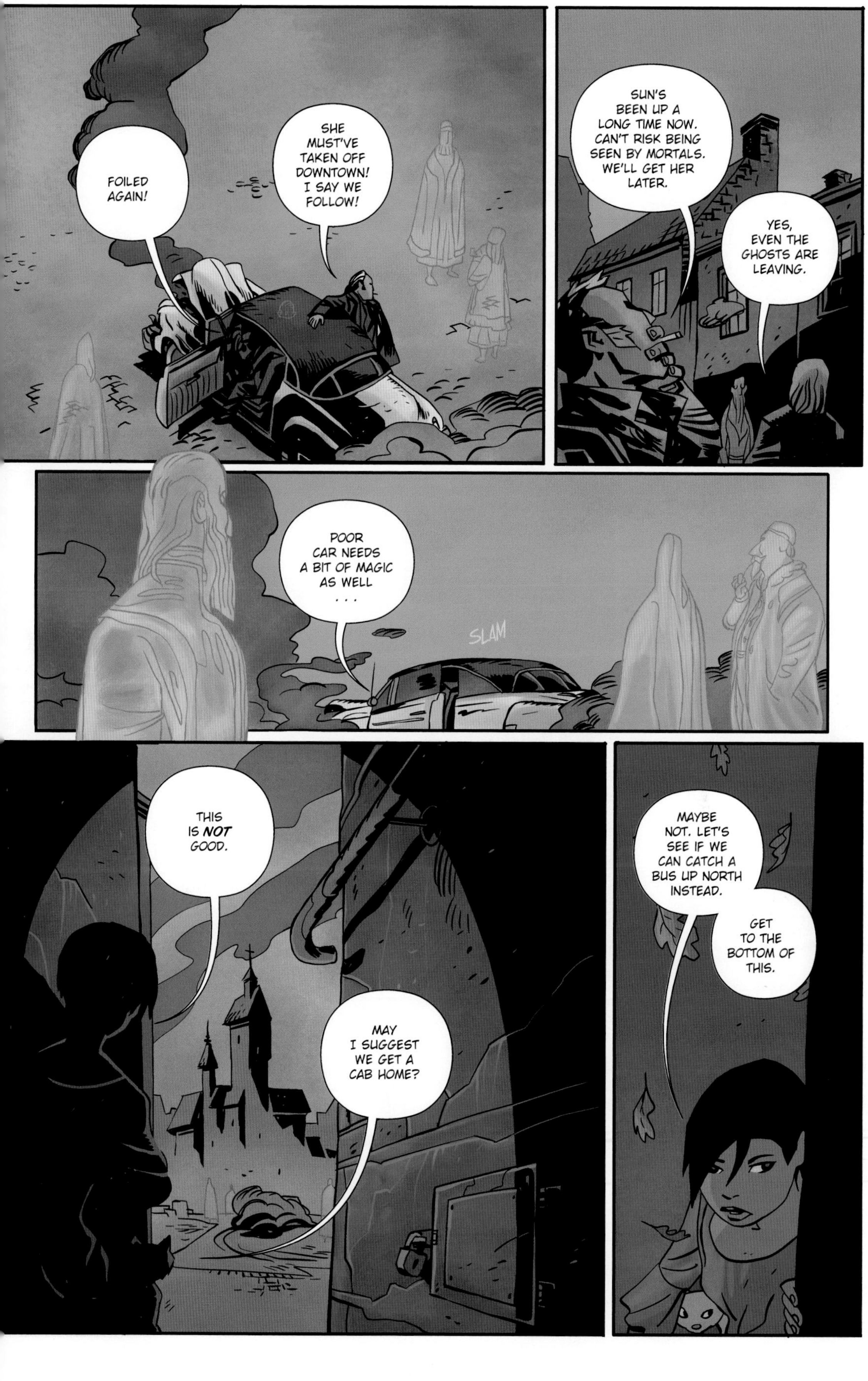
FOILED AGAIN!
SHE MUST'VE TAKEN OFF DOWNTOWN! I SAY WE FOLLOW!
SUN'S BEEN UP A LONG TIME NOW. CAN'T RISK BEING SEEN BY MORTALS. WE'LL GET HER LATER.
YES, EVEN THE GHOSTS ARE LEAVING.
POOR CAR NEEDS A BIT OF MAGIC AS WELL . . .
SLAM
THIS IS NOT GOOD.
MAY I SUGGEST WE GET A CAB HOME?
MAYBE NOT. LET'S SEE IF WE CAN CATCH A BUS UP NORTH INSTEAD.
GET TO THE BOTTOM OF THIS.

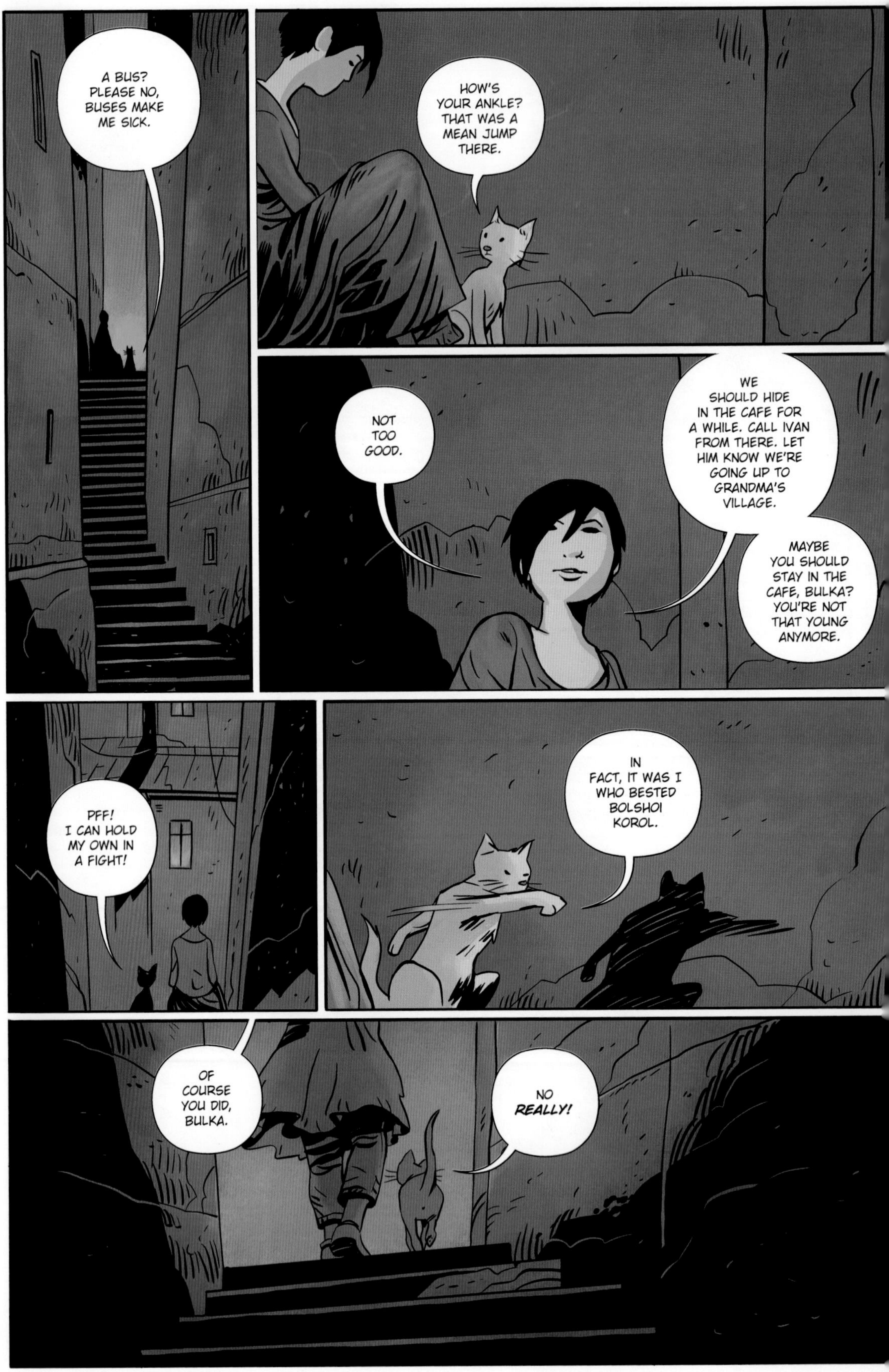
A BUS? PLEASE NO, BUSES MAKE ME SICK.
HOW'S YOUR ANKLE? THAT WAS A MEAN JUMP THERE.
NOT TOO GOOD.
WE SHOULD HIDE IN THE CAFE FOR A WHILE. CALL IVAN FROM THERE. LET HIM KNOW WE'RE GOING UP TO GRANDMA'S VILLAGE.
MAYBE YOU SHOULD STAY IN THE CAFE, BULKA? YOU'RE NOT THAT YOUNG ANYMORE.
PFF! I CAN HOLD MY OWN IN A FIGHT!
IN FACT, IT WAS I WHO BESTED BOLSHOI KOROL.
OF COURSE YOU DID, BULKA.
NO *REALLY!*

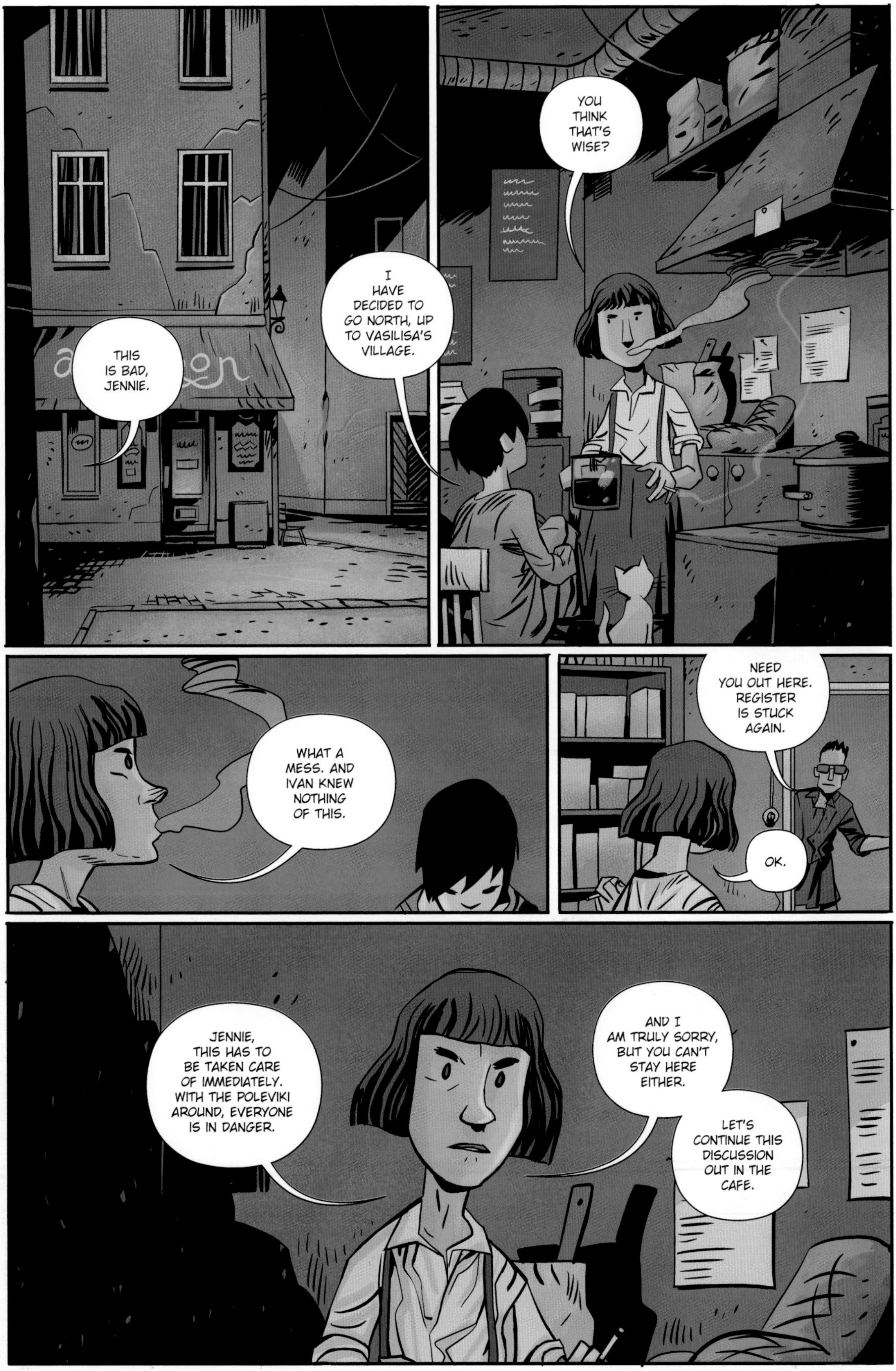
THIS IS BAD, JENNIE.
I HAVE DECIDED TO GO NORTH, UP TO VASILISA'S VILLAGE.
YOU THINK THAT'S WISE?
WHAT A MESS. AND IVAN KNEW NOTHING OF THIS.
NEED YOU OUT HERE. REGISTER IS STUCK AGAIN.
OK.
JENNIE, THIS HAS TO BE TAKEN CARE OF IMMEDIATELY. WITH THE POLEVIKI AROUND, EVERYONE IS IN DANGER.
AND I AM TRULY SORRY, BUT YOU CAN'T STAY HERE EITHER.
LET'S CONTINUE THIS DISCUSSION OUT IN THE CAFE.

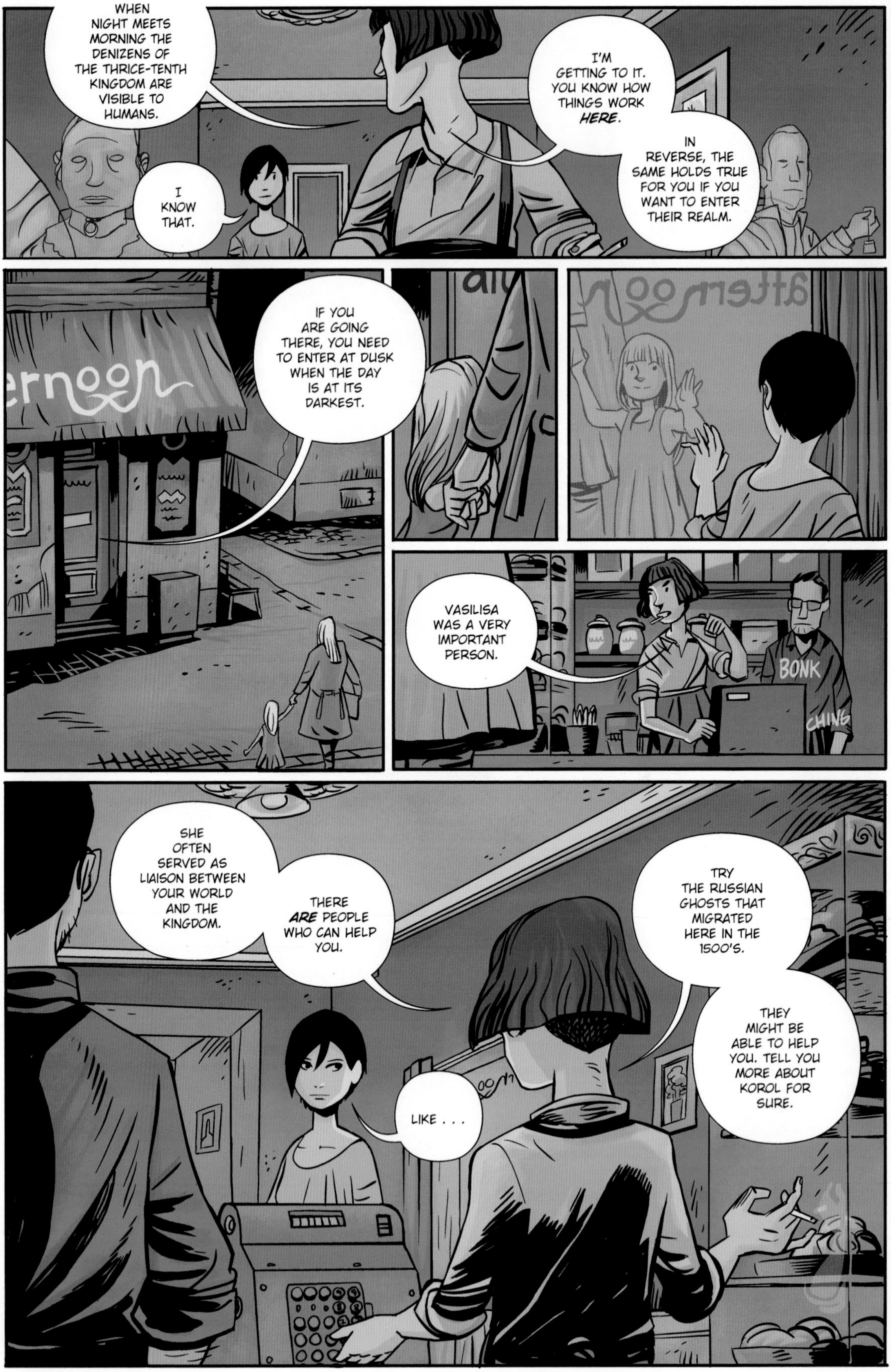
WHEN NIGHT MEETS MORNING THE DENIZENS OF THE THRICE-TENTH KINGDOM ARE VISIBLE TO HUMANS.
I KNOW THAT.
I'M GETTING TO IT. YOU KNOW HOW THINGS WORK *HERE*.
IN REVERSE, THE SAME HOLDS TRUE FOR YOU IF YOU WANT TO ENTER THEIR REALM.
ernoon
IF YOU ARE GOING THERE, YOU NEED TO ENTER AT DUSK WHEN THE DAY IS AT ITS DARKEST.
afternoon
VASILISA WAS A VERY IMPORTANT PERSON.
BONK
CHING
SHE OFTEN SERVED AS LIAISON BETWEEN YOUR WORLD AND THE KINGDOM.
THERE *ARE* PEOPLE WHO CAN HELP YOU.
TRY THE RUSSIAN GHOSTS THAT MIGRATED HERE IN THE 1500'S.
THEY MIGHT BE ABLE TO HELP YOU. TELL YOU MORE ABOUT KOROL FOR SURE.
LIKE . . .

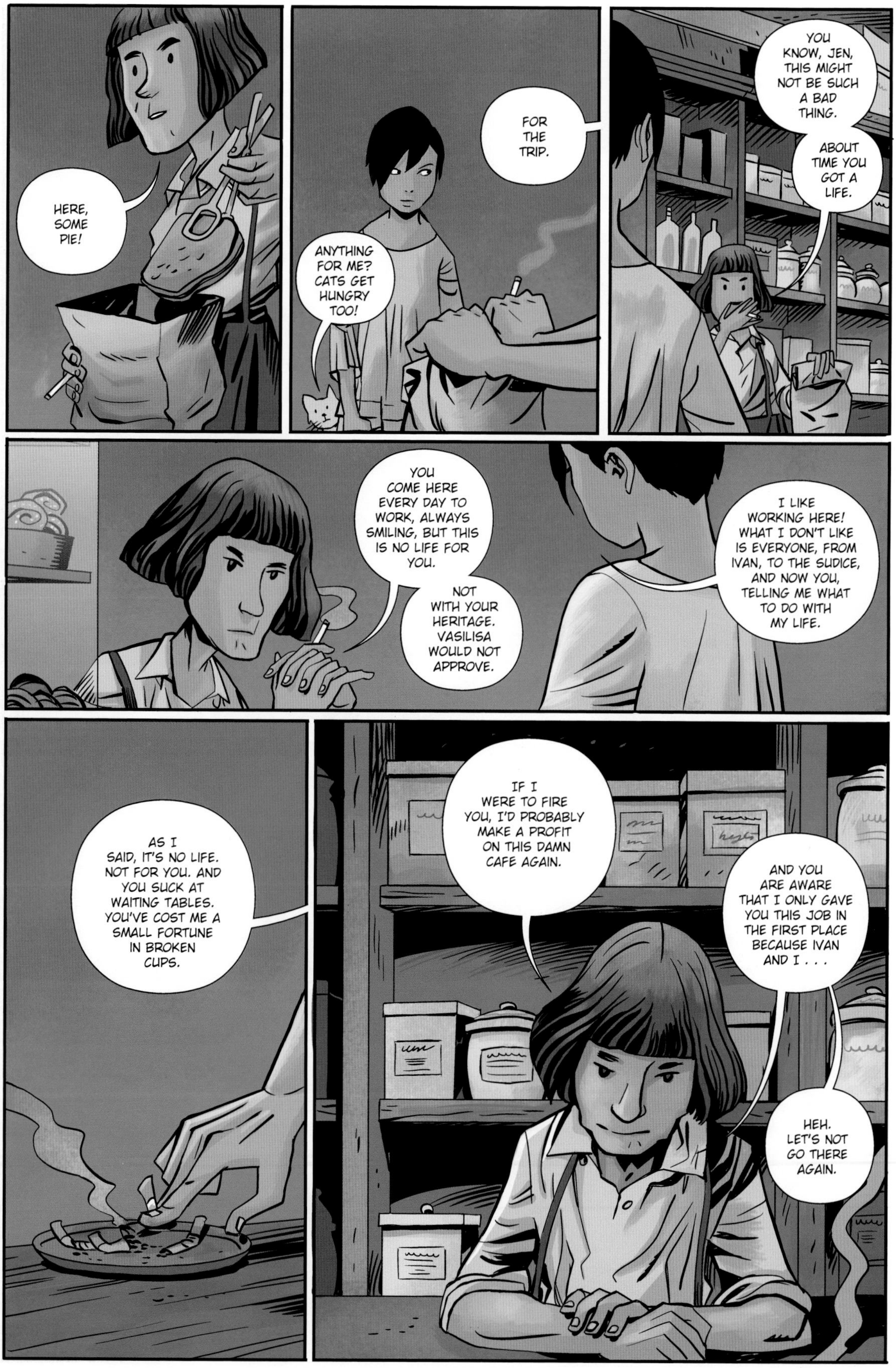
HERE, SOME PIE!
FOR THE TRIP.
ANYTHING FOR ME? CATS GET HUNGRY TOO!
YOU KNOW, JEN, THIS MIGHT NOT BE SUCH A BAD THING.
ABOUT TIME YOU GOT A LIFE.
YOU COME HERE EVERY DAY TO WORK, ALWAYS SMILING, BUT THIS IS NO LIFE FOR YOU.
NOT WITH YOUR HERITAGE. VASILISA WOULD NOT APPROVE.
I LIKE WORKING HERE! WHAT I DON'T LIKE IS EVERYONE, FROM IVAN, TO THE SUDICE, AND NOW YOU, TELLING ME WHAT TO DO WITH MY LIFE.
AS I SAID, IT'S NO LIFE. NOT FOR YOU. AND YOU SUCK AT WAITING TABLES. YOU'VE COST ME A SMALL FORTUNE IN BROKEN CUPS.
IF I WERE TO FIRE YOU, I'D PROBABLY MAKE A PROFIT ON THIS DAMN CAFE AGAIN.
AND YOU ARE AWARE THAT I ONLY GAVE YOU THIS JOB IN THE FIRST PLACE BECAUSE IVAN AND I . . .
HEH. LET'S NOT GO THERE AGAIN.

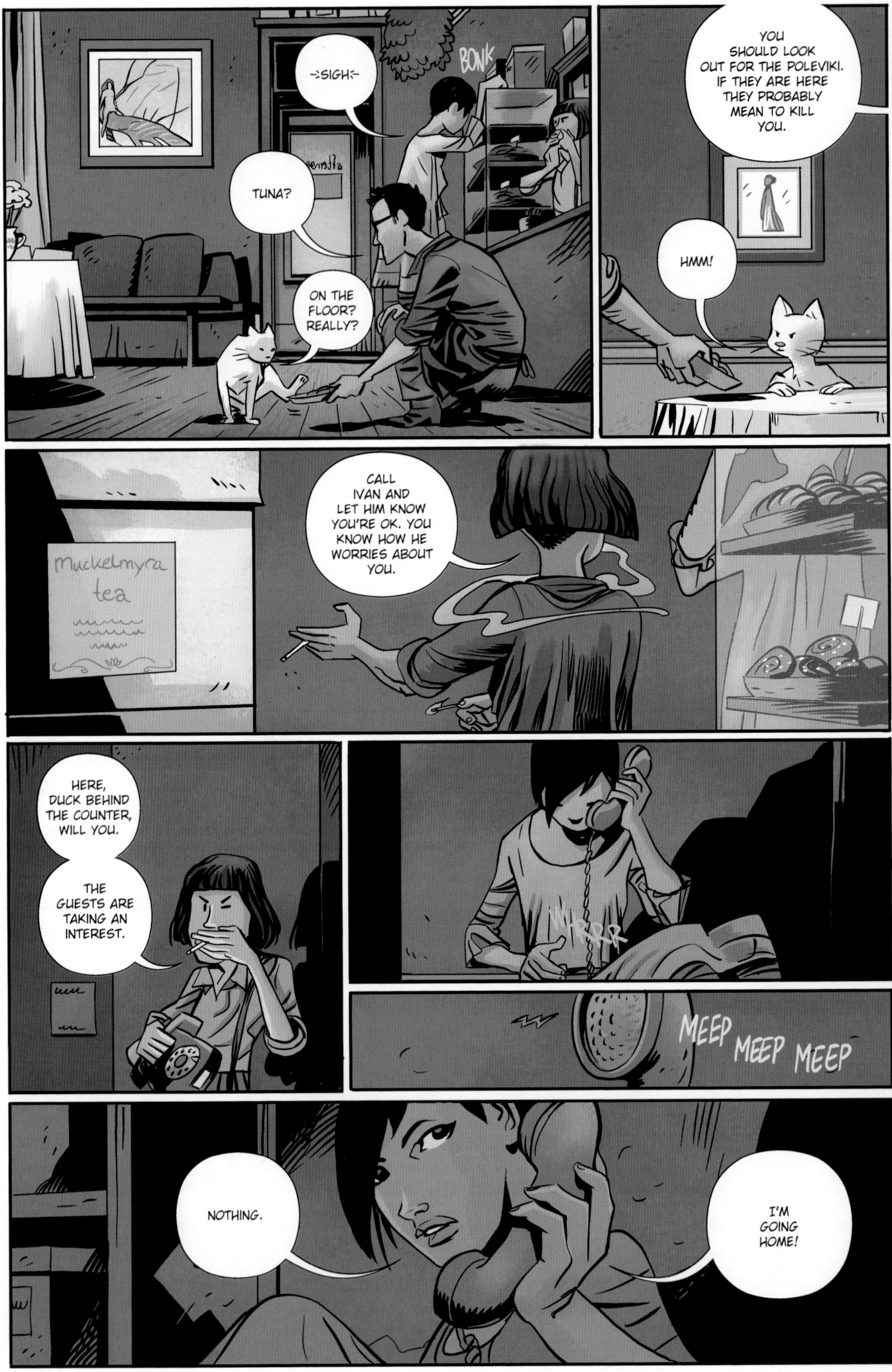
~SIGH~
BONK
TUNA?
ON THE FLOOR? REALLY?
YOU SHOULD LOOK OUT FOR THE POLEVIKI. IF THEY ARE HERE THEY PROBABLY MEAN TO KILL YOU.
HMM!
muckelmyra tea
CALL IVAN AND LET HIM KNOW YOU'RE OK. YOU KNOW HOW HE WORRIES ABOUT YOU.
HERE, DUCK BEHIND THE COUNTER, WILL YOU.
THE GUESTS ARE TAKING AN INTEREST.
WHRRR
MEEP MEEP MEEP
NOTHING.
I'M GOING HOME!

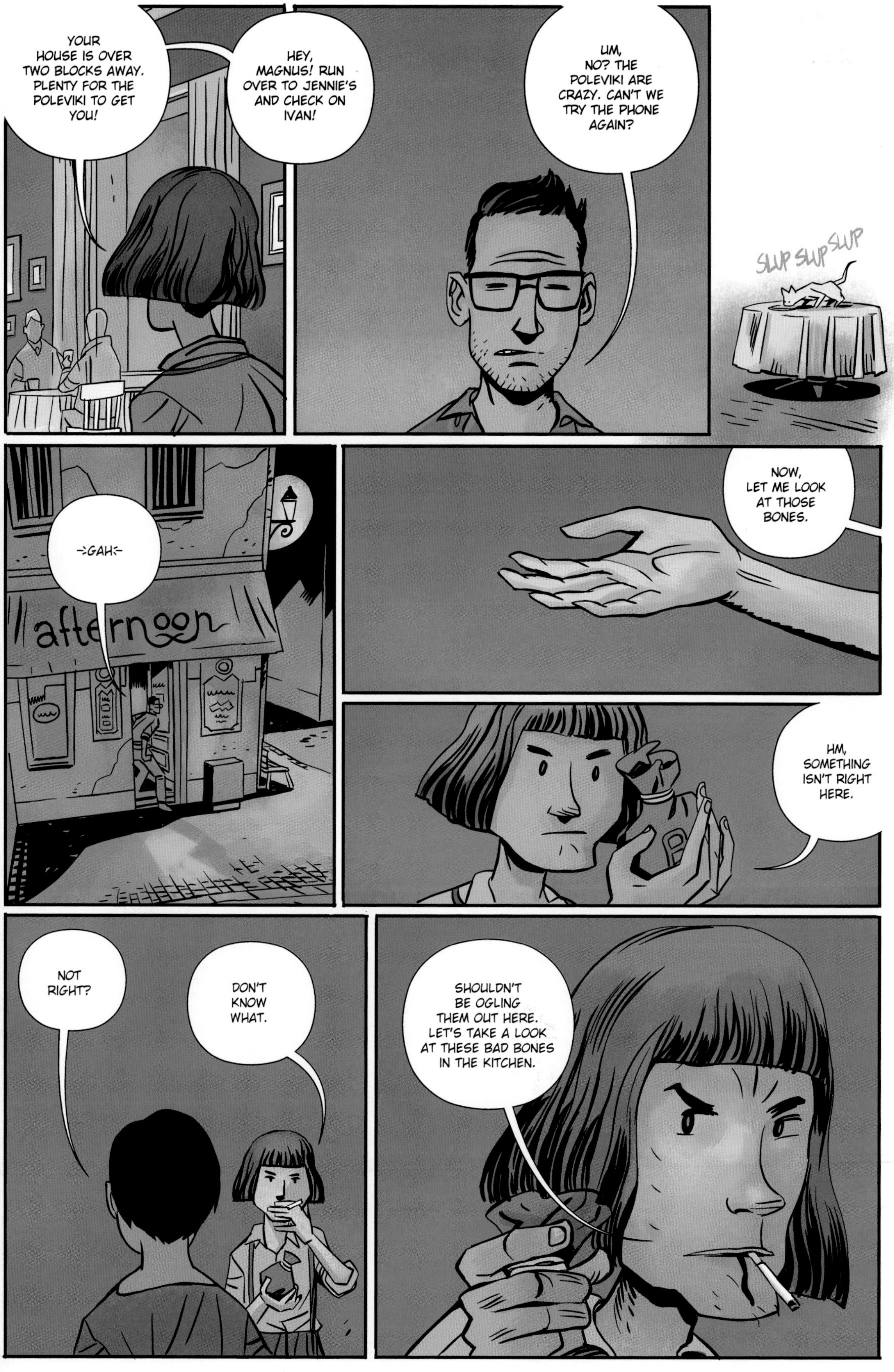
YOUR HOUSE IS OVER TWO BLOCKS AWAY. PLENTY FOR THE POLEVIKI TO GET YOU!
HEY, MAGNUS! RUN OVER TO JENNIE'S AND CHECK ON IVAN!
UM, NO? THE POLEVIKI ARE CRAZY. CAN'T WE TRY THE PHONE AGAIN?
SLUP SLUP SLUP
afternoon
-GAH-
NOW, LET ME LOOK AT THOSE BONES.
HM, SOMETHING ISN'T RIGHT HERE.
NOT RIGHT?
DON'T KNOW WHAT.
SHOULDN'T BE OGLING THEM OUT HERE. LET'S TAKE A LOOK AT THESE BAD BONES IN THE KITCHEN.

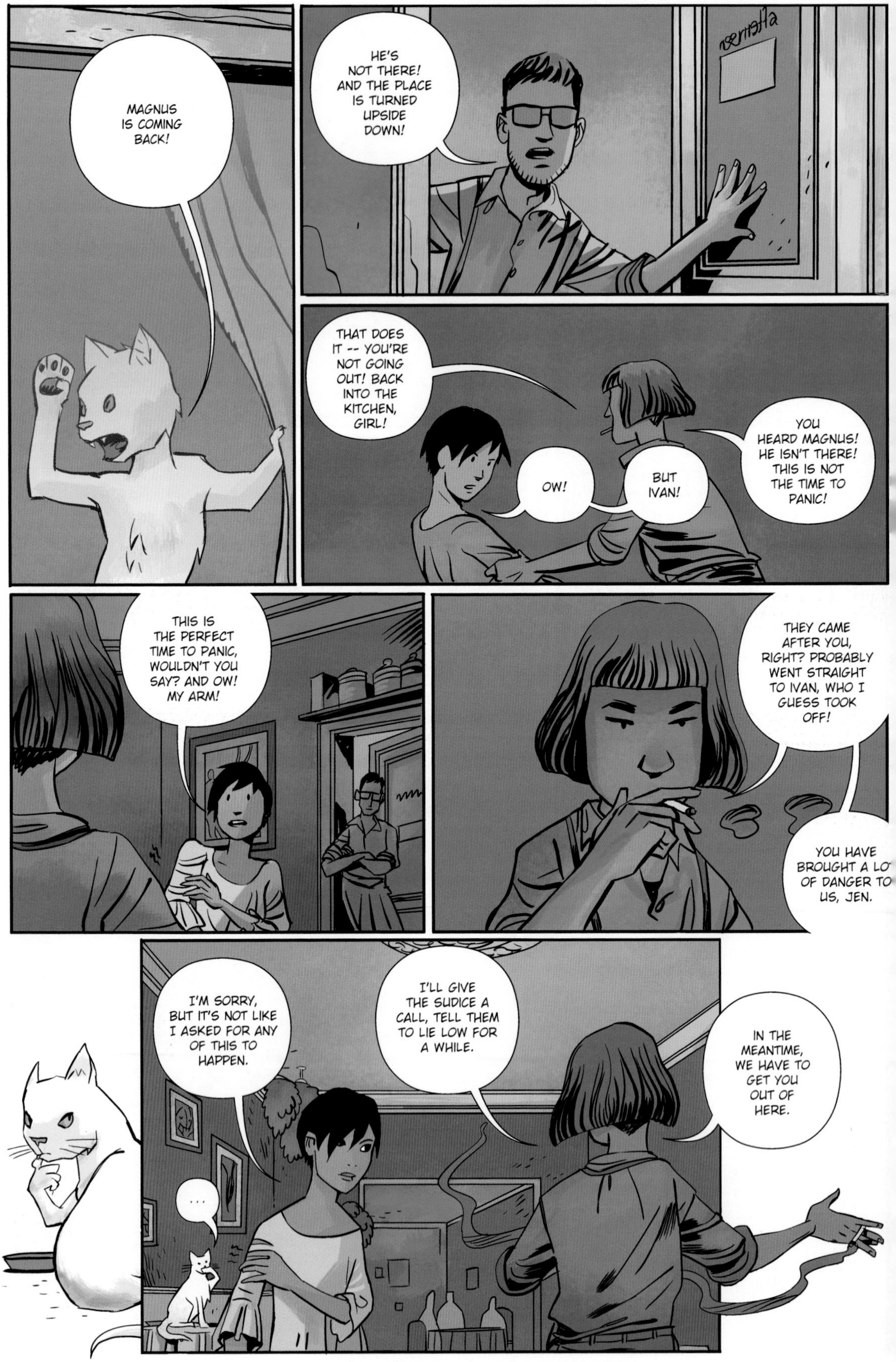
MAGNUS IS COMING BACK!
HE'S NOT THERE! AND THE PLACE IS TURNED UPSIDE DOWN!
THAT DOES IT -- YOU'RE NOT GOING OUT! BACK INTO THE KITCHEN, GIRL!
OW!
BUT IVAN!
YOU HEARD MAGNUS! HE ISN'T THERE! THIS IS NOT THE TIME TO PANIC!
THIS IS THE PERFECT TIME TO PANIC, WOULDN'T YOU SAY? AND OW! MY ARM!
THEY CAME AFTER YOU, RIGHT? PROBABLY WENT STRAIGHT TO IVAN, WHO I GUESS TOOK OFF!
YOU HAVE BROUGHT A LOT OF DANGER TO US, JEN.
I'M SORRY, BUT IT'S NOT LIKE I ASKED FOR ANY OF THIS TO HAPPEN.
I'LL GIVE THE SUDICE A CALL, TELL THEM TO LIE LOW FOR A WHILE.
IN THE MEANTIME, WE HAVE TO GET YOU OUT OF HERE.
...

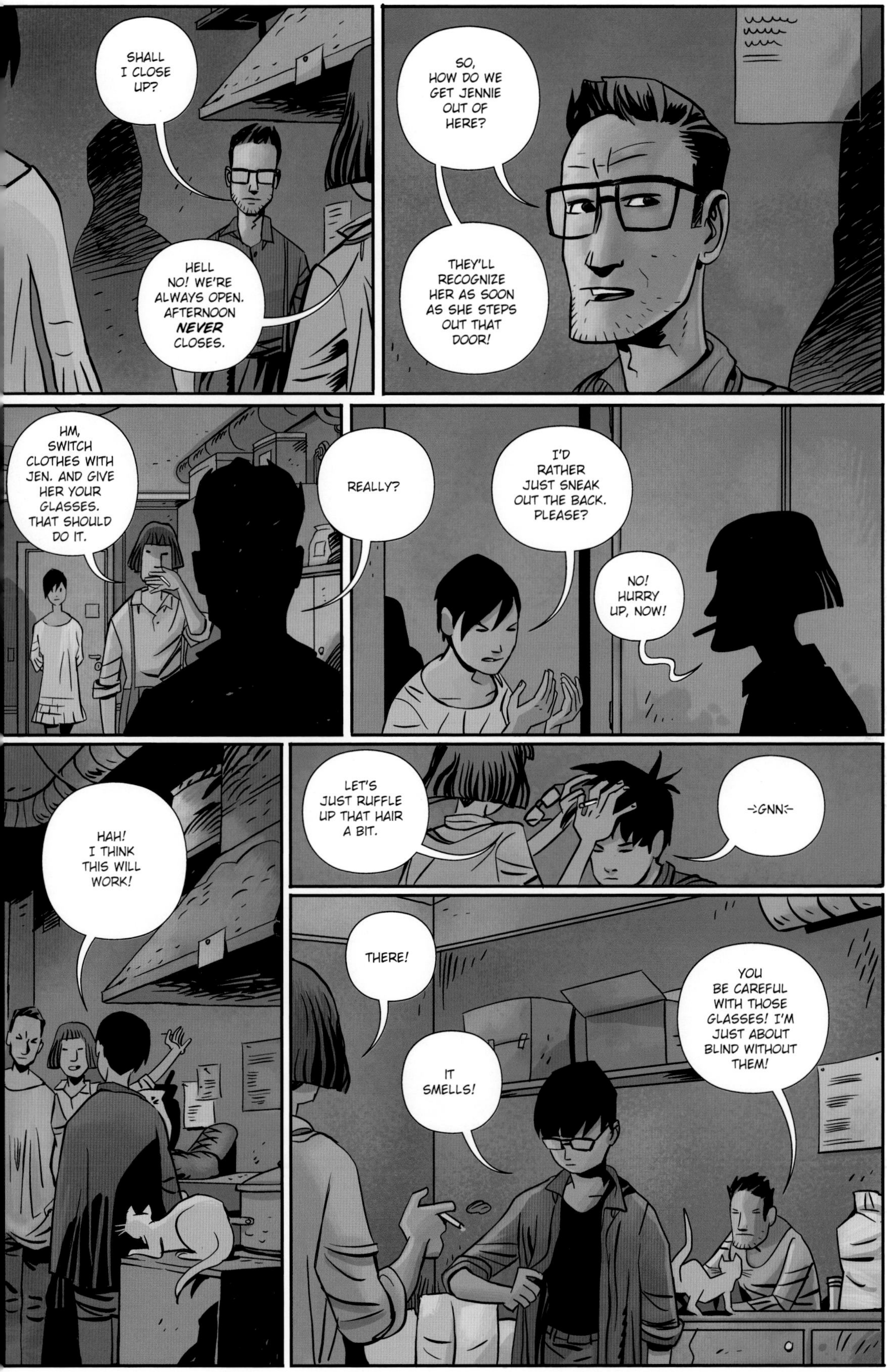
SHALL I CLOSE UP?
HELL NO! WE'RE ALWAYS OPEN. AFTERNOON **NEVER** CLOSES.
SO, HOW DO WE GET JENNIE OUT OF HERE?
THEY'LL RECOGNIZE HER AS SOON AS SHE STEPS OUT THAT DOOR!
HM, SWITCH CLOTHES WITH JEN. AND GIVE HER YOUR GLASSES. THAT SHOULD DO IT.
REALLY?
I'D RATHER JUST SNEAK OUT THE BACK. PLEASE?
NO! HURRY UP, NOW!
HAH! I THINK THIS WILL WORK!
LET'S JUST RUFFLE UP THAT HAIR A BIT.
-GNN-
THERE!
IT SMELLS!
YOU BE CAREFUL WITH THOSE GLASSES! I'M JUST ABOUT BLIND WITHOUT THEM!

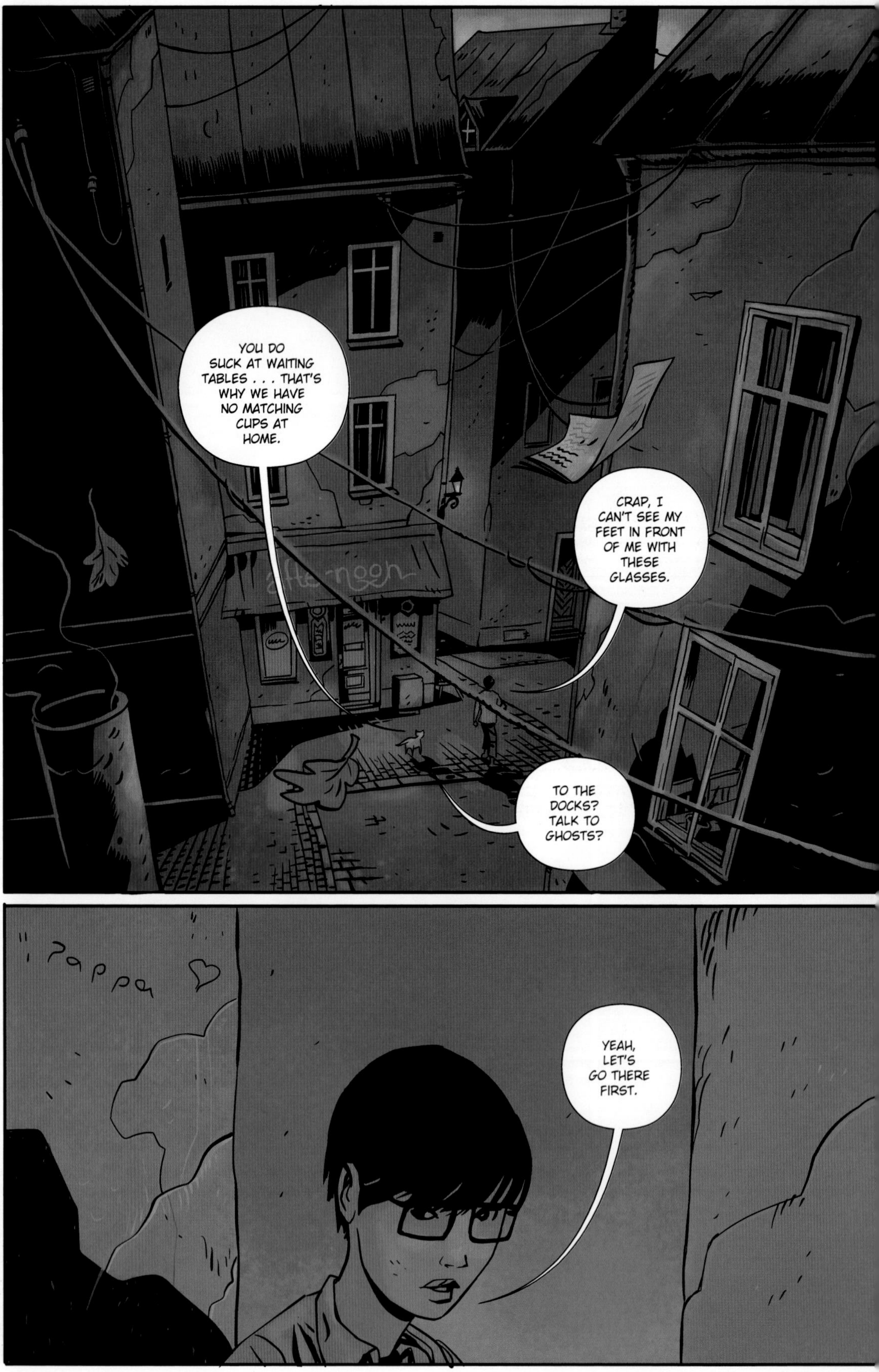
YOU DO SUCK AT WAITING TABLES . . . THAT'S WHY WE HAVE NO MATCHING CUPS AT HOME.
CRAP, I CAN'T SEE MY FEET IN FRONT OF ME WITH THESE GLASSES.
TO THE DOCKS? TALK TO GHOSTS?
YEAH, LET'S GO THERE FIRST.

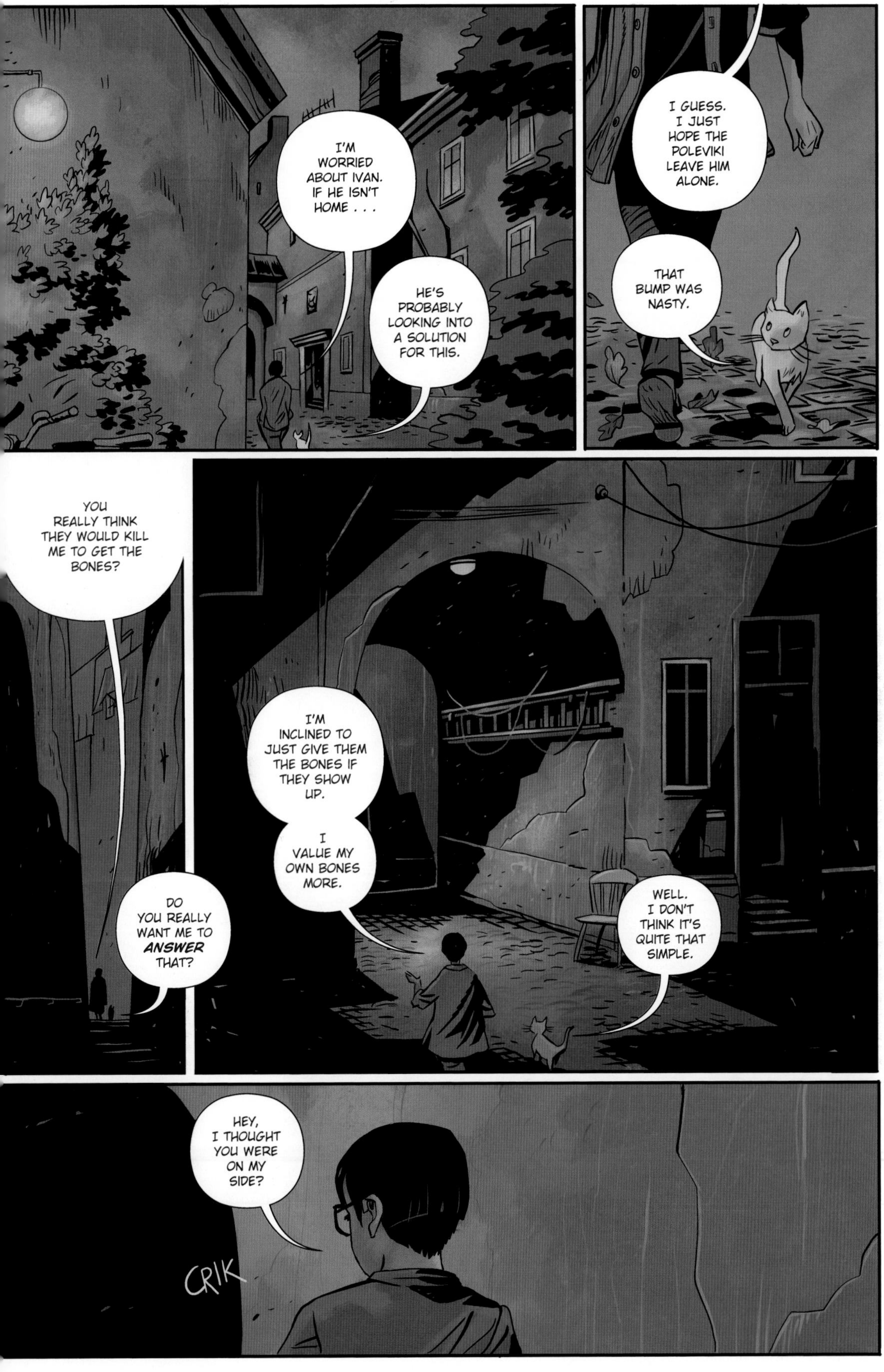
I'M WORRIED ABOUT IVAN. IF HE ISN'T HOME . . .
HE'S PROBABLY LOOKING INTO A SOLUTION FOR THIS.
I GUESS. I JUST HOPE THE POLEVIKI LEAVE HIM ALONE.
THAT BUMP WAS NASTY.
YOU REALLY THINK THEY WOULD KILL ME TO GET THE BONES?
DO YOU REALLY WANT ME TO ***ANSWER*** THAT?
I'M INCLINED TO JUST GIVE THEM THE BONES IF THEY SHOW UP.
I VALUE MY OWN BONES MORE.
WELL. I DON'T THINK IT'S QUITE THAT SIMPLE.
HEY, I THOUGHT YOU WERE ON MY SIDE?
CRIK

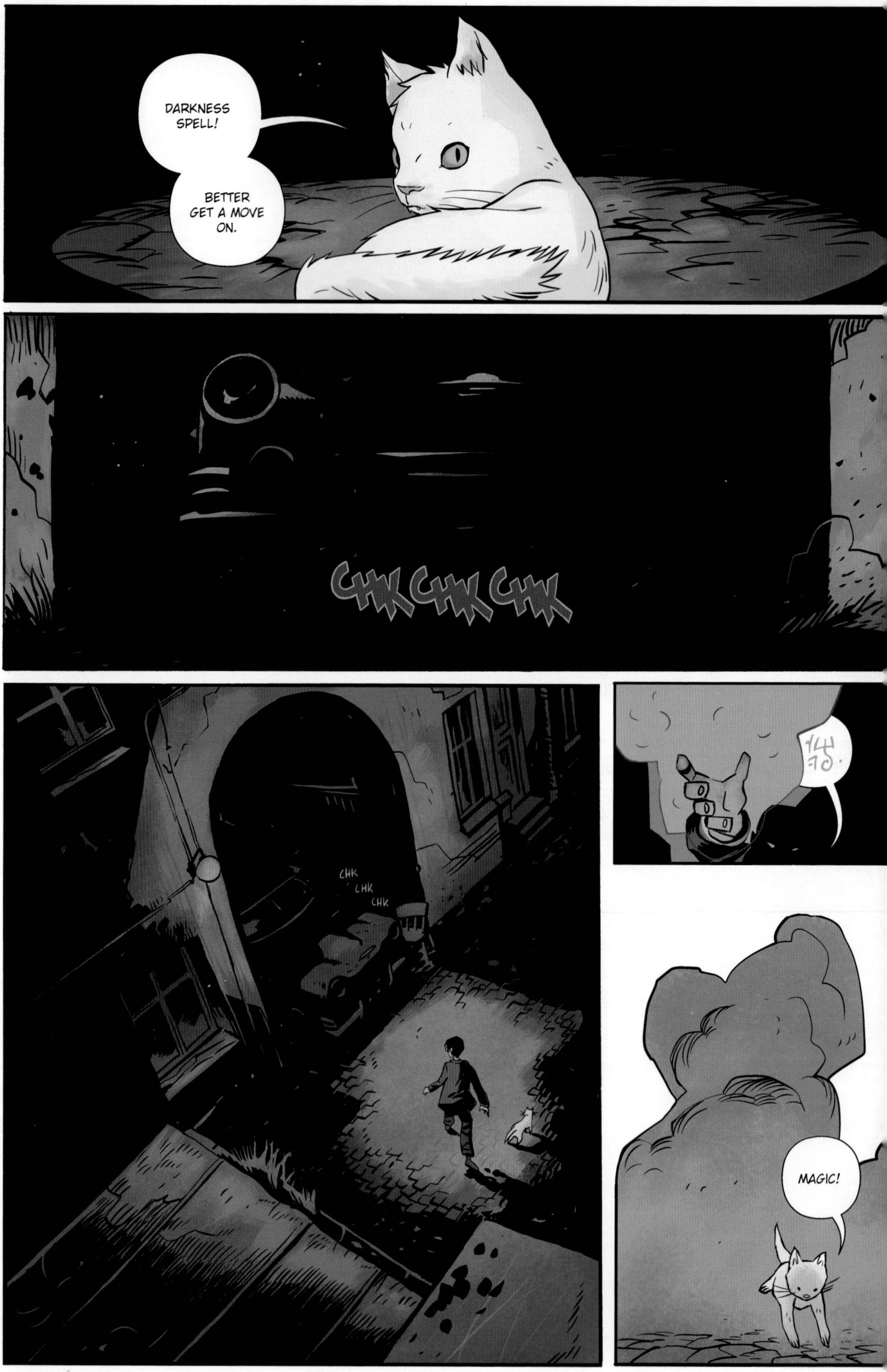
DARKNESS SPELL!
BETTER GET A MOVE ON.
CHK CHK CHK
CHK CHK CHK
MAGIC!

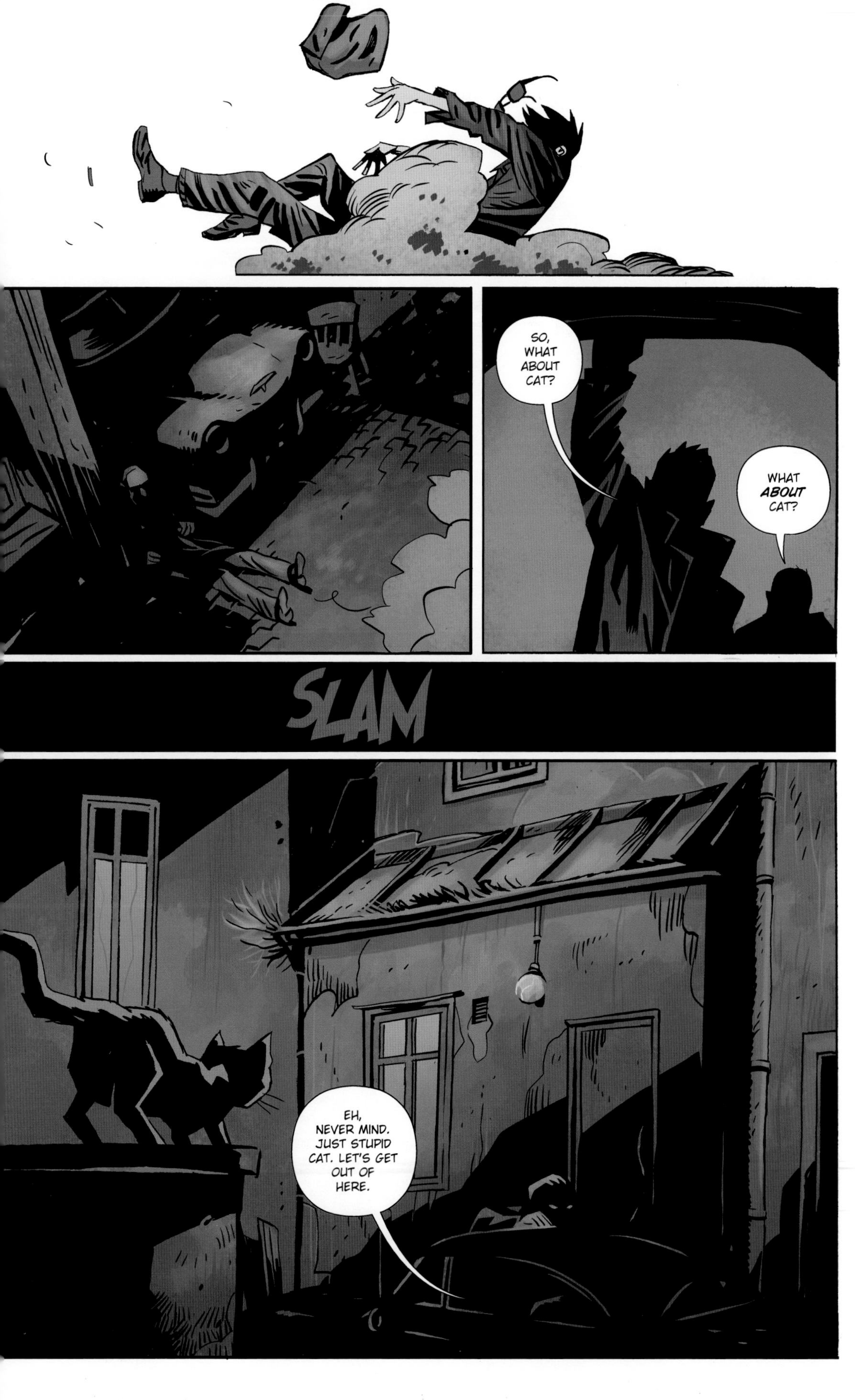
SO, WHAT ABOUT CAT?
WHAT ABOUT CAT?
SLAM
EH, NEVER MIND. JUST STUPID CAT. LET'S GET OUT OF HERE.

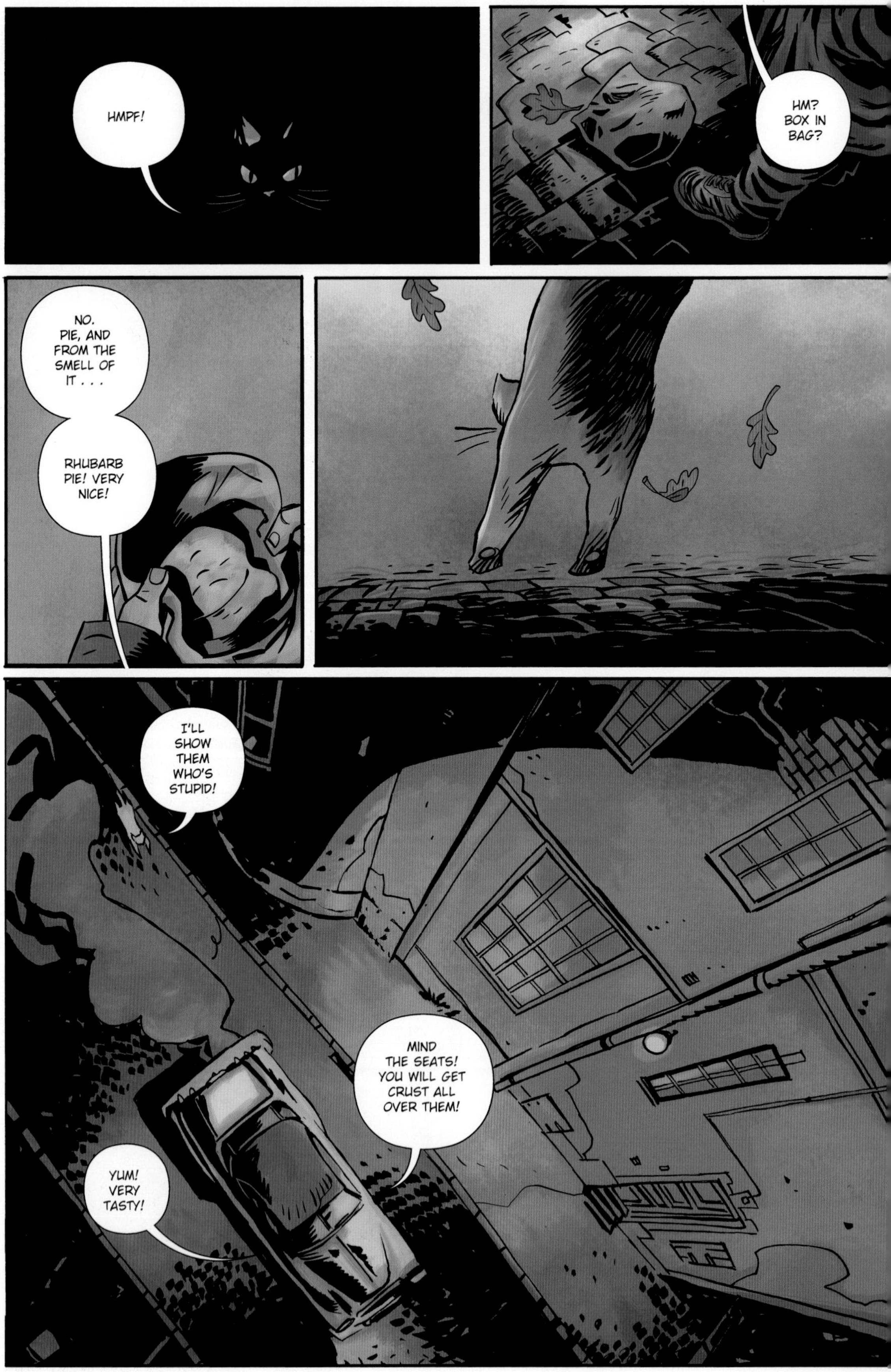
HMPF!
HM? BOX IN BAG?
NO. PIE, AND FROM THE SMELL OF IT . . .
RHUBARB PIE! VERY NICE!
I'LL SHOW THEM WHO'S STUPID!
MIND THE SEATS! YOU WILL GET CRUST ALL OVER THEM!
YUM! VERY TASTY!

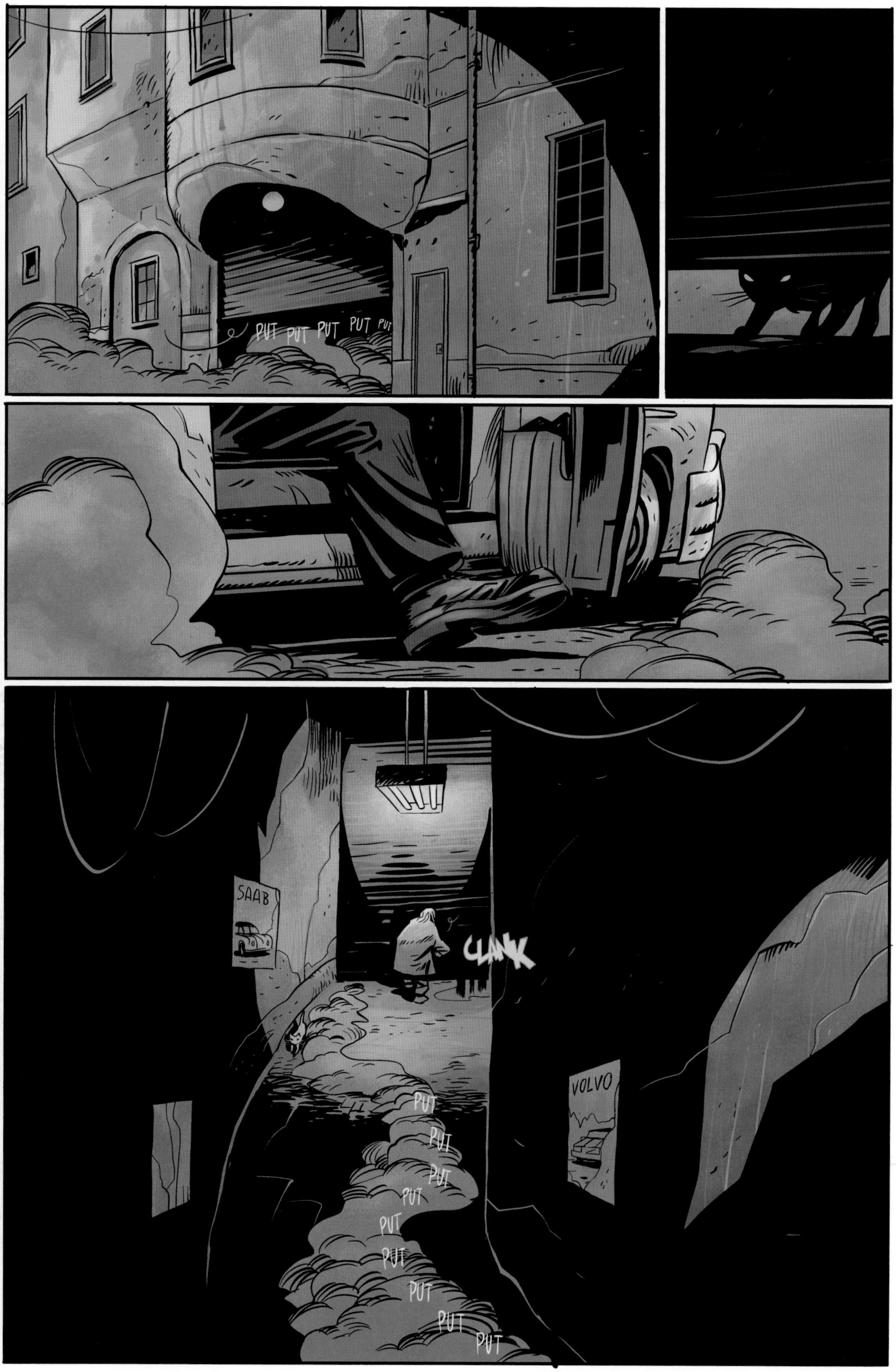

PUT PUT PUT PUT PUT
SAAB
CLANK
VOLVO
PUT
PUT
PUT
PUT
PUT
PUT
PUT
PUT
PUT

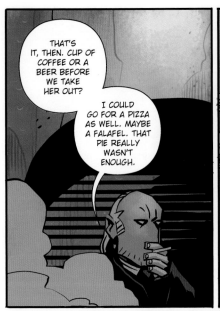

THAT'S IT, THEN. CUP OF COFFEE OR A BEER BEFORE WE TAKE HER OUT?

I COULD GO FOR A PIZZA AS WELL. MAYBE A FALAFEL. THAT PIE REALLY WASN'T ENOUGH.

AND WHO SERVES RHUBARB PIE WITHOUT PASTRY CUSTARD?

YAOW!

BLOODY CAT! GET IT OFF ME!

GAH!

MIAO!

THIS IS NOT OVER! YOU *OPEN* THAT TRUNK!

OR I WILL UNLEASH *THE FURY!*

OW!

EASY THERE, CAT! YOU WINGED HIM. HE GOT MESSAGE. RELAX.

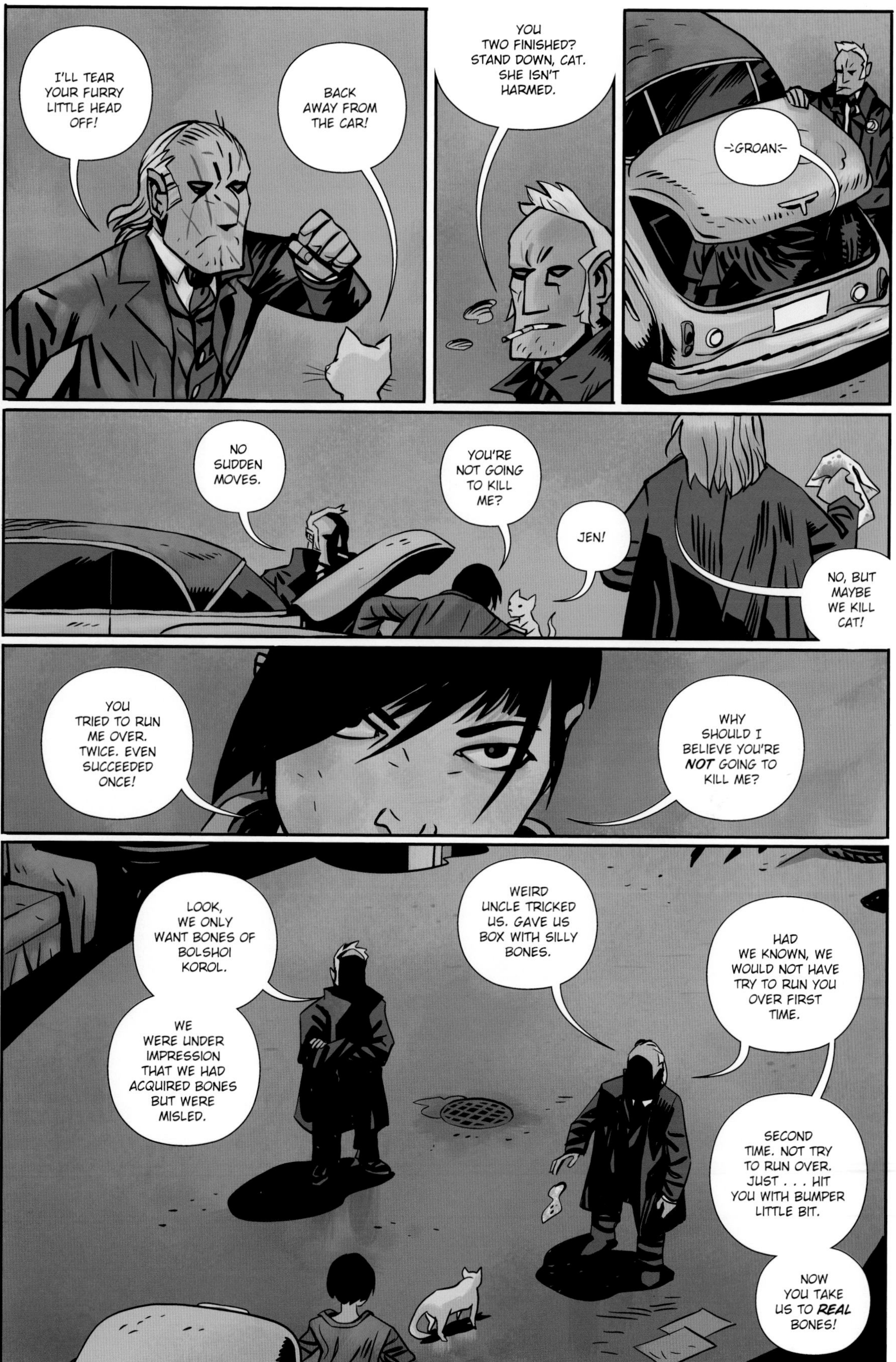
I'LL TEAR YOUR FURRY LITTLE HEAD OFF!
BACK AWAY FROM THE CAR!
YOU TWO FINISHED? STAND DOWN, CAT. SHE ISN'T HARMED.
-GROAN-
NO SUDDEN MOVES.
YOU'RE NOT GOING TO KILL ME?
JEN!
NO, BUT MAYBE WE KILL CAT!
YOU TRIED TO RUN ME OVER. TWICE. EVEN SUCCEEDED ONCE!
WHY SHOULD I BELIEVE YOU'RE NOT GOING TO KILL ME?
LOOK, WE ONLY WANT BONES OF BOLSHOI KOROL.
WE WERE UNDER IMPRESSION THAT WE HAD ACQUIRED BONES BUT WERE MISLED.
WEIRD UNCLE TRICKED US. GAVE US BOX WITH SILLY BONES.
HAD WE KNOWN, WE WOULD NOT HAVE TRY TO RUN YOU OVER FIRST TIME.
SECOND TIME. NOT TRY TO RUN OVER. JUST . . . HIT YOU WITH BUMPER LITTLE BIT.
NOW YOU TAKE US TO REAL BONES!

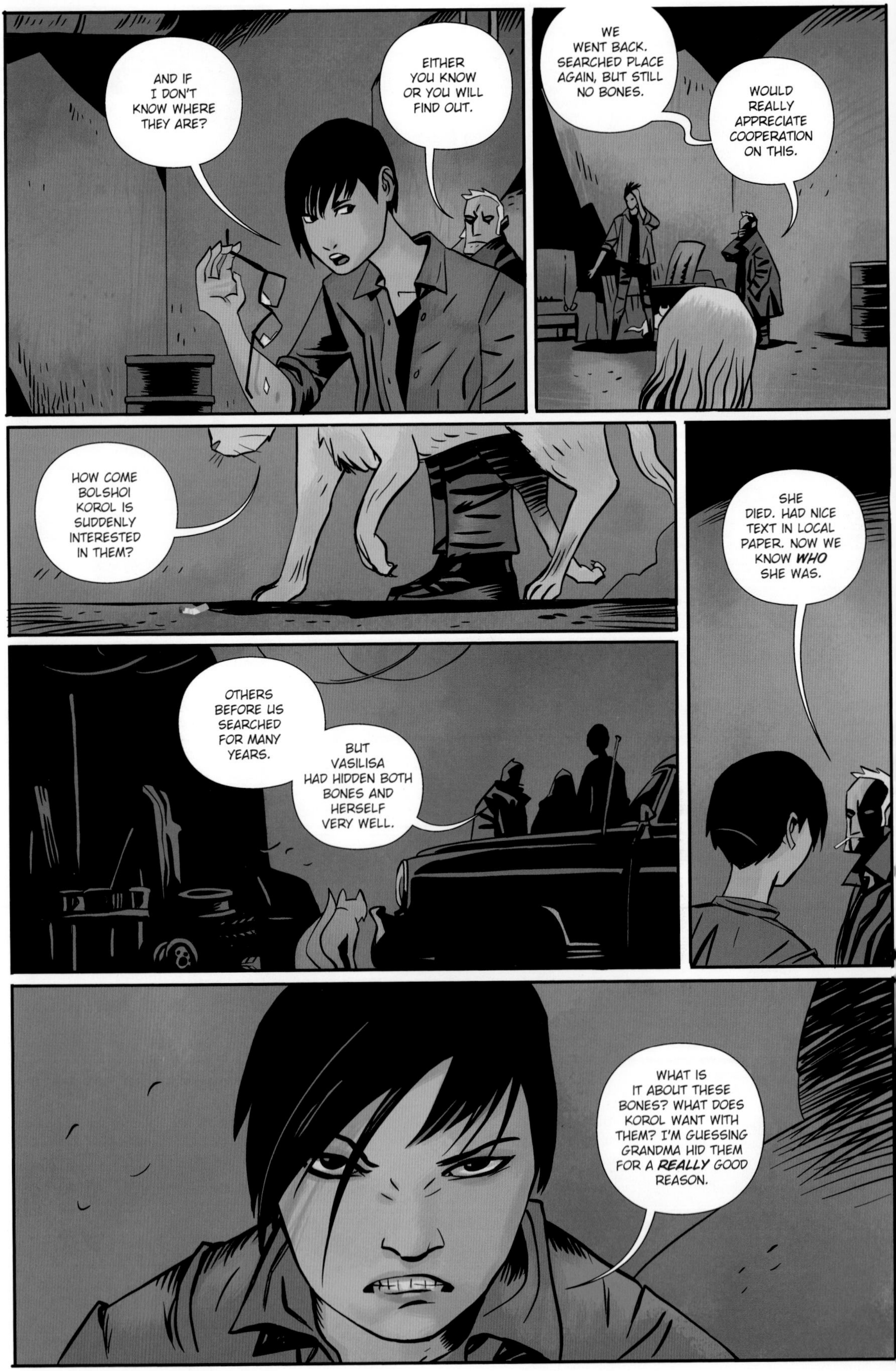
AND IF I DON'T KNOW WHERE THEY ARE?
EITHER YOU KNOW OR YOU WILL FIND OUT.
WE WENT BACK. SEARCHED PLACE AGAIN, BUT STILL NO BONES.
WOULD REALLY APPRECIATE COOPERATION ON THIS.
HOW COME BOLSHOI KOROL IS SUDDENLY INTERESTED IN THEM?
SHE DIED. HAD NICE TEXT IN LOCAL PAPER. NOW WE KNOW WHO SHE WAS.
OTHERS BEFORE US SEARCHED FOR MANY YEARS.
BUT VASILISA HAD HIDDEN BOTH BONES AND HERSELF VERY WELL.
WHAT IS IT ABOUT THESE BONES? WHAT DOES KOROL WANT WITH THEM? I'M GUESSING GRANDMA HID THEM FOR A REALLY GOOD REASON.

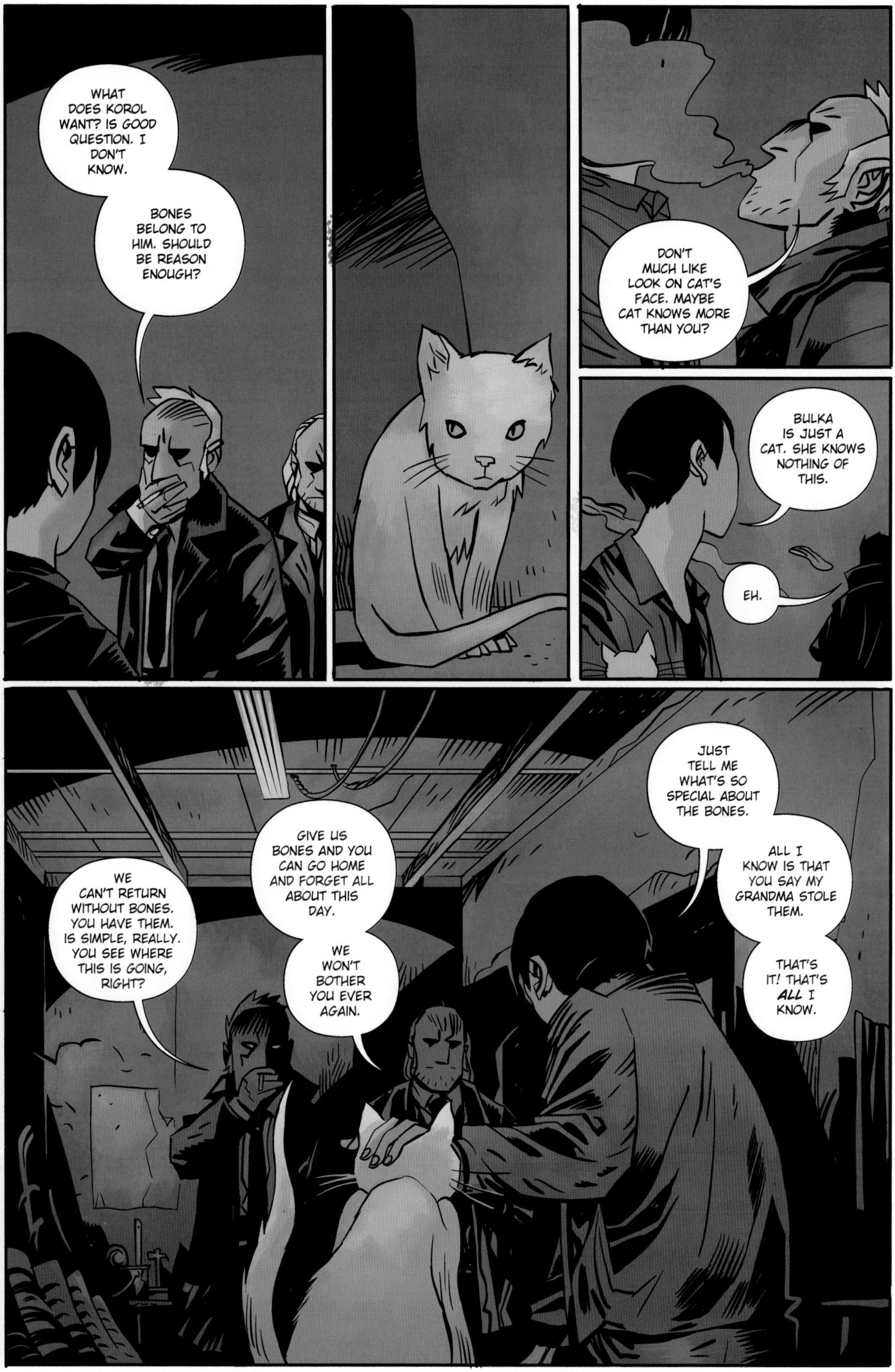
WHAT DOES KOROL WANT? IS GOOD QUESTION. I DON'T KNOW.
BONES BELONG TO HIM. SHOULD BE REASON ENOUGH?
DON'T MUCH LIKE LOOK ON CAT'S FACE. MAYBE CAT KNOWS MORE THAN YOU?
BULKA IS JUST A CAT. SHE KNOWS NOTHING OF THIS.
EH.
JUST TELL ME WHAT'S SO SPECIAL ABOUT THE BONES.
ALL I KNOW IS THAT YOU SAY MY GRANDMA STOLE THEM.
THAT'S IT! THAT'S ALL I KNOW.
WE CAN'T RETURN WITHOUT BONES. YOU HAVE THEM. IS SIMPLE, REALLY. YOU SEE WHERE THIS IS GOING, RIGHT?
GIVE US BONES AND YOU CAN GO HOME AND FORGET ALL ABOUT THIS DAY.
WE WON'T BOTHER YOU EVER AGAIN.

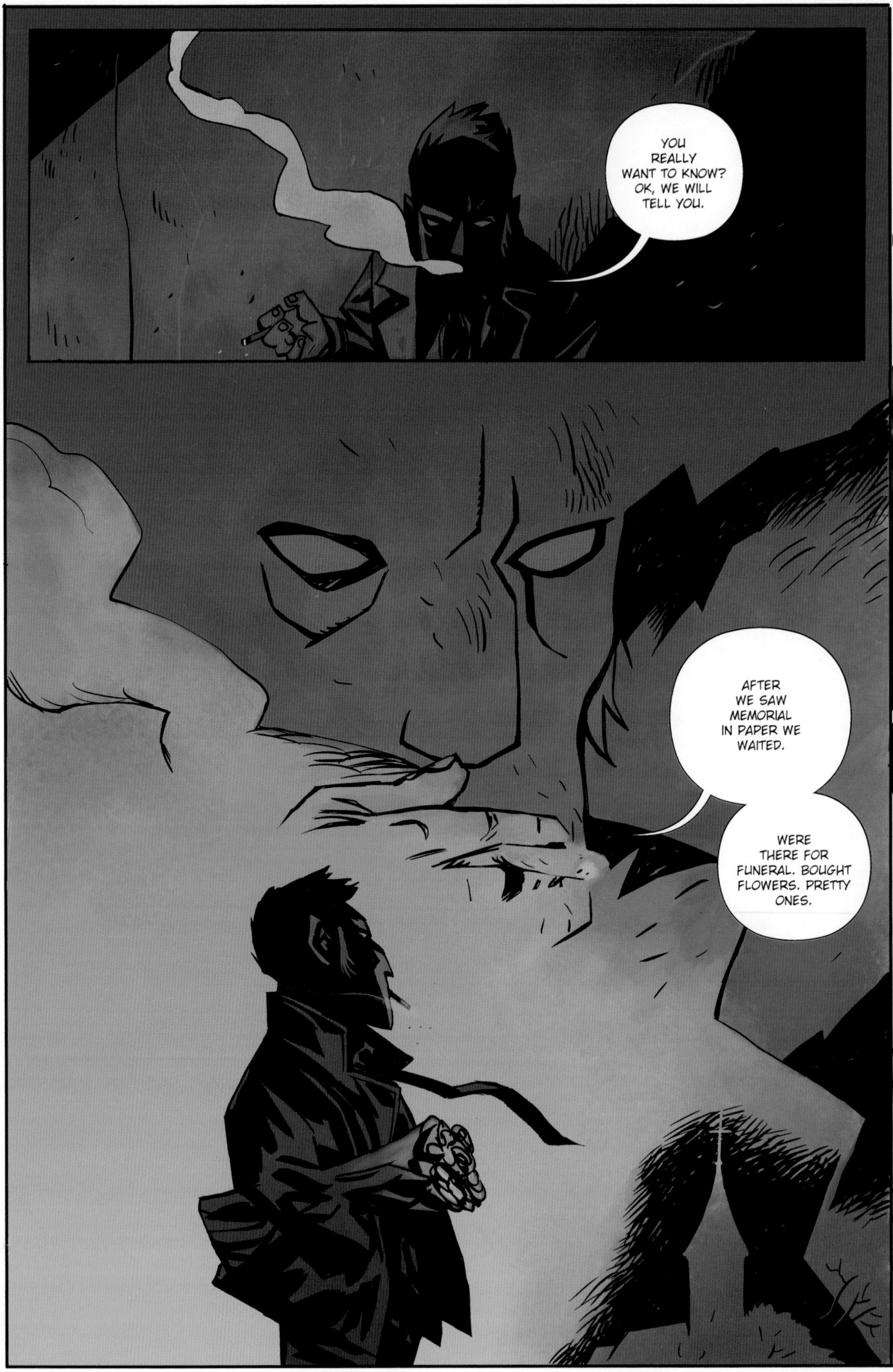
YOU REALLY WANT TO KNOW? OK, WE WILL TELL YOU.
AFTER WE SAW MEMORIAL IN PAPER WE WAITED.
WERE THERE FOR FUNERAL. BOUGHT FLOWERS. PRETTY ONES.

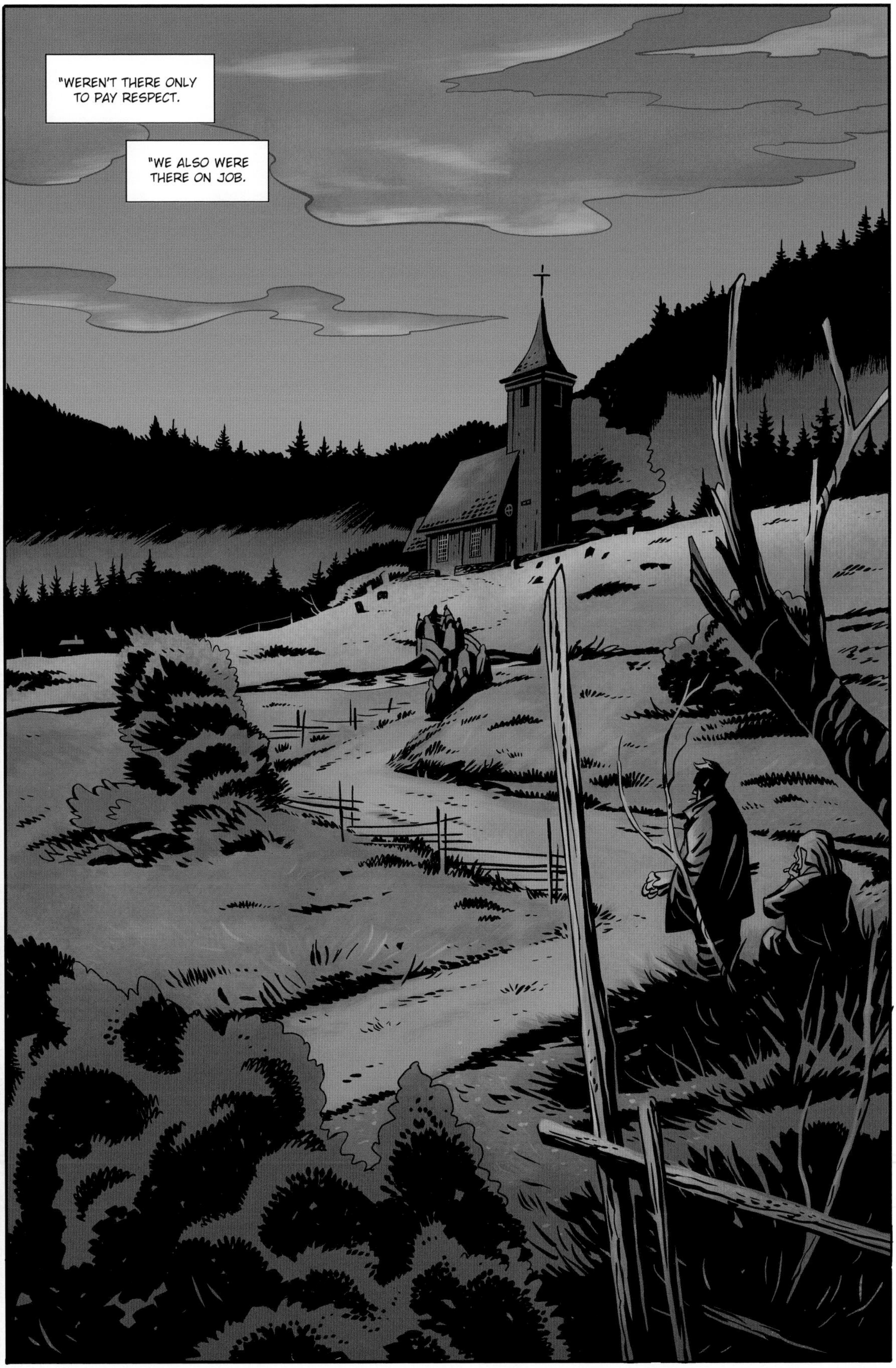
"WEREN'T THERE ONLY TO PAY RESPECT.
"WE ALSO WERE THERE ON JOB.

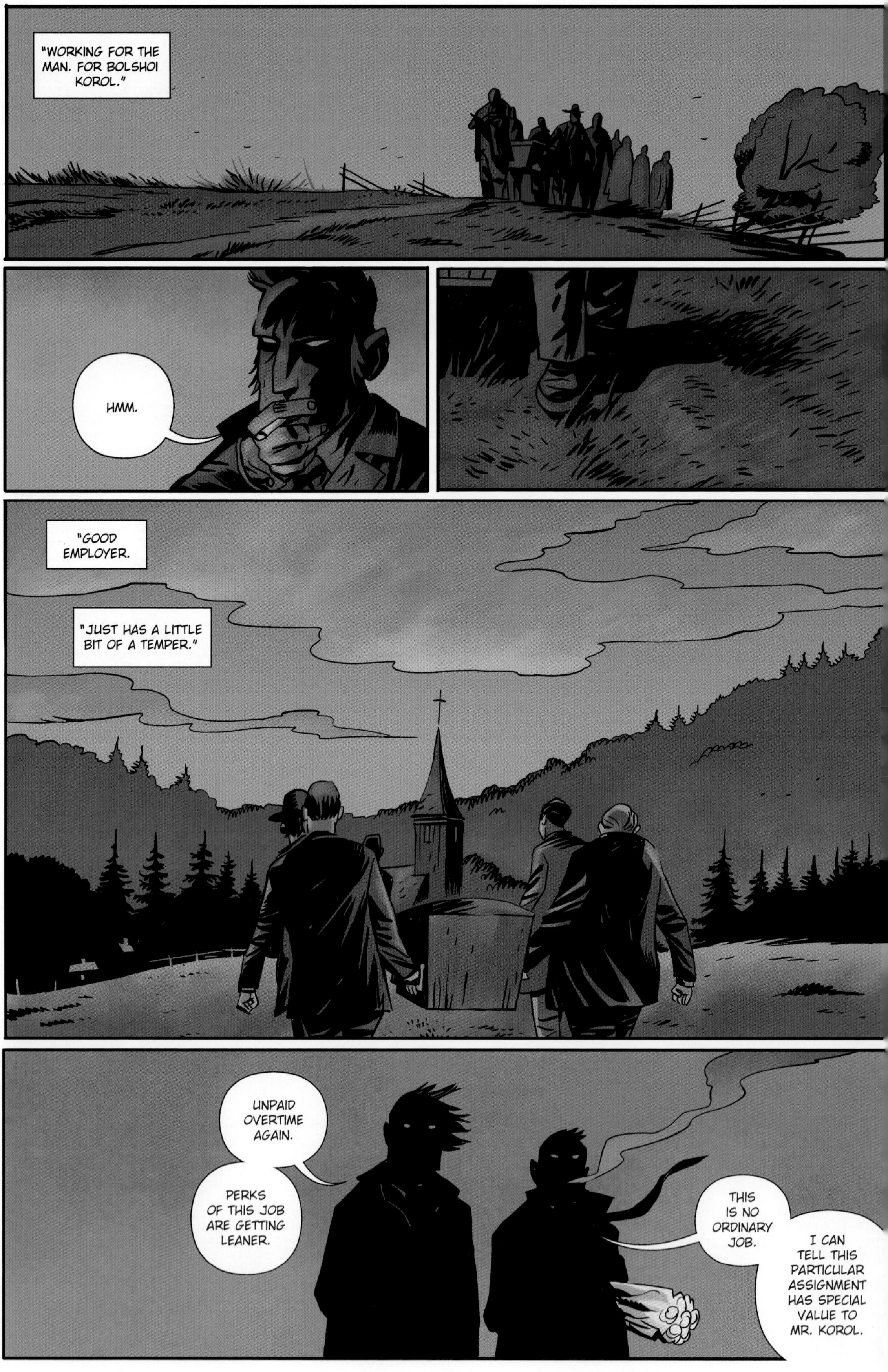
"WORKING FOR THE MAN. FOR BOLSHOI KOROL."
HMM.
"GOOD EMPLOYER.
"JUST HAS A LITTLE BIT OF A TEMPER."
UNPAID OVERTIME AGAIN.
PERKS OF THIS JOB ARE GETTING LEANER.
THIS IS NO ORDINARY JOB.
I CAN TELL THIS PARTICULAR ASSIGNMENT HAS SPECIAL VALUE TO MR. KOROL.

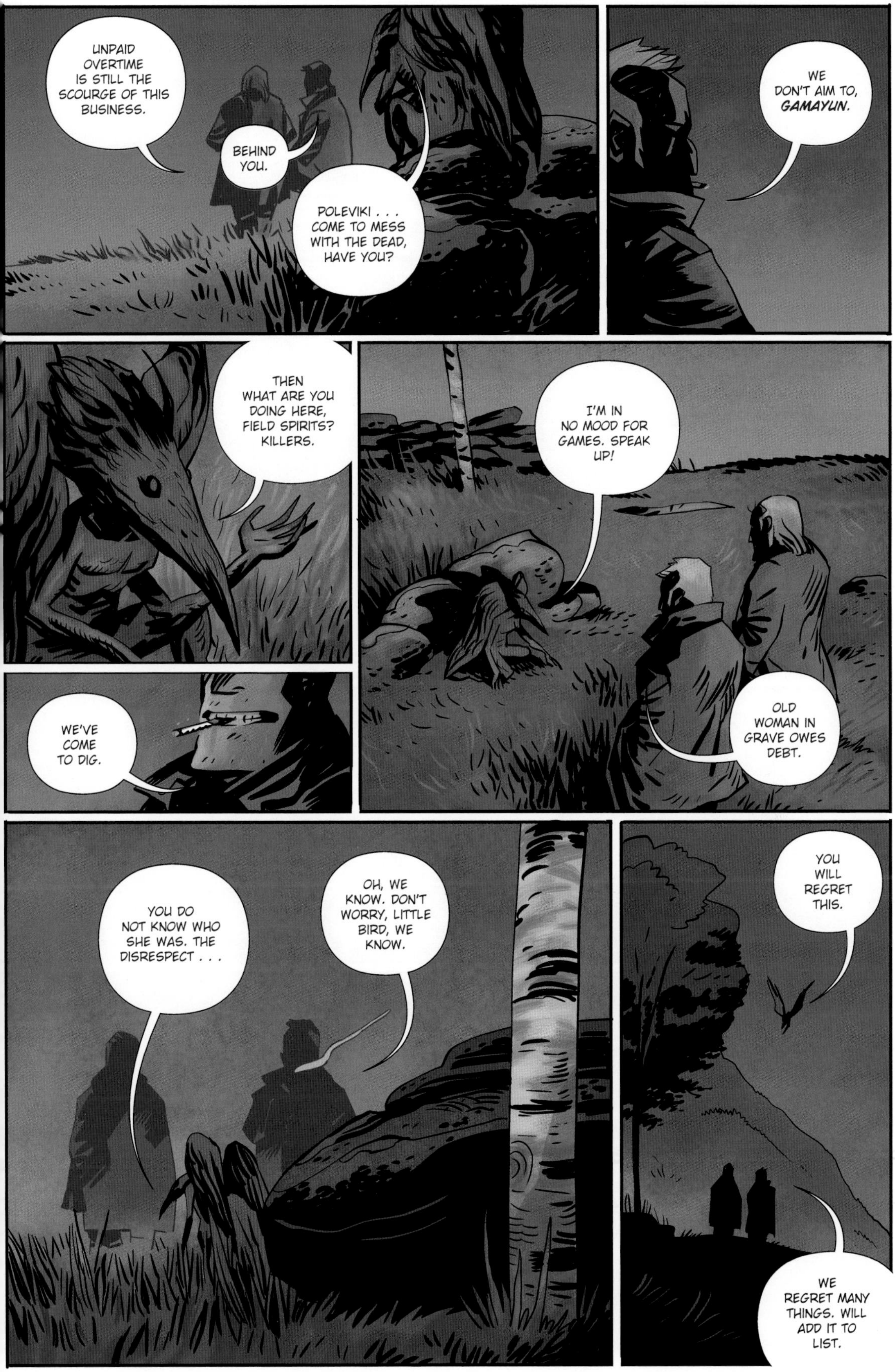
UNPAID OVERTIME IS STILL THE SCOURGE OF THIS BUSINESS.
BEHIND YOU.
POLEVIKI . . . COME TO MESS WITH THE DEAD, HAVE YOU?
WE DON'T AIM TO, GAMAYUN.
THEN WHAT ARE YOU DOING HERE, FIELD SPIRITS? KILLERS.
WE'VE COME TO DIG.
I'M IN NO MOOD FOR GAMES. SPEAK UP!
OLD WOMAN IN GRAVE OWES DEBT.
YOU DO NOT KNOW WHO SHE WAS. THE DISRESPECT . . .
OH, WE KNOW. DON'T WORRY, LITTLE BIRD, WE KNOW.
YOU WILL REGRET THIS.
WE REGRET MANY THINGS. WILL ADD IT TO LIST.

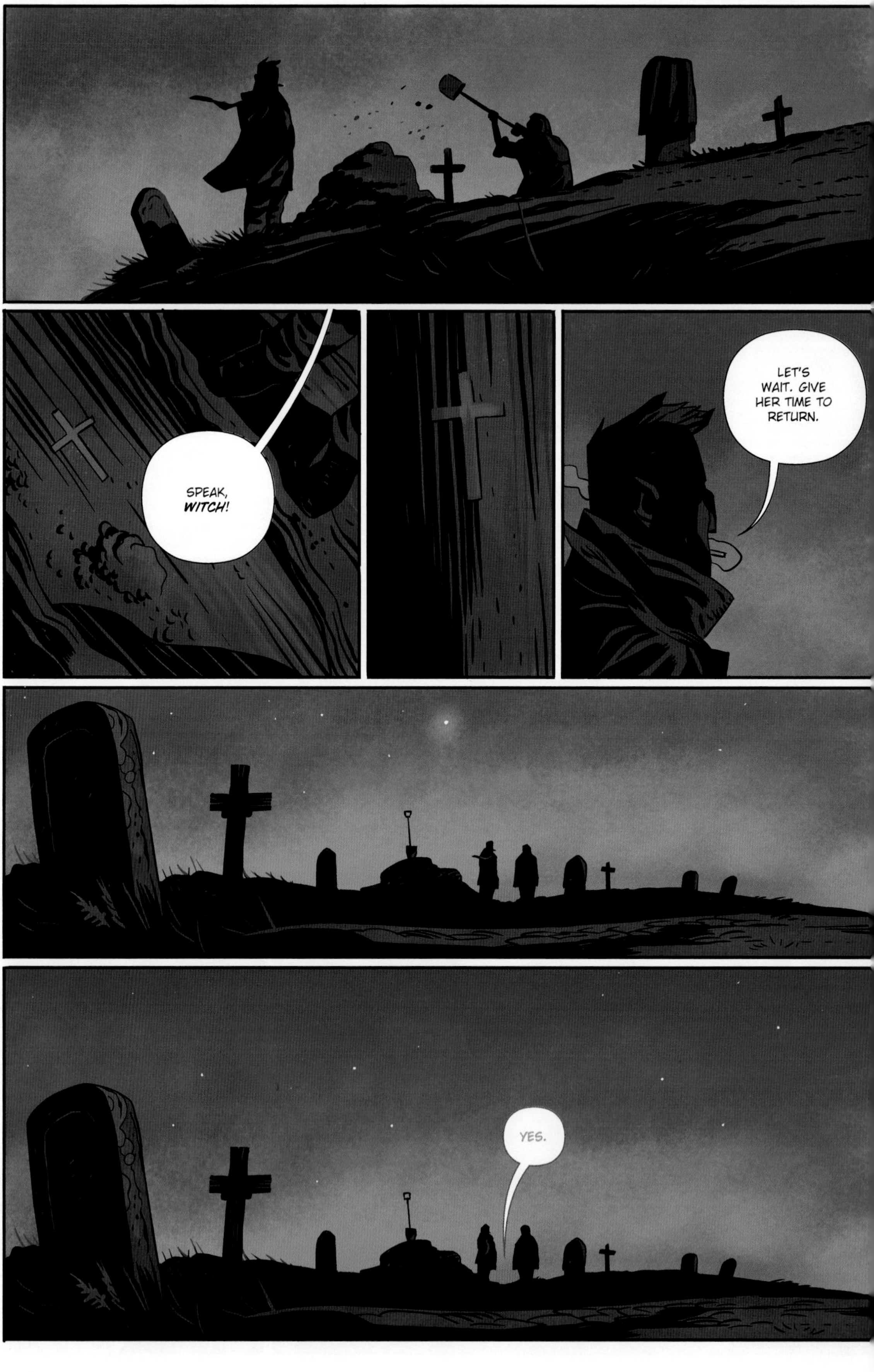
SPEAK, WITCH!
LET'S WAIT. GIVE HER TIME TO RETURN.
YES.

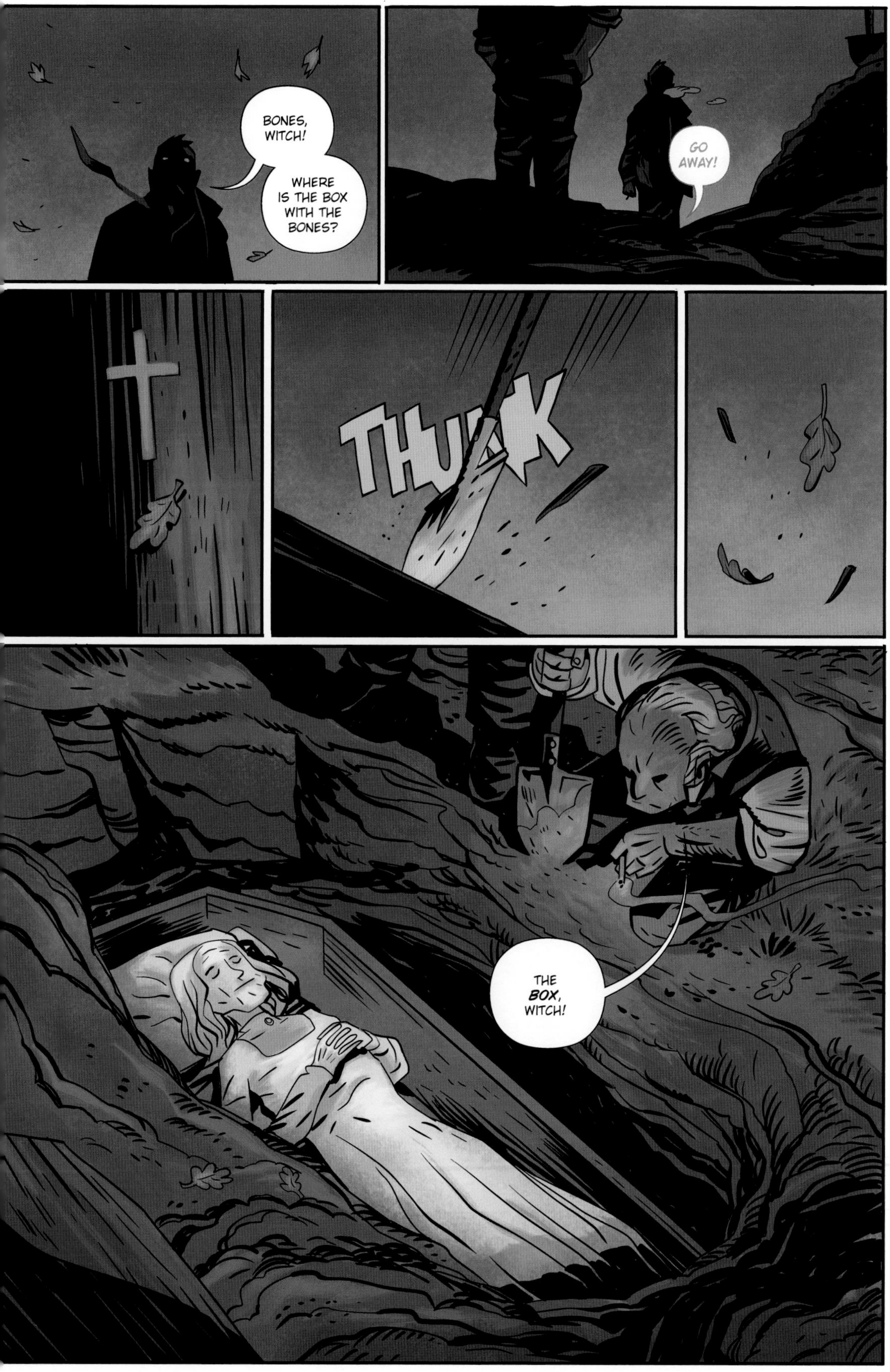
BONES, WITCH!
WHERE IS THE BOX WITH THE BONES?
GO AWAY!
THUNK
THE *BOX*, WITCH!

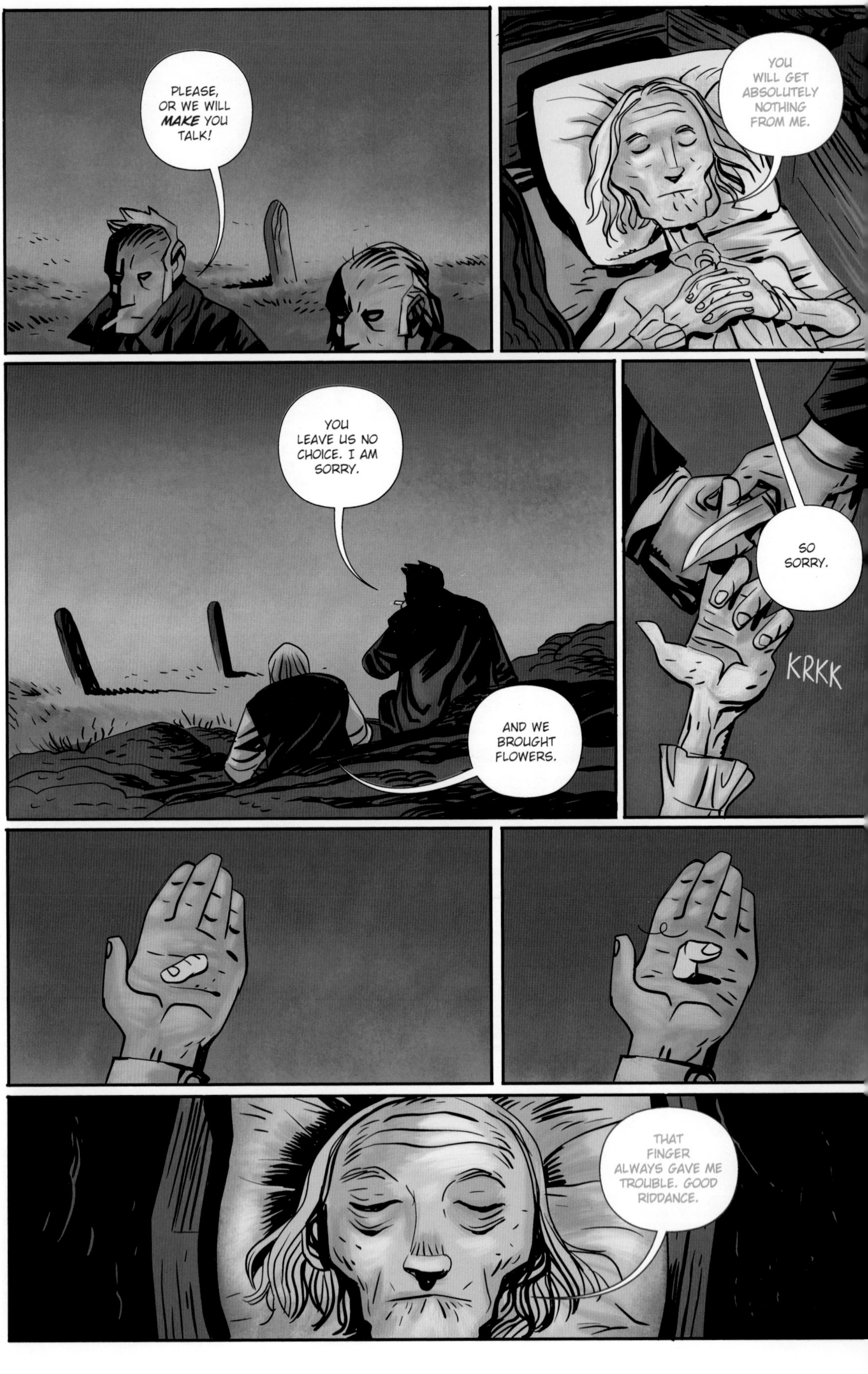
PLEASE, OR WE WILL MAKE YOU TALK!
YOU WILL GET ABSOLUTELY NOTHING FROM ME.
YOU LEAVE US NO CHOICE. I AM SORRY.
AND WE BROUGHT FLOWERS.
SO SORRY.
KRKK
THAT FINGER ALWAYS GAVE ME TROUBLE. GOOD RIDDANCE.

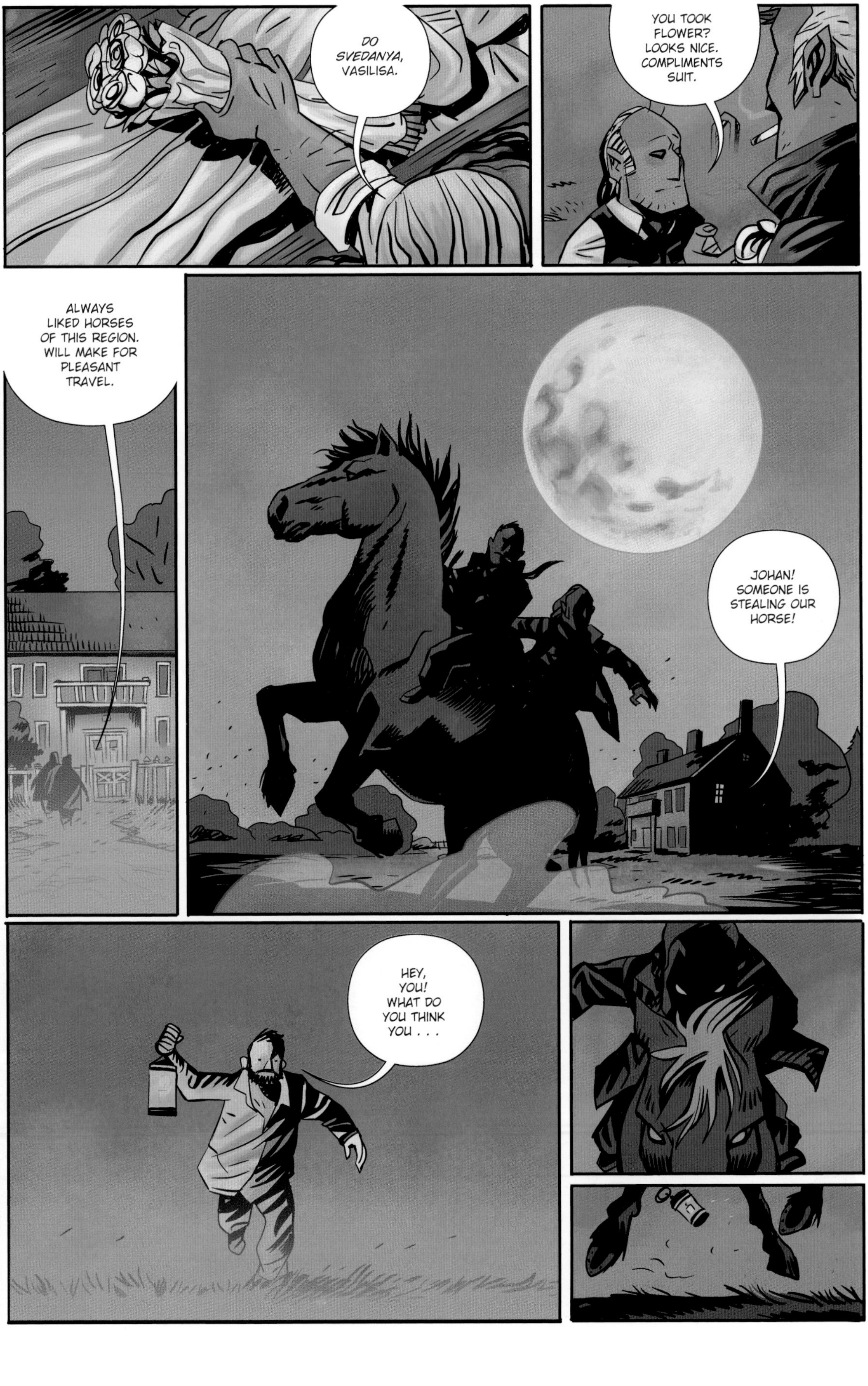
DO SVEDANYA, VASILISA.
YOU TOOK FLOWER? LOOKS NICE. COMPLIMENTS SUIT.
ALWAYS LIKED HORSES OF THIS REGION. WILL MAKE FOR PLEASANT TRAVEL.
JOHAN! SOMEONE IS STEALING OUR HORSE!
HEY, YOU! WHAT DO YOU THINK YOU . . .

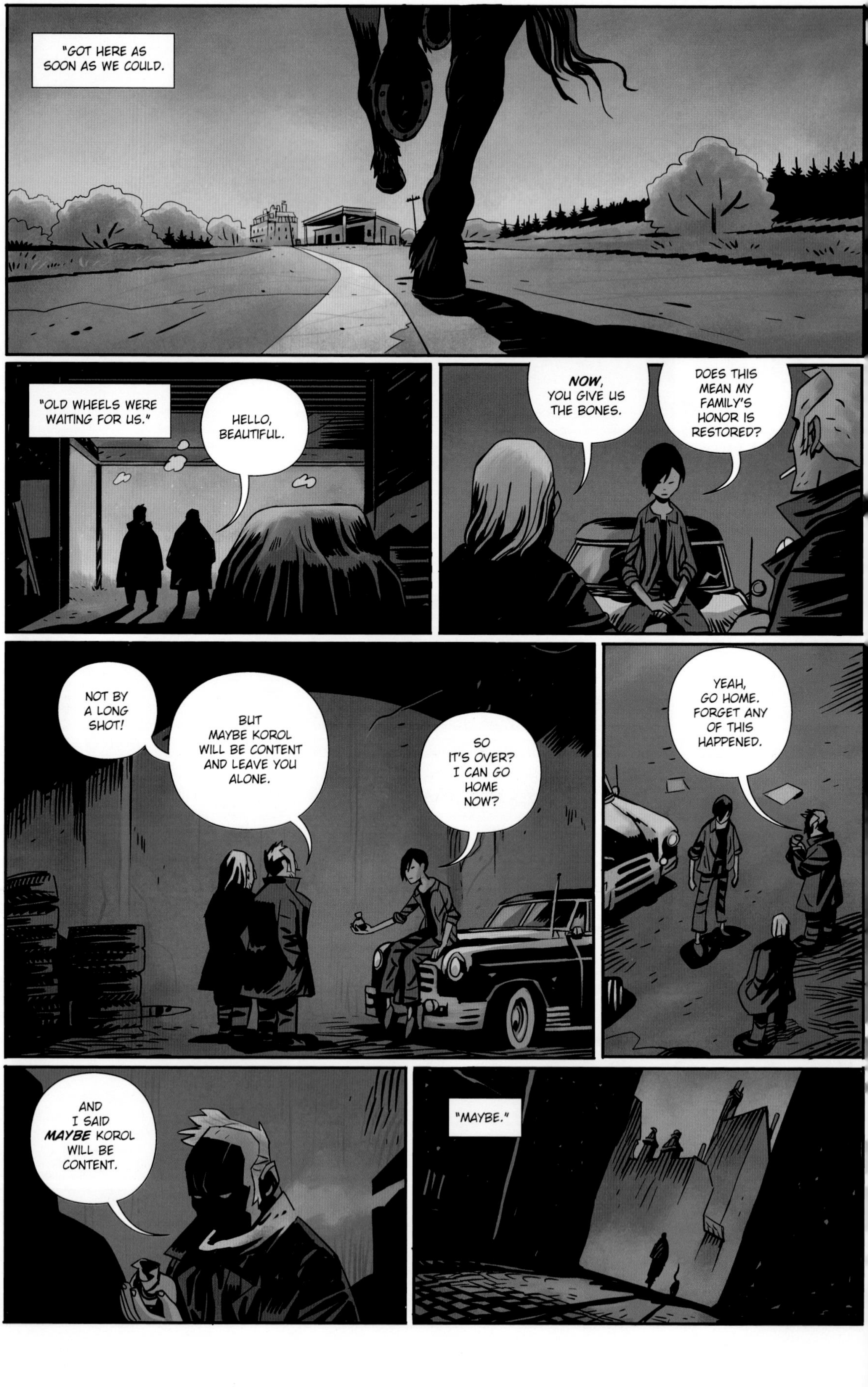
"GOT HERE AS SOON AS WE COULD.
"OLD WHEELS WERE WAITING FOR US."
HELLO, BEAUTIFUL.
NOW, YOU GIVE US THE BONES.
DOES THIS MEAN MY FAMILY'S HONOR IS RESTORED?
NOT BY A LONG SHOT!
BUT MAYBE KOROL WILL BE CONTENT AND LEAVE YOU ALONE.
SO IT'S OVER? I CAN GO HOME NOW?
YEAH, GO HOME. FORGET ANY OF THIS HAPPENED.
AND I SAID MAYBE KOROL WILL BE CONTENT.
"MAYBE."

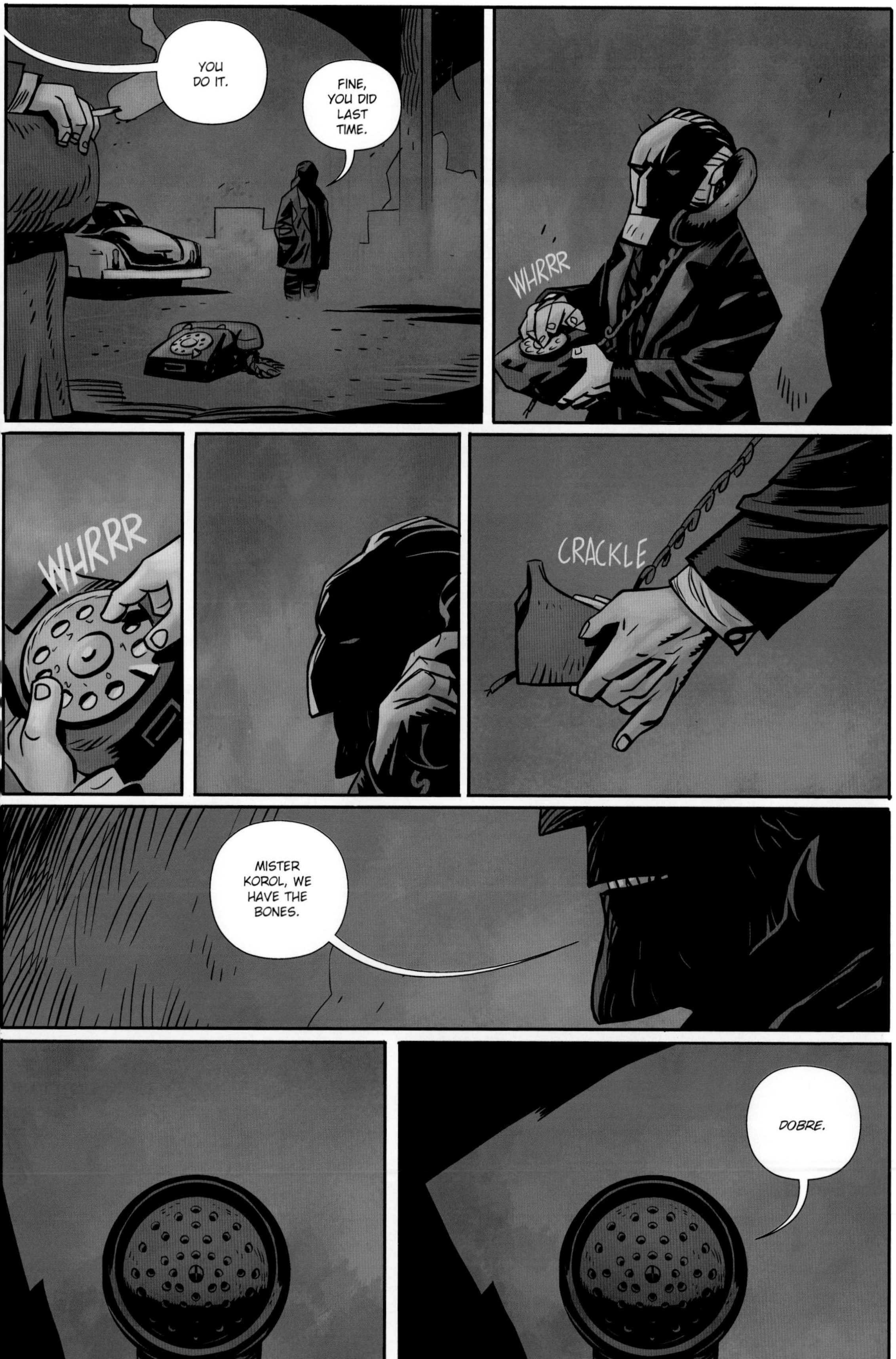
YOU DO IT.
FINE, YOU DID LAST TIME.
WHRRR
WHRRR
CRACKLE
MISTER KOROL, WE HAVE THE BONES.
DOBRE.

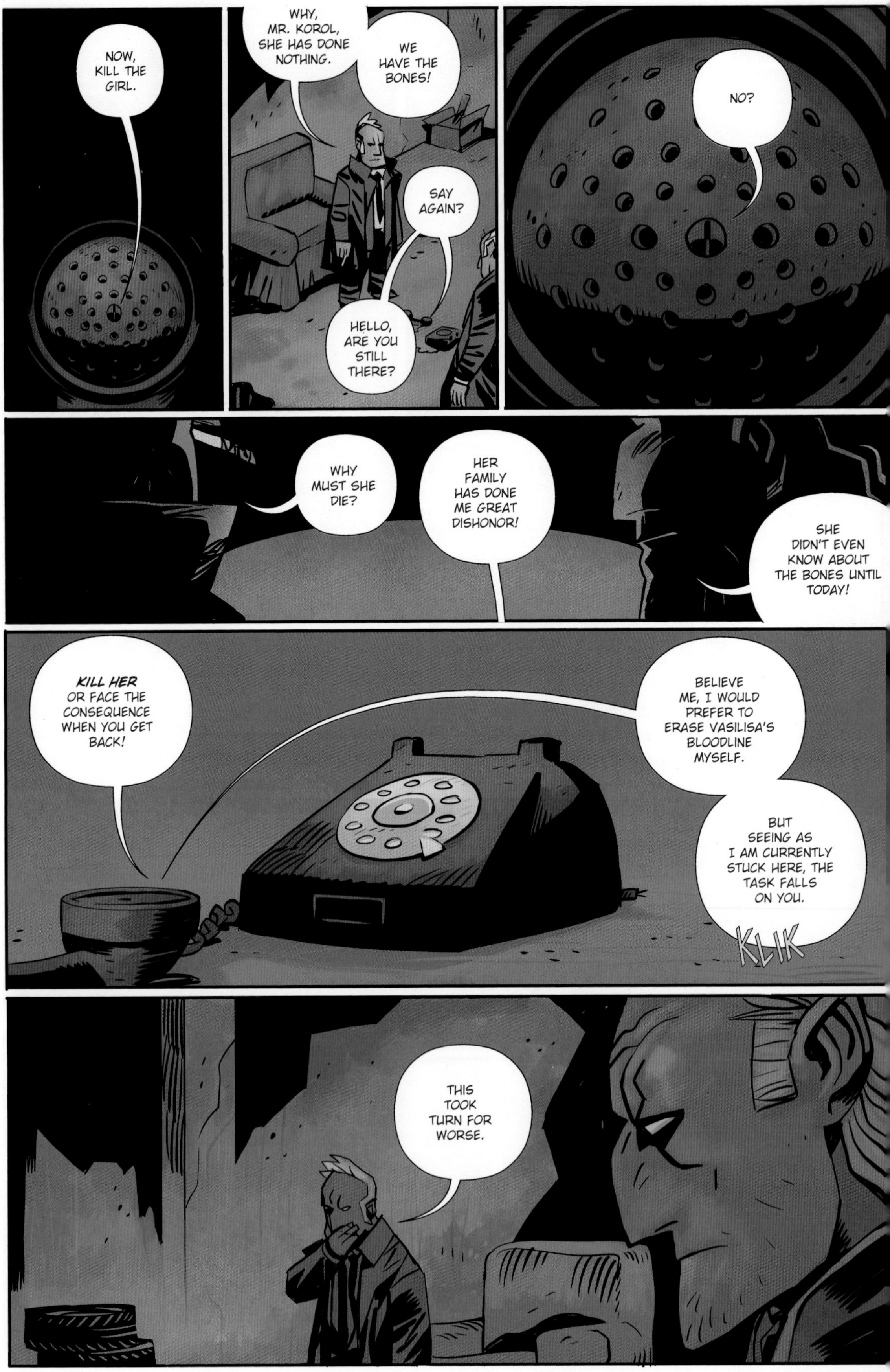
NOW, KILL THE GIRL.
WHY, MR. KOROL, SHE HAS DONE NOTHING.
WE HAVE THE BONES!
SAY AGAIN?
HELLO, ARE YOU STILL THERE?
NO?
WHY MUST SHE DIE?
HER FAMILY HAS DONE ME GREAT DISHONOR!
SHE DIDN'T EVEN KNOW ABOUT THE BONES UNTIL TODAY!
KILL HER OR FACE THE CONSEQUENCE WHEN YOU GET BACK!
BELIEVE ME, I WOULD PREFER TO ERASE VASILISA'S BLOODLINE MYSELF.
BUT SEEING AS I AM CURRENTLY STUCK HERE, THE TASK FALLS ON YOU.
KLIK
THIS TOOK TURN FOR WORSE.

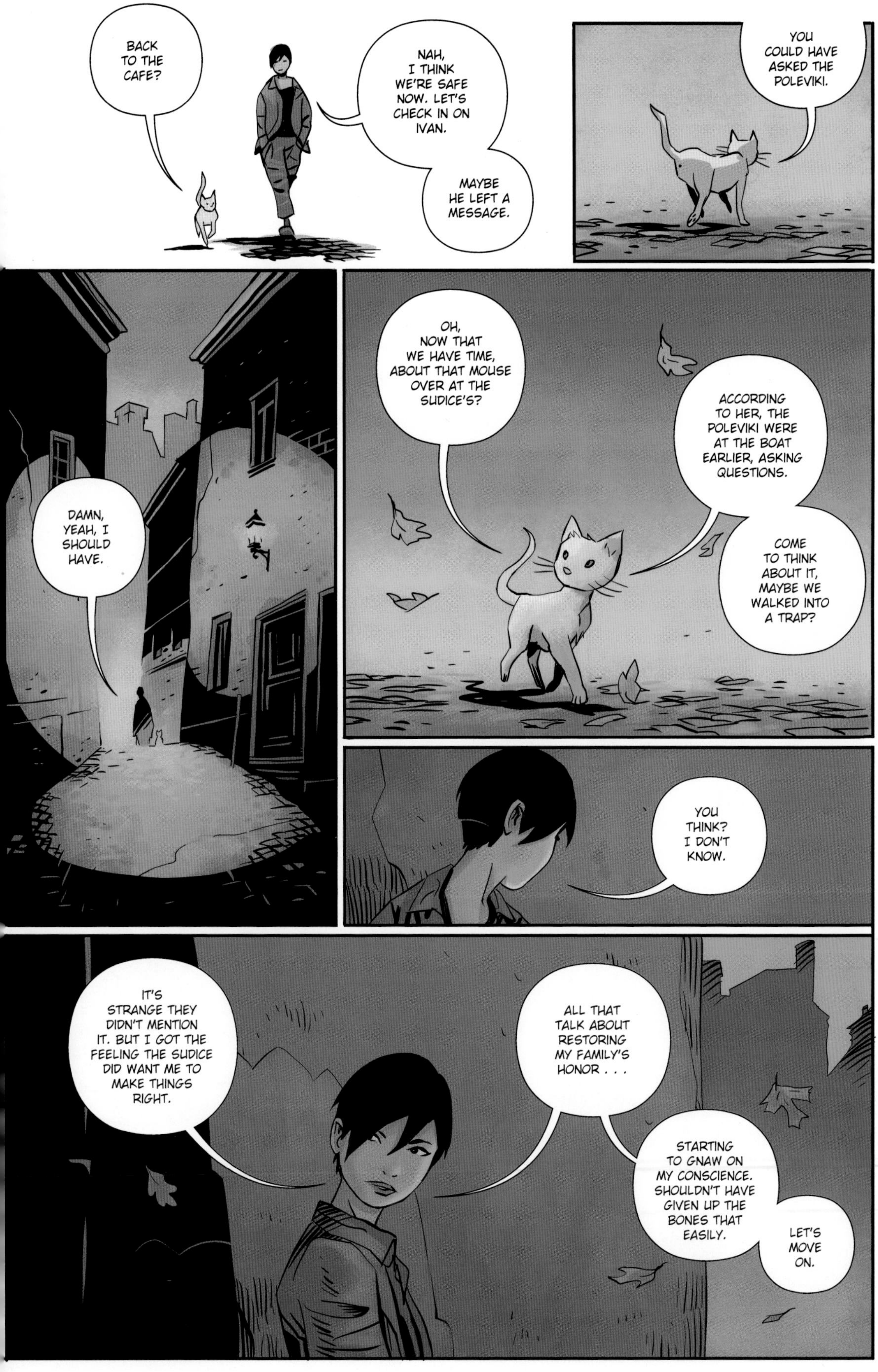
BACK TO THE CAFE?
NAH, I THINK WE'RE SAFE NOW. LET'S CHECK IN ON IVAN.
MAYBE HE LEFT A MESSAGE.
YOU COULD HAVE ASKED THE POLEVIKI.
DAMN, YEAH, I SHOULD HAVE.
OH, NOW THAT WE HAVE TIME, ABOUT THAT MOUSE OVER AT THE SUDICE'S?
ACCORDING TO HER, THE POLEVIKI WERE AT THE BOAT EARLIER, ASKING QUESTIONS.
COME TO THINK ABOUT IT, MAYBE WE WALKED INTO A TRAP?
YOU THINK? I DON'T KNOW.
IT'S STRANGE THEY DIDN'T MENTION IT. BUT I GOT THE FEELING THE SUDICE DID WANT ME TO MAKE THINGS RIGHT.
ALL THAT TALK ABOUT RESTORING MY FAMILY'S HONOR . . .
STARTING TO GNAW ON MY CONSCIENCE. SHOULDN'T HAVE GIVEN UP THE BONES THAT EASILY.
LET'S MOVE ON.

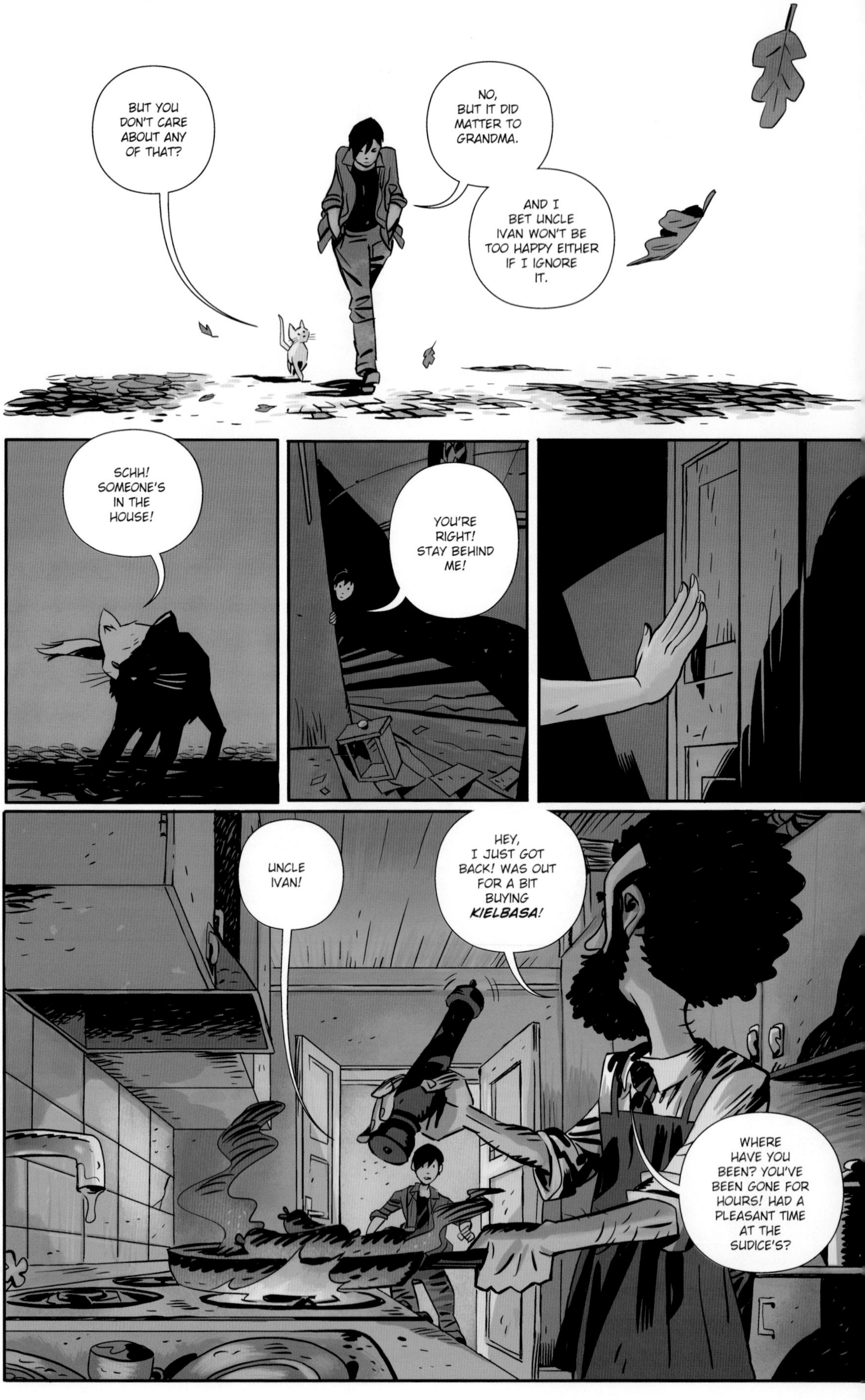
BUT YOU DON'T CARE ABOUT ANY OF THAT?
NO, BUT IT DID MATTER TO GRANDMA.
AND I BET UNCLE IVAN WON'T BE TOO HAPPY EITHER IF I IGNORE IT.
SCHH! SOMEONE'S IN THE HOUSE!
YOU'RE RIGHT! STAY BEHIND ME!
UNCLE IVAN!
HEY, I JUST GOT BACK! WAS OUT FOR A BIT BUYING KIELBASA!
WHERE HAVE YOU BEEN? YOU'VE BEEN GONE FOR HOURS! HAD A PLEASANT TIME AT THE SUDICE'S?

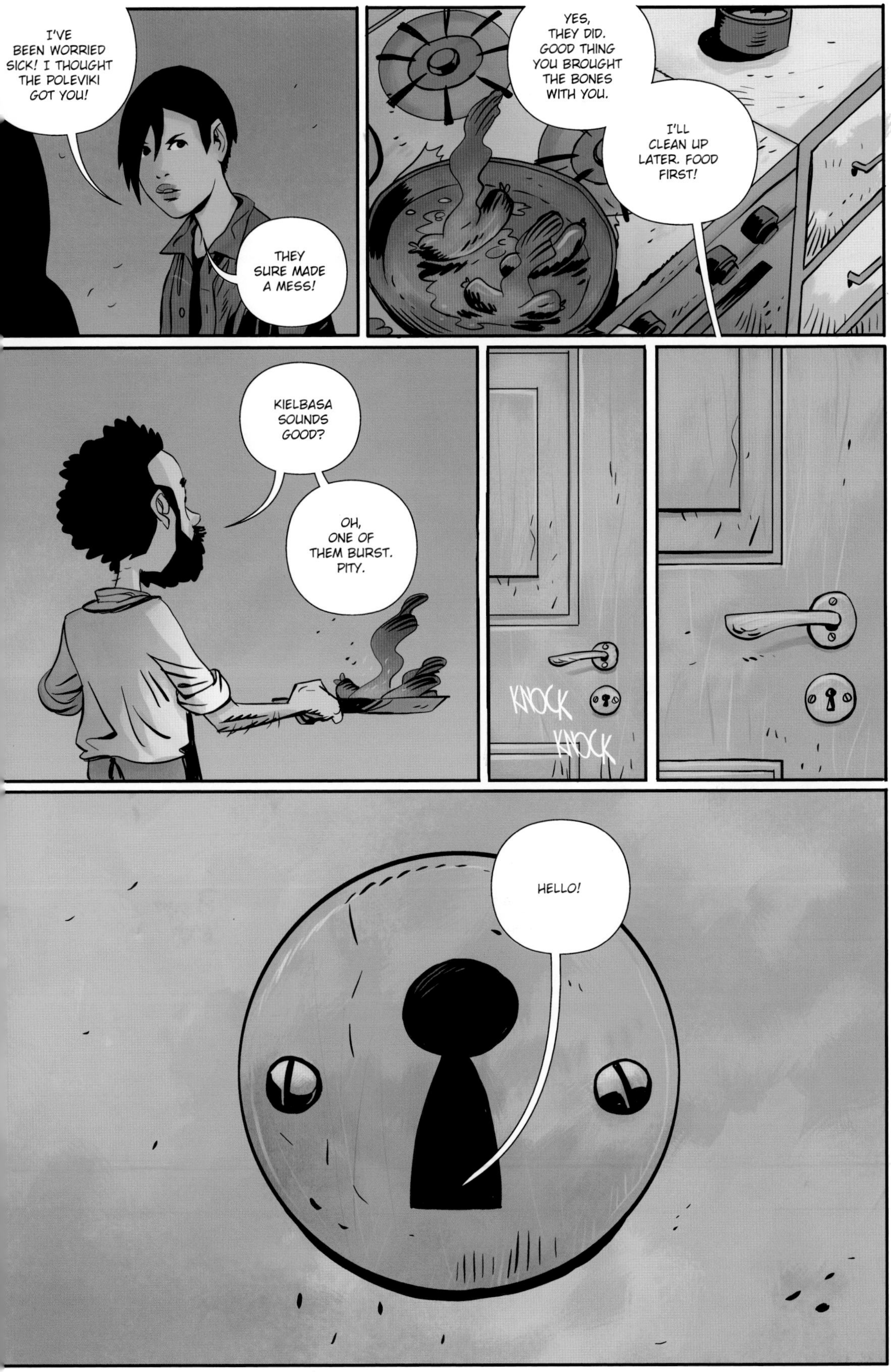
I'VE BEEN WORRIED SICK! I THOUGHT THE POLEVIKI GOT YOU!
THEY SURE MADE A MESS!
YES, THEY DID. GOOD THING YOU BROUGHT THE BONES WITH YOU.
I'LL CLEAN UP LATER. FOOD FIRST!
KIELBASA SOUNDS GOOD?
OH, ONE OF THEM BURST. PITY.
KNOCK
KNOCK
HELLO!

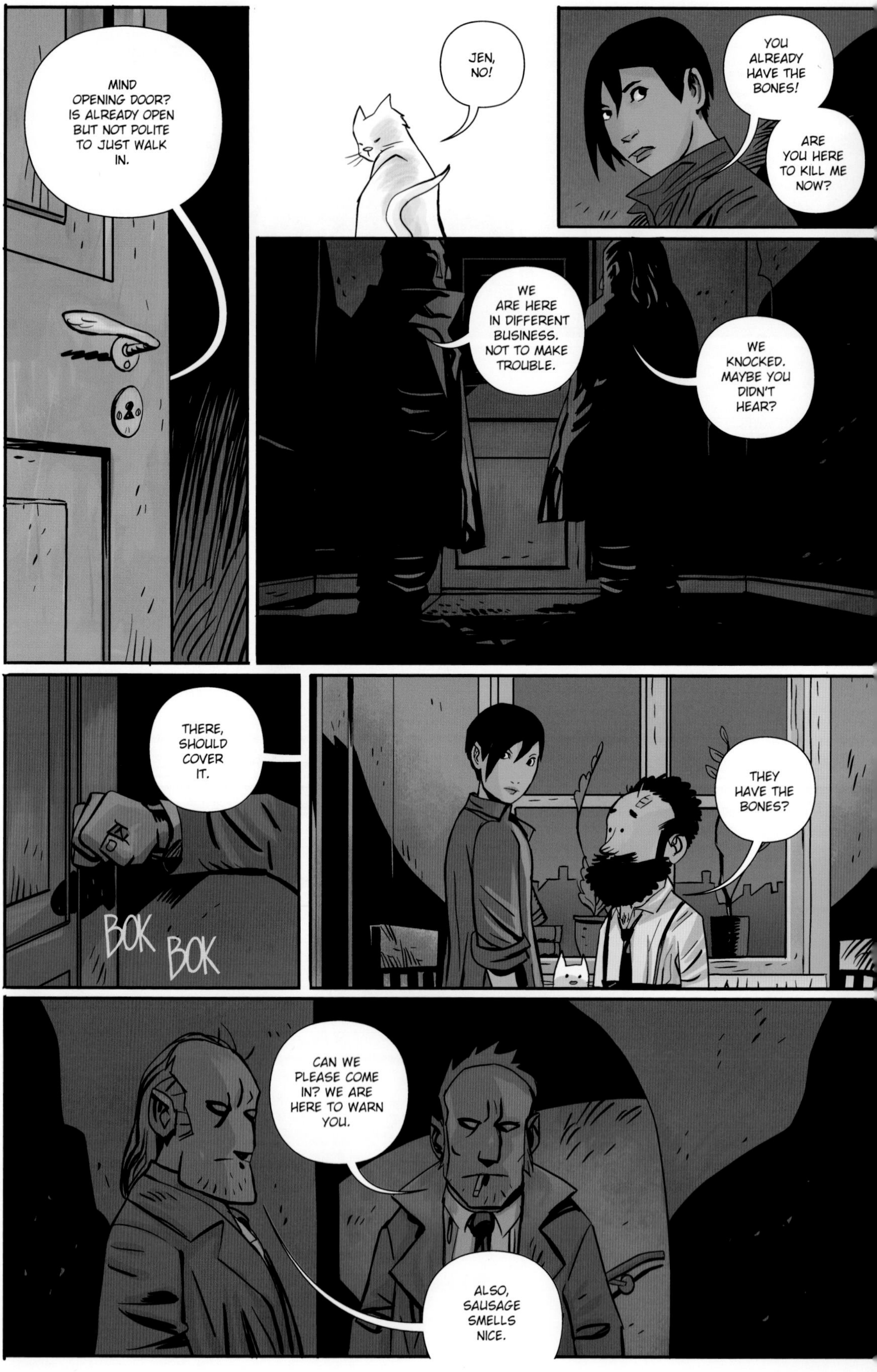
MIND OPENING DOOR? IS ALREADY OPEN BUT NOT POLITE TO JUST WALK IN.
JEN, NO!
YOU ALREADY HAVE THE BONES!
ARE YOU HERE TO KILL ME NOW?
WE ARE HERE IN DIFFERENT BUSINESS. NOT TO MAKE TROUBLE.
WE KNOCKED. MAYBE YOU DIDN'T HEAR?
THERE, SHOULD COVER IT.
BOK BOK
THEY HAVE THE BONES?
CAN WE PLEASE COME IN? WE ARE HERE TO WARN YOU.
ALSO, SAUSAGE SMELLS NICE.

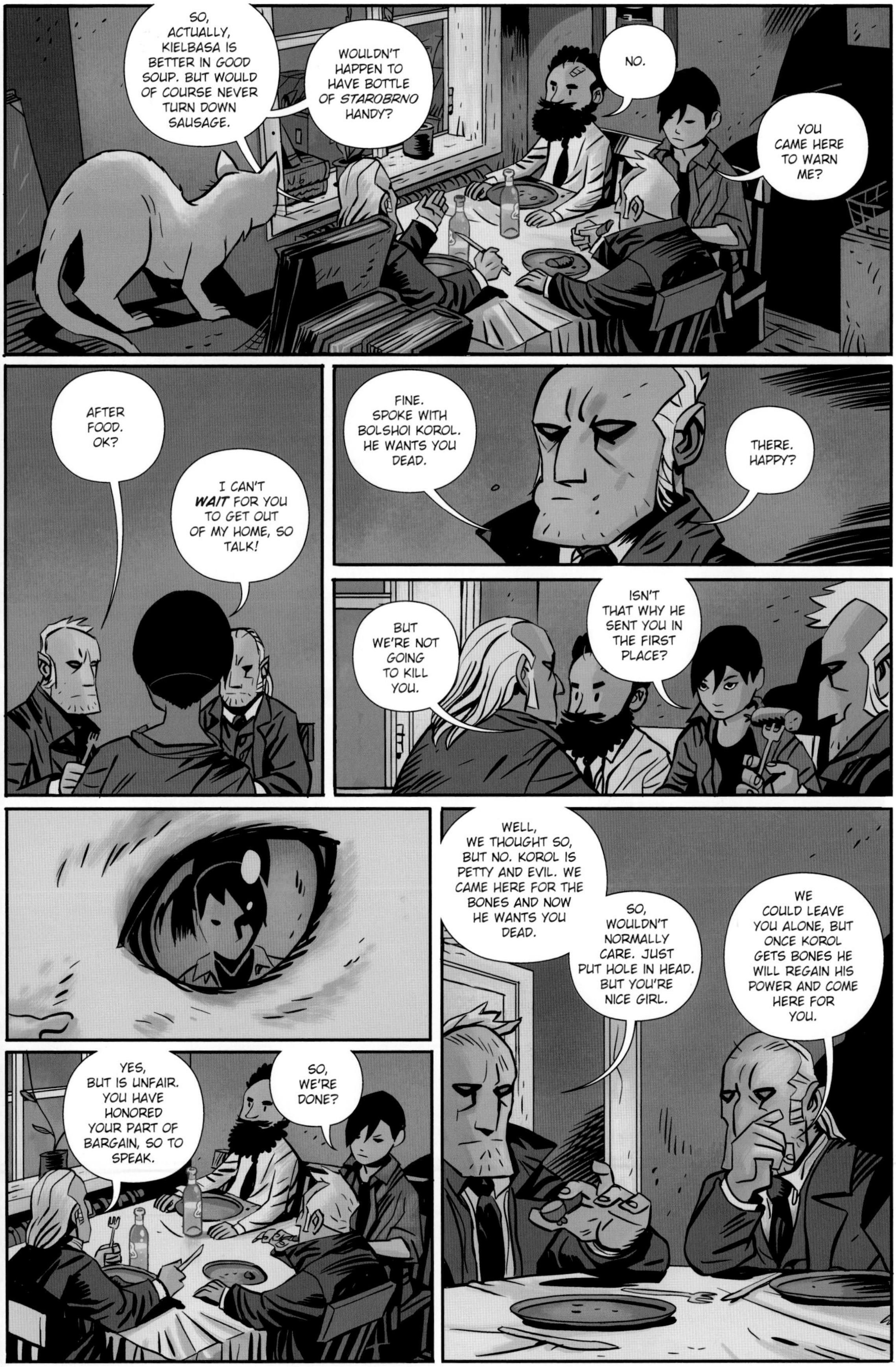
SO, ACTUALLY, KIELBASA IS BETTER IN GOOD SOUP. BUT WOULD OF COURSE NEVER TURN DOWN SAUSAGE.
WOULDN'T HAPPEN TO HAVE BOTTLE OF *STAROBRNO* HANDY?
NO.
YOU CAME HERE TO WARN ME?
AFTER FOOD. OK?
I CAN'T ***WAIT*** FOR YOU TO GET OUT OF MY HOME, SO TALK!
FINE. SPOKE WITH BOLSHOI KOROL. HE WANTS YOU DEAD.
THERE. HAPPY?
BUT WE'RE NOT GOING TO KILL YOU.
ISN'T THAT WHY HE SENT YOU IN THE FIRST PLACE?
WELL, WE THOUGHT SO, BUT NO. KOROL IS PETTY AND EVIL. WE CAME HERE FOR THE BONES AND NOW HE WANTS YOU DEAD.
SO, WOULDN'T NORMALLY CARE. JUST PUT HOLE IN HEAD. BUT YOU'RE NICE GIRL.
WE COULD LEAVE YOU ALONE, BUT ONCE KOROL GETS BONES HE WILL REGAIN HIS POWER AND COME HERE FOR YOU.
YES, BUT IS UNFAIR. YOU HAVE HONORED YOUR PART OF BARGAIN, SO TO SPEAK.
SO, WE'RE DONE?

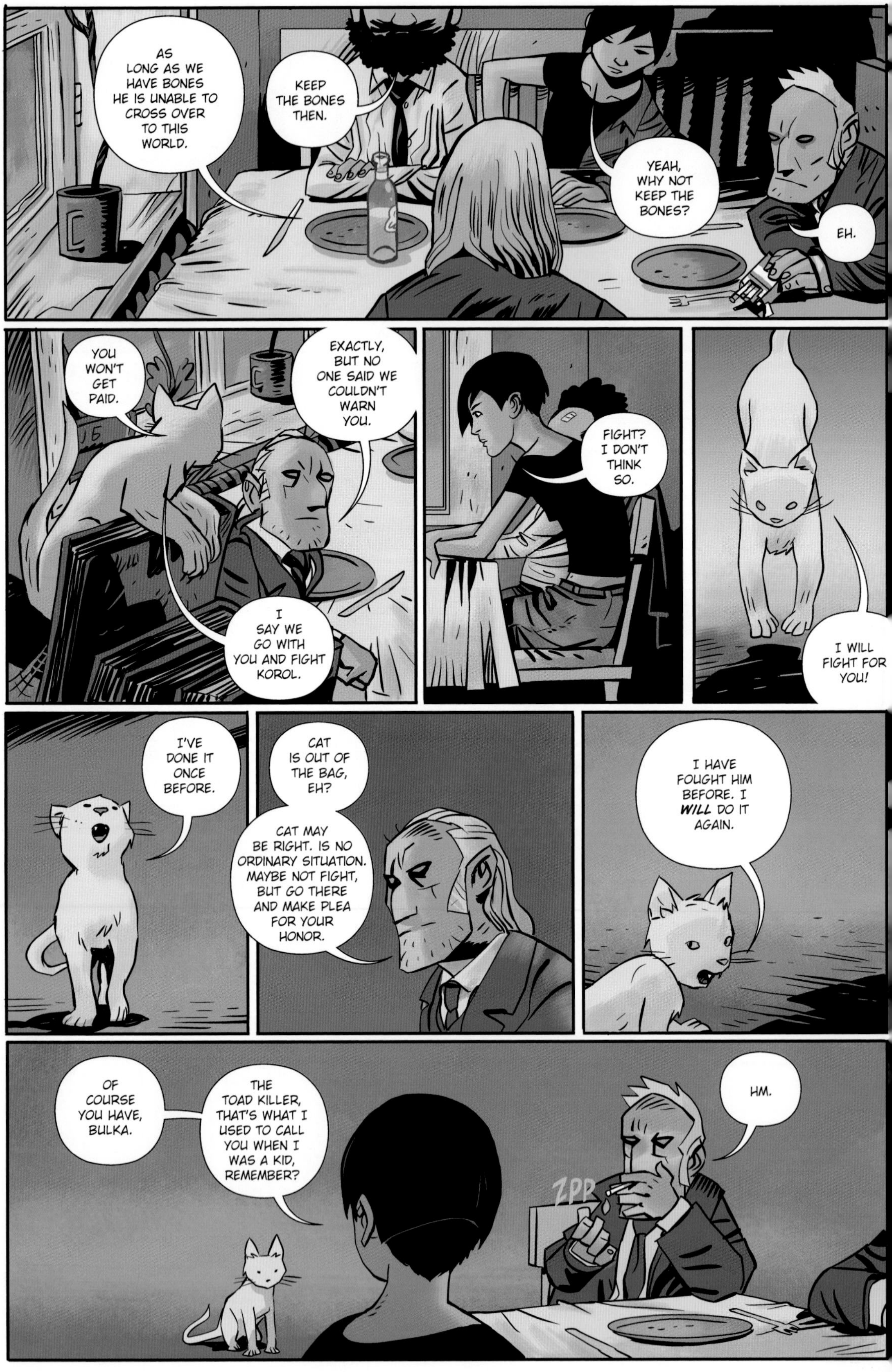
AS LONG AS WE HAVE BONES HE IS UNABLE TO CROSS OVER TO THIS WORLD.
KEEP THE BONES THEN.
YEAH, WHY NOT KEEP THE BONES?
EH.
YOU WON'T GET PAID.
EXACTLY, BUT NO ONE SAID WE COULDN'T WARN YOU.
I SAY WE GO WITH YOU AND FIGHT KOROL.
FIGHT? I DON'T THINK SO.
I WILL FIGHT FOR YOU!
I'VE DONE IT ONCE BEFORE.
CAT IS OUT OF THE BAG, EH?
CAT MAY BE RIGHT. IS NO ORDINARY SITUATION. MAYBE NOT FIGHT, BUT GO THERE AND MAKE PLEA FOR YOUR HONOR.
I HAVE FOUGHT HIM BEFORE. I WILL DO IT AGAIN.
OF COURSE YOU HAVE, BULKA.
THE TOAD KILLER, THAT'S WHAT I USED TO CALL YOU WHEN I WAS A KID, REMEMBER?
HM.
ZPP

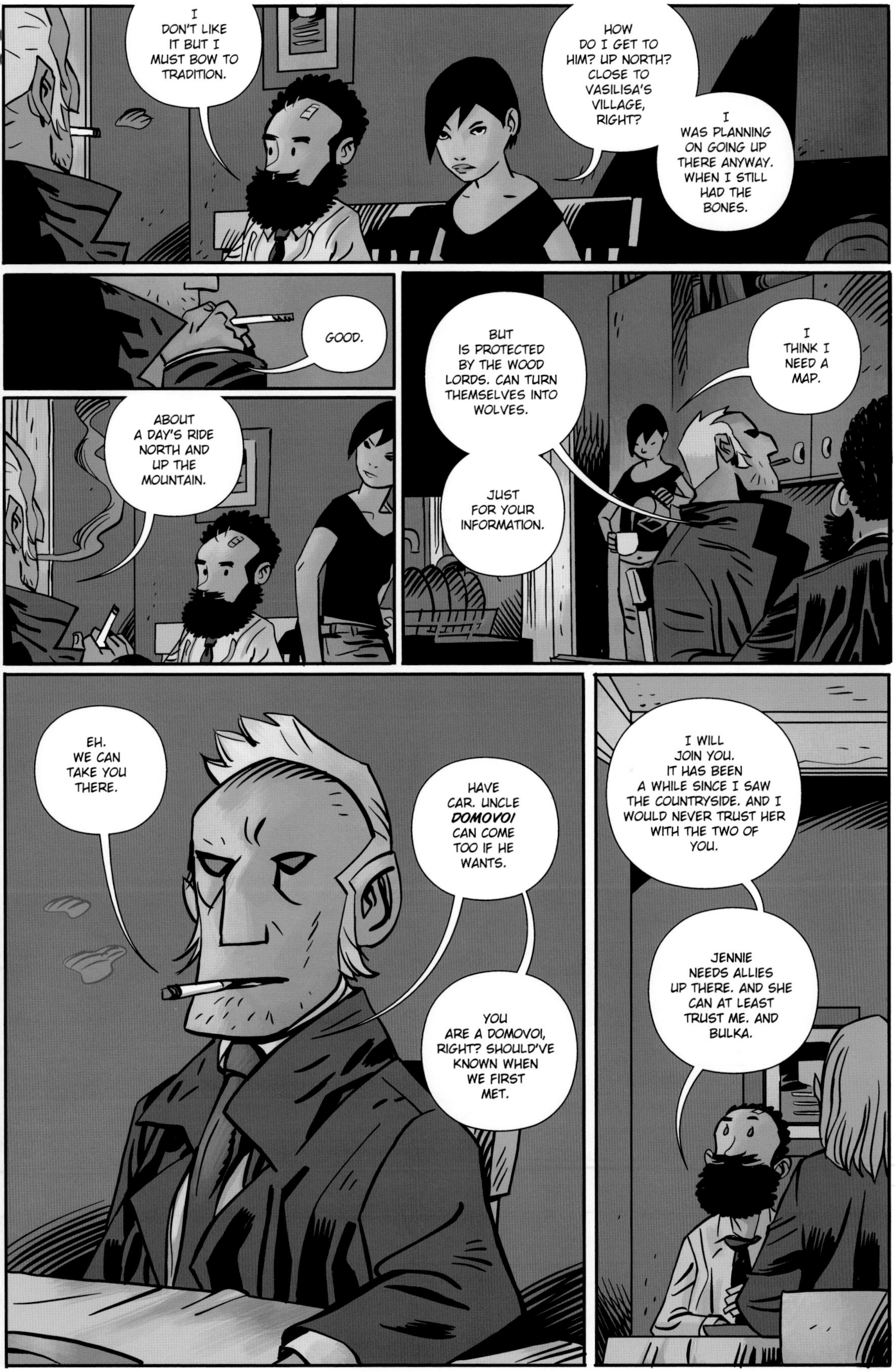
I DON'T LIKE IT BUT I MUST BOW TO TRADITION.
HOW DO I GET TO HIM? UP NORTH? CLOSE TO VASILISA'S VILLAGE, RIGHT?
I WAS PLANNING ON GOING UP THERE ANYWAY. WHEN I STILL HAD THE BONES.
GOOD.
ABOUT A DAY'S RIDE NORTH AND UP THE MOUNTAIN.
BUT IS PROTECTED BY THE WOOD LORDS. CAN TURN THEMSELVES INTO WOLVES.
JUST FOR YOUR INFORMATION.
I THINK I NEED A MAP.
EH. WE CAN TAKE YOU THERE.
HAVE CAR. UNCLE DOMOVOI CAN COME TOO IF HE WANTS.
YOU ARE A DOMOVOI, RIGHT? SHOULD'VE KNOWN WHEN WE FIRST MET.
I WILL JOIN YOU. IT HAS BEEN A WHILE SINCE I SAW THE COUNTRYSIDE. AND I WOULD NEVER TRUST HER WITH THE TWO OF YOU.
JENNIE NEEDS ALLIES UP THERE. AND SHE CAN AT LEAST TRUST ME. AND BULKA.

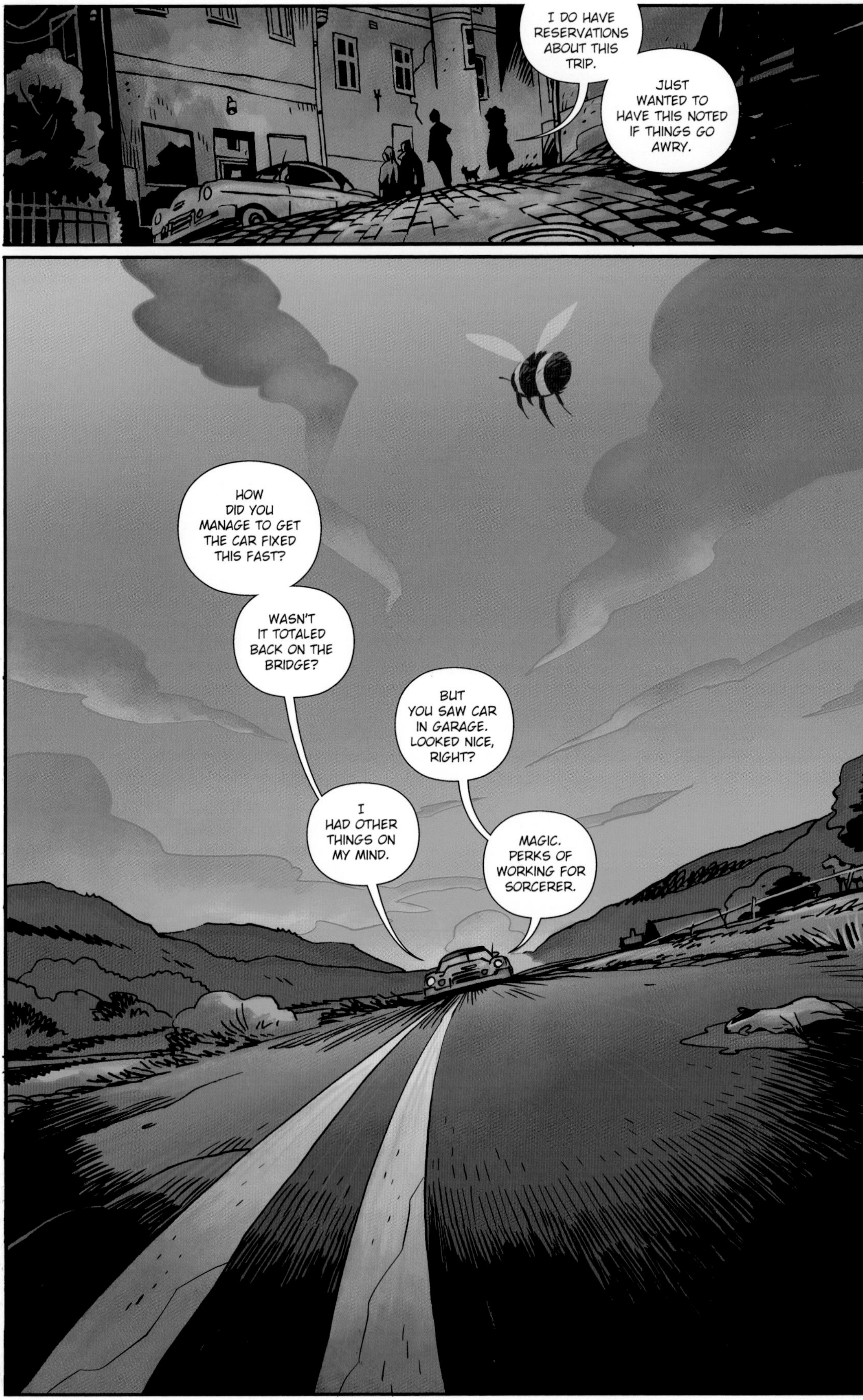

I DO HAVE RESERVATIONS ABOUT THIS TRIP.
JUST WANTED TO HAVE THIS NOTED IF THINGS GO AWRY.
HOW DID YOU MANAGE TO GET THE CAR FIXED THIS FAST?
WASN'T IT TOTALED BACK ON THE BRIDGE?
BUT YOU SAW CAR IN GARAGE. LOOKED NICE, RIGHT?
I HAD OTHER THINGS ON MY MIND.
MAGIC. PERKS OF WORKING FOR SORCERER.

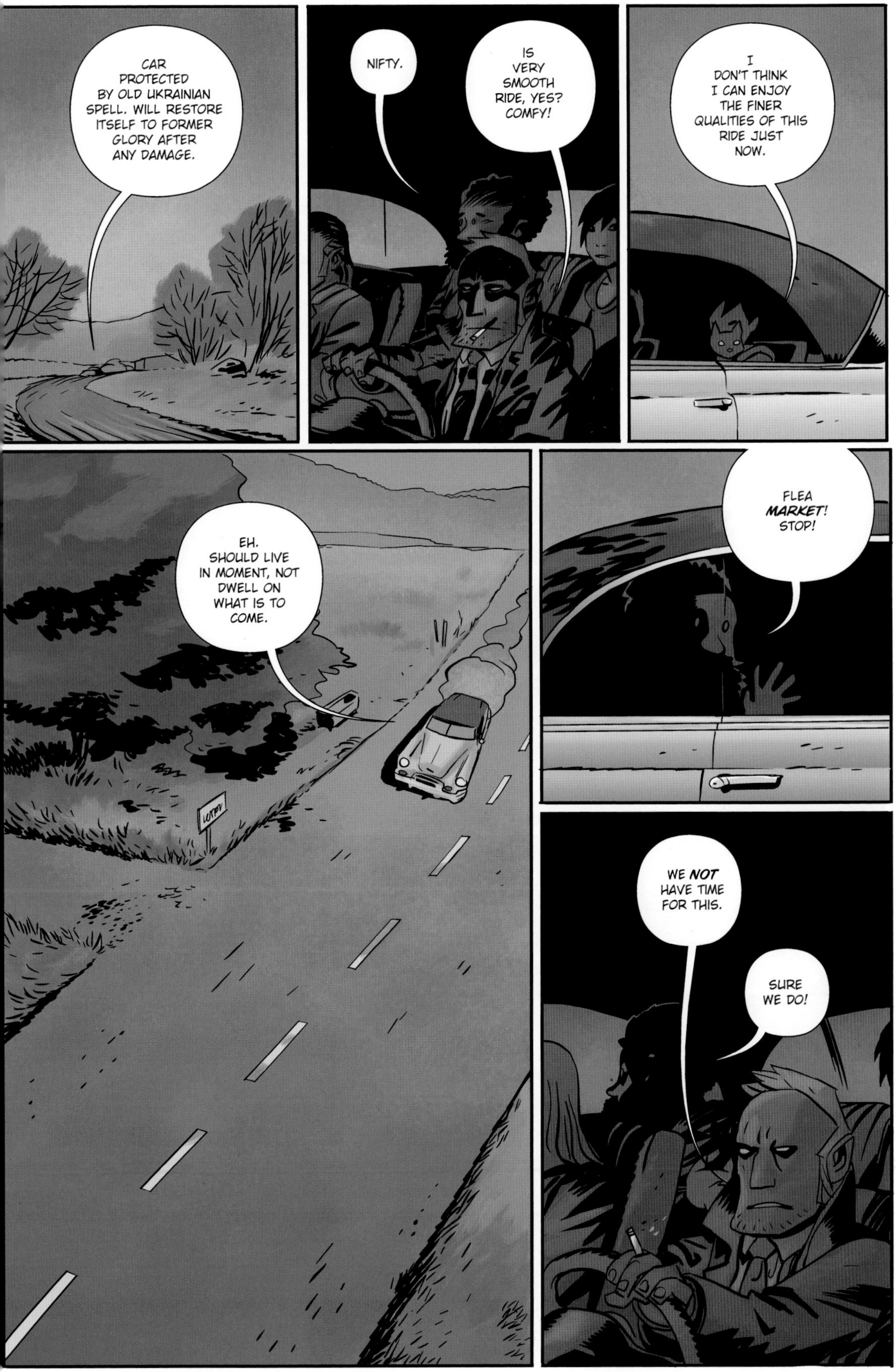
CAR PROTECTED BY OLD UKRAINIAN SPELL. WILL RESTORE ITSELF TO FORMER GLORY AFTER ANY DAMAGE.
NIFTY.
IS VERY SMOOTH RIDE, YES? COMFY!
I DON'T THINK I CAN ENJOY THE FINER QUALITIES OF THIS RIDE JUST NOW.
EH. SHOULD LIVE IN MOMENT, NOT DWELL ON WHAT IS TO COME.
FLEA MARKET! STOP!
WE NOT HAVE TIME FOR THIS.
SURE WE DO!

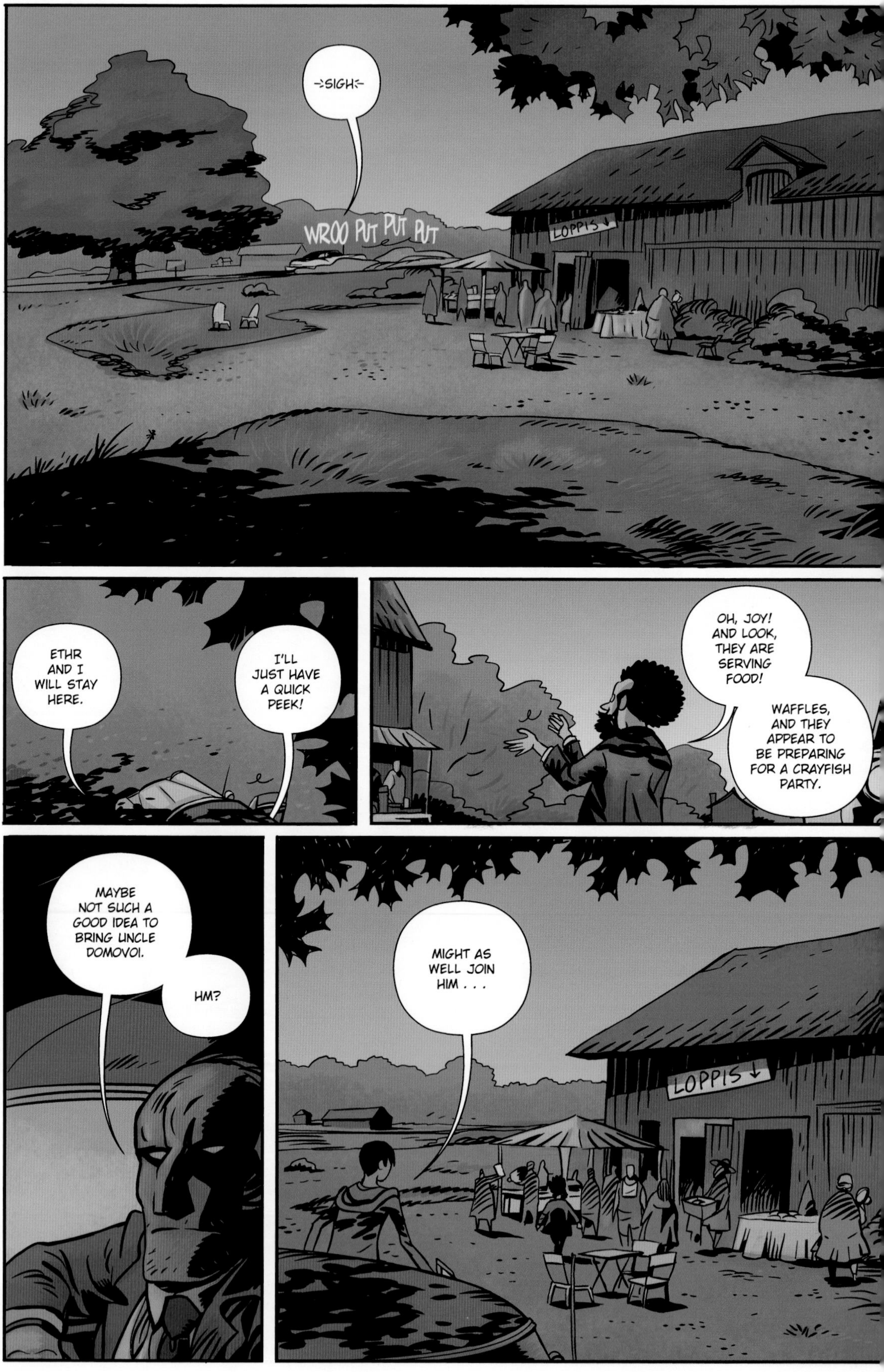

-SIGH-
WROO PUT PUT PUT
LOPPIS ↓
ETHR AND I WILL STAY HERE.
I'LL JUST HAVE A QUICK PEEK!
OH, JOY! AND LOOK, THEY ARE SERVING FOOD!
WAFFLES, AND THEY APPEAR TO BE PREPARING FOR A CRAYFISH PARTY.
MAYBE NOT SUCH A GOOD IDEA TO BRING UNCLE DOMOVOI.
HM?
MIGHT AS WELL JOIN HIM . . .
LOPPIS ↓

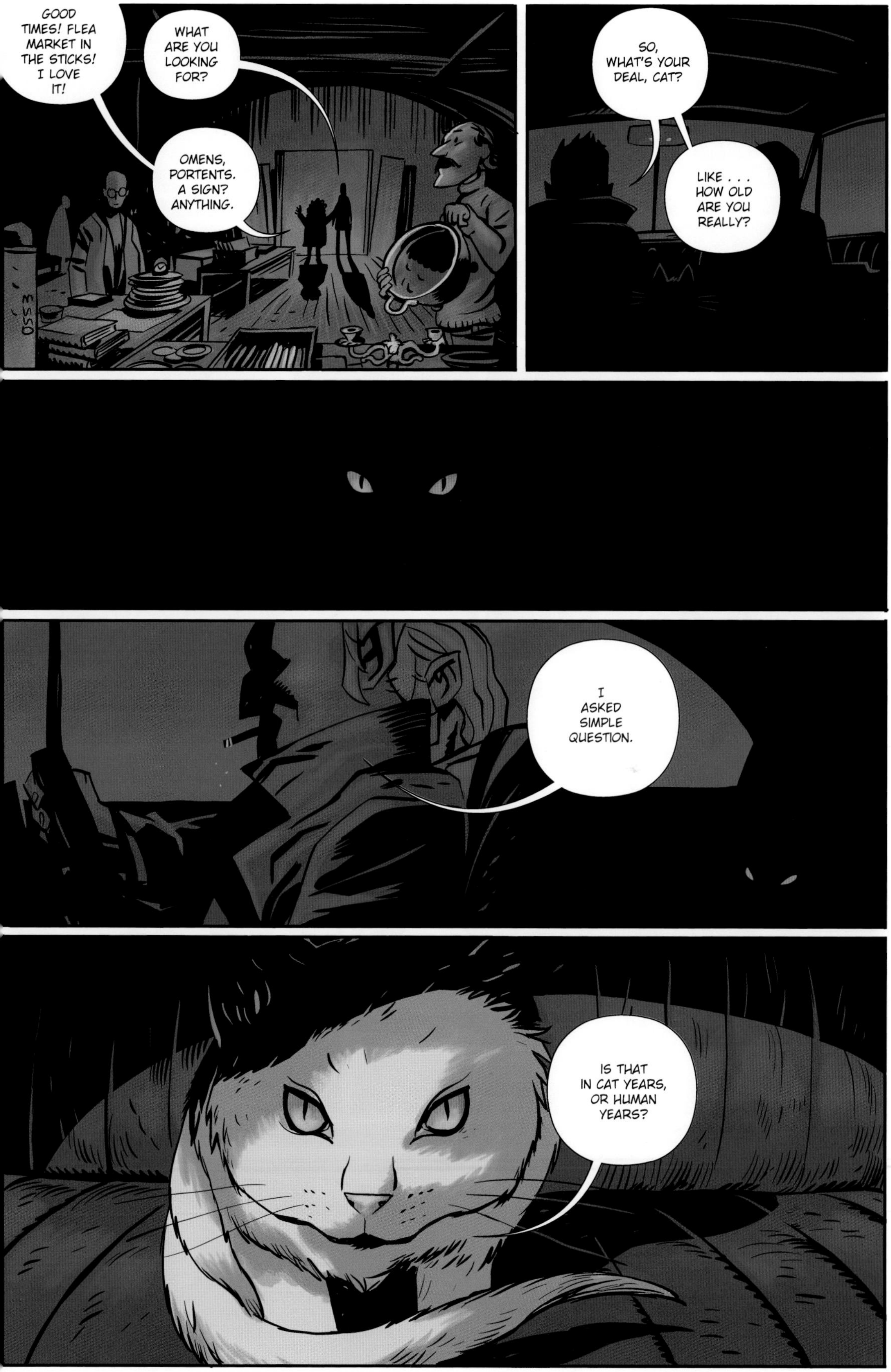
GOOD TIMES! FLEA MARKET IN THE STICKS! I LOVE IT!
WHAT ARE YOU LOOKING FOR?
OMENS, PORTENTS. A SIGN? ANYTHING.
SO, WHAT'S YOUR DEAL, CAT?
LIKE . . . HOW OLD ARE YOU REALLY?
I ASKED SIMPLE QUESTION.
IS THAT IN CAT YEARS, OR HUMAN YEARS?

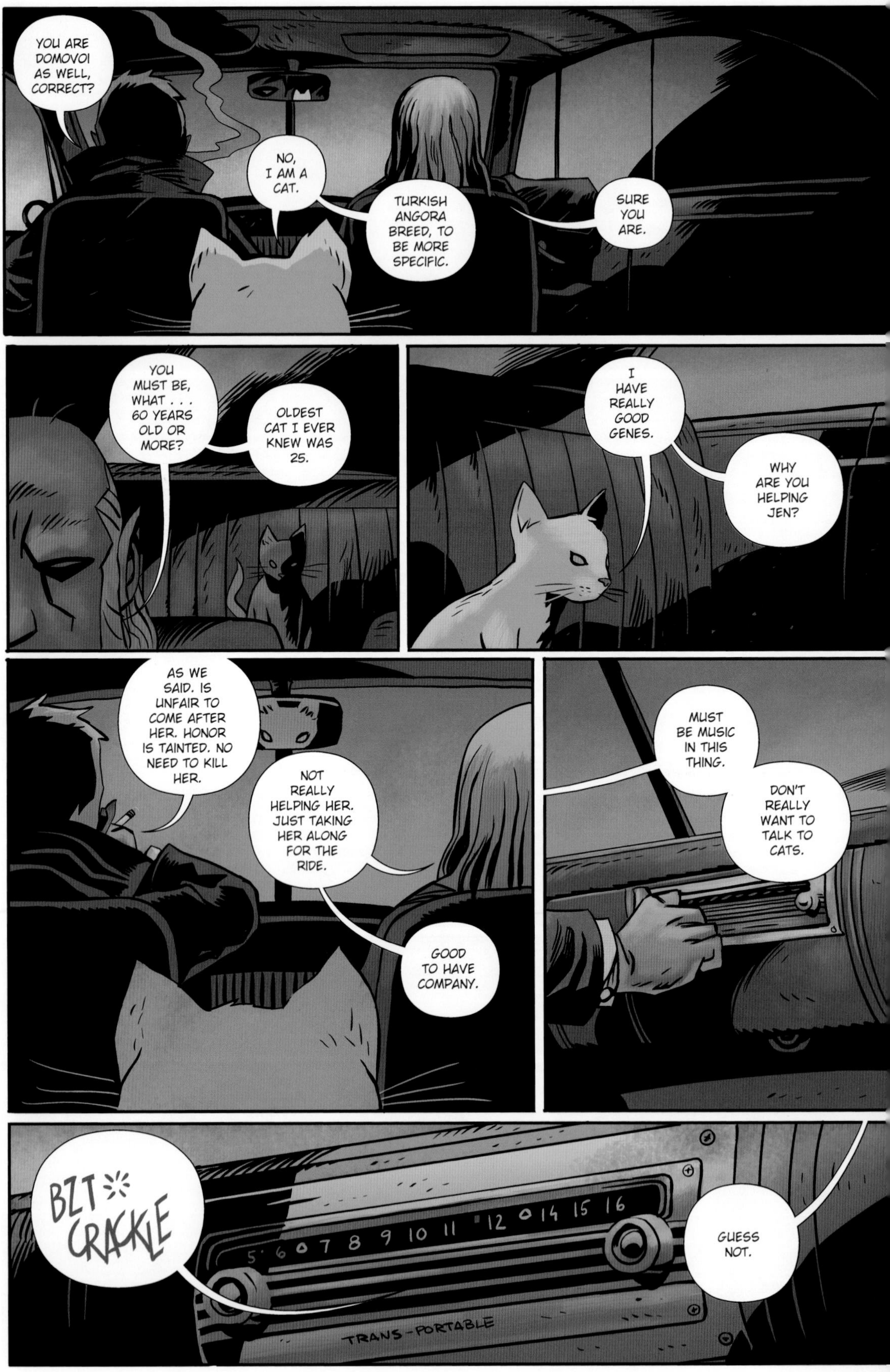
YOU ARE DOMOVOI AS WELL, CORRECT?
NO, I AM A CAT.
TURKISH ANGORA BREED, TO BE MORE SPECIFIC.
SURE YOU ARE.
YOU MUST BE, WHAT . . . 60 YEARS OLD OR MORE?
OLDEST CAT I EVER KNEW WAS 25.
I HAVE REALLY GOOD GENES.
WHY ARE YOU HELPING JEN?
AS WE SAID. IS UNFAIR TO COME AFTER HER. HONOR IS TAINTED. NO NEED TO KILL HER.
NOT REALLY HELPING HER. JUST TAKING HER ALONG FOR THE RIDE.
GOOD TO HAVE COMPANY.
MUST BE MUSIC IN THIS THING.
DON'T REALLY WANT TO TALK TO CATS.
BZT CRACKLE
GUESS NOT.
TRANS-PORTABLE

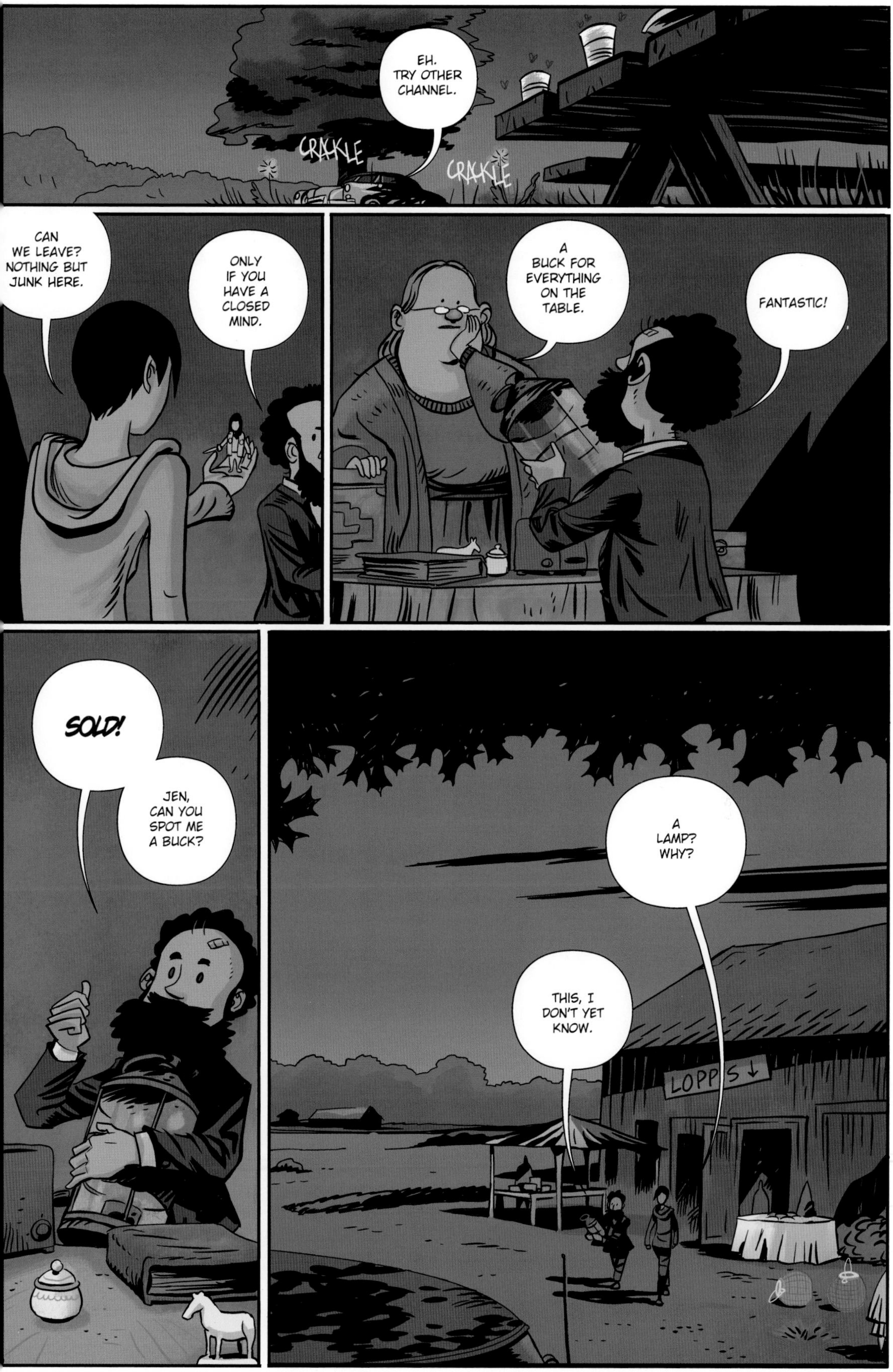
EH. TRY OTHER CHANNEL.
CRACKLE
CRACKLE
CAN WE LEAVE? NOTHING BUT JUNK HERE.
ONLY IF YOU HAVE A CLOSED MIND.
A BUCK FOR EVERYTHING ON THE TABLE.
FANTASTIC!
SOLD!
JEN, CAN YOU SPOT ME A BUCK?
A LAMP? WHY?
THIS, I DON'T YET KNOW.
LOPPIS ↓

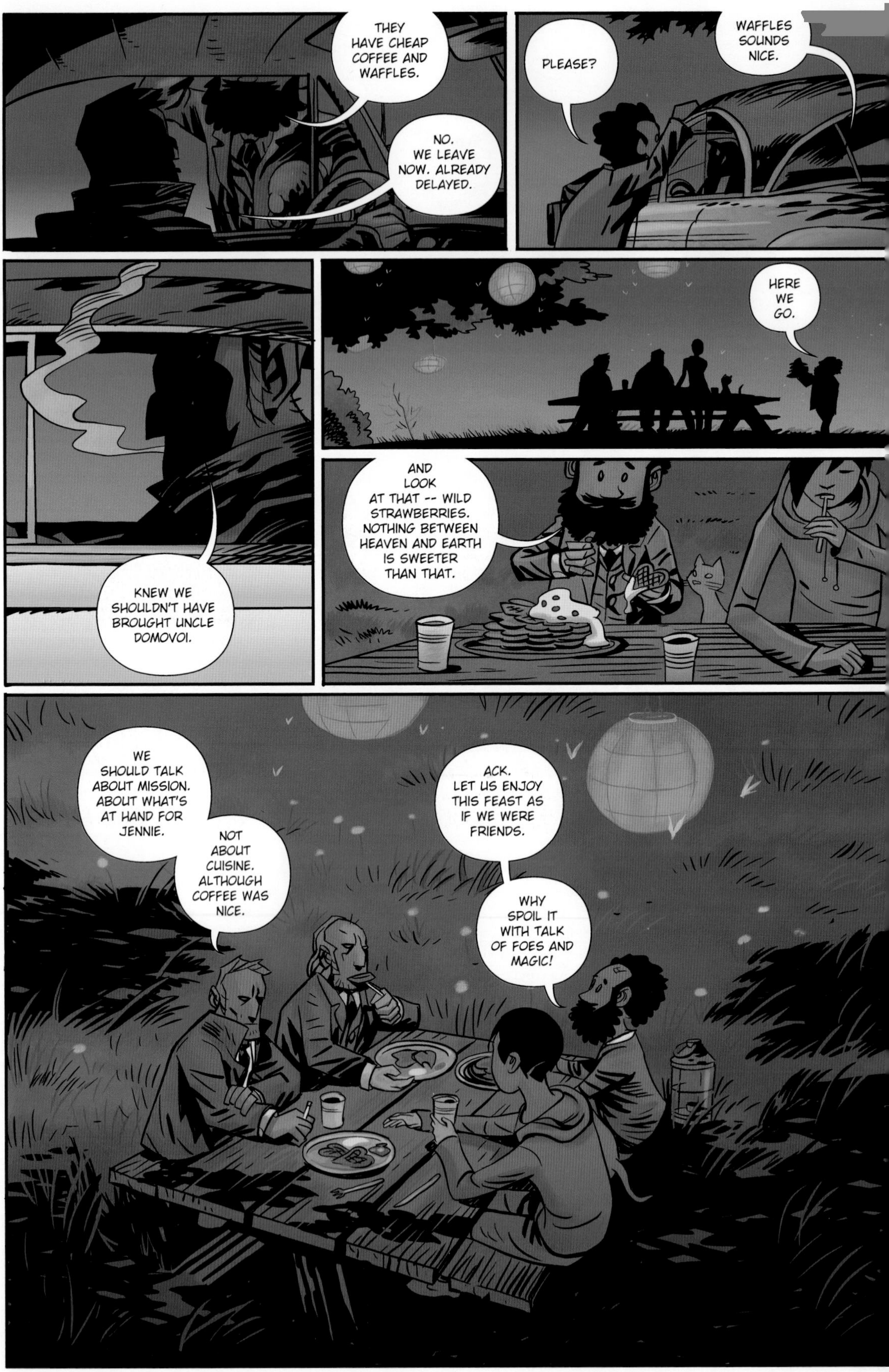
THEY HAVE CHEAP COFFEE AND WAFFLES.
NO. WE LEAVE NOW. ALREADY DELAYED.
PLEASE?
WAFFLES SOUNDS NICE.
KNEW WE SHOULDN'T HAVE BROUGHT UNCLE DOMOVOI.
HERE WE GO.
AND LOOK AT THAT -- WILD STRAWBERRIES. NOTHING BETWEEN HEAVEN AND EARTH IS SWEETER THAN THAT.
WE SHOULD TALK ABOUT MISSION. ABOUT WHAT'S AT HAND FOR JENNIE.
NOT ABOUT CUISINE. ALTHOUGH COFFEE WAS NICE.
ACK. LET US ENJOY THIS FEAST AS IF WE WERE FRIENDS.
WHY SPOIL IT WITH TALK OF FOES AND MAGIC!

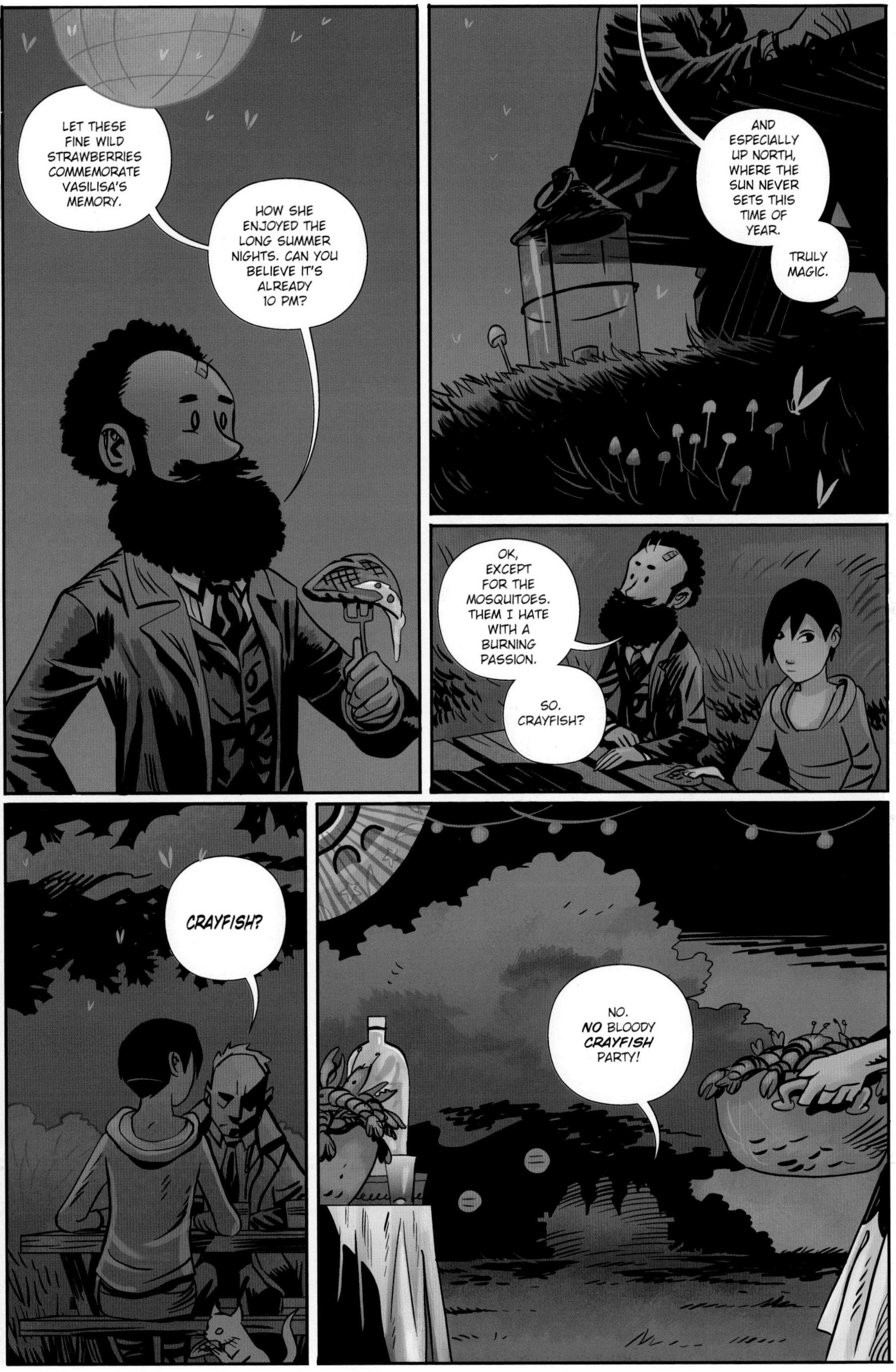
LET THESE FINE WILD STRAWBERRIES COMMEMORATE VASILISA'S MEMORY.
HOW SHE ENJOYED THE LONG SUMMER NIGHTS. CAN YOU BELIEVE IT'S ALREADY 10 PM?
AND ESPECIALLY UP NORTH, WHERE THE SUN NEVER SETS THIS TIME OF YEAR.
TRULY MAGIC.
OK, EXCEPT FOR THE MOSQUITOES. THEM I HATE WITH A BURNING PASSION.
SO. CRAYFISH?
CRAYFISH?
NO. NO BLOODY CRAYFISH PARTY!

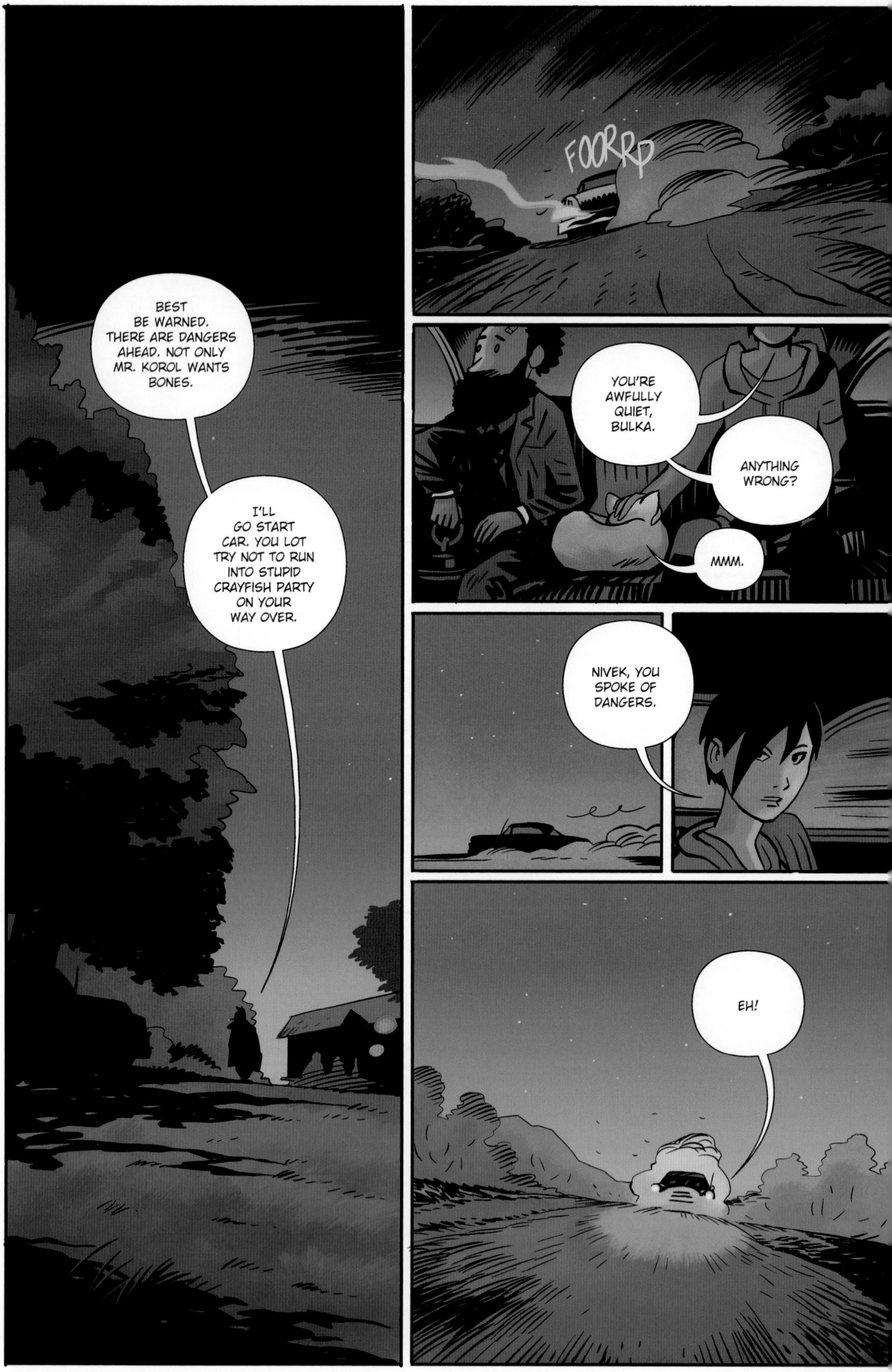
BEST BE WARNED. THERE ARE DANGERS AHEAD. NOT ONLY MR. KOROL WANTS BONES.
I'LL GO START CAR. YOU LOT TRY NOT TO RUN INTO STUPID CRAYFISH PARTY ON YOUR WAY OVER.
FOORRP
YOU'RE AWFULLY QUIET, BULKA.
ANYTHING WRONG?
MMM.
NIVEK, YOU SPOKE OF DANGERS.
EH!

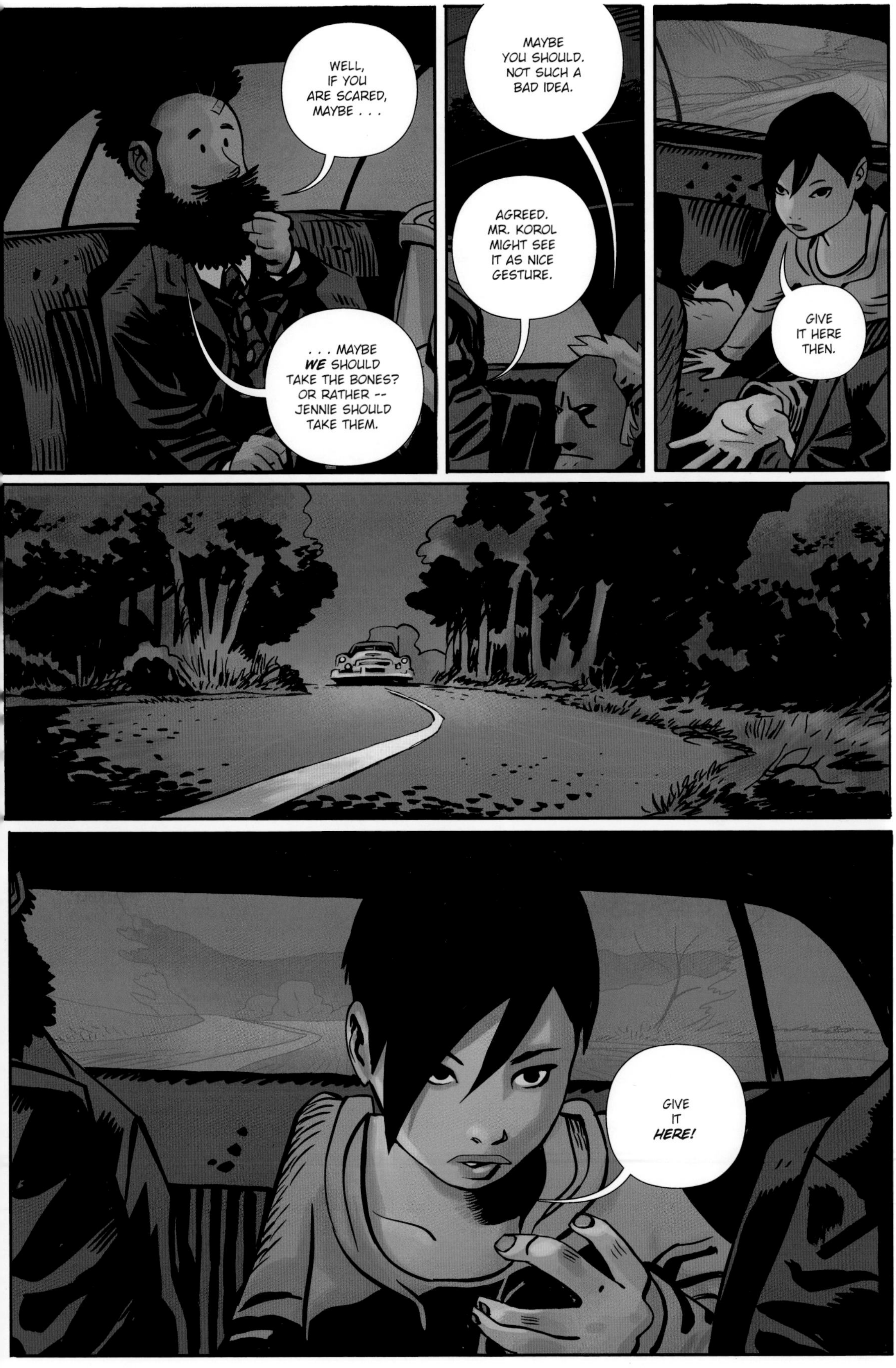
WELL, IF YOU ARE SCARED, MAYBE . . .
. . . MAYBE **WE** SHOULD TAKE THE BONES? OR RATHER -- JENNIE SHOULD TAKE THEM.
MAYBE YOU SHOULD. NOT SUCH A BAD IDEA.
AGREED. MR. KOROL MIGHT SEE IT AS NICE GESTURE.
GIVE IT HERE THEN.
GIVE IT ***HERE!***

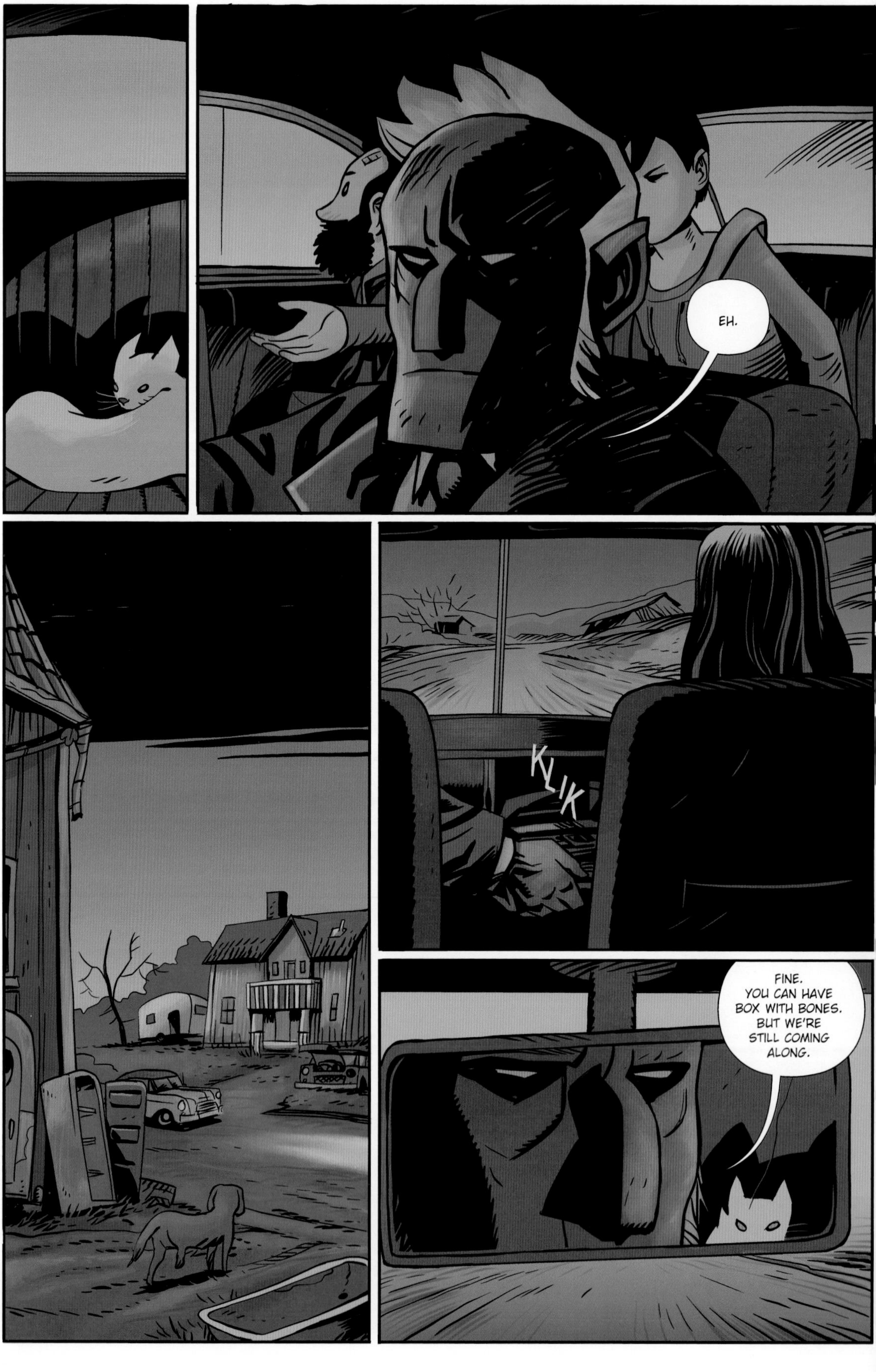
EH.
KLIK
FINE. YOU CAN HAVE BOX WITH BONES. BUT WE'RE STILL COMING ALONG.

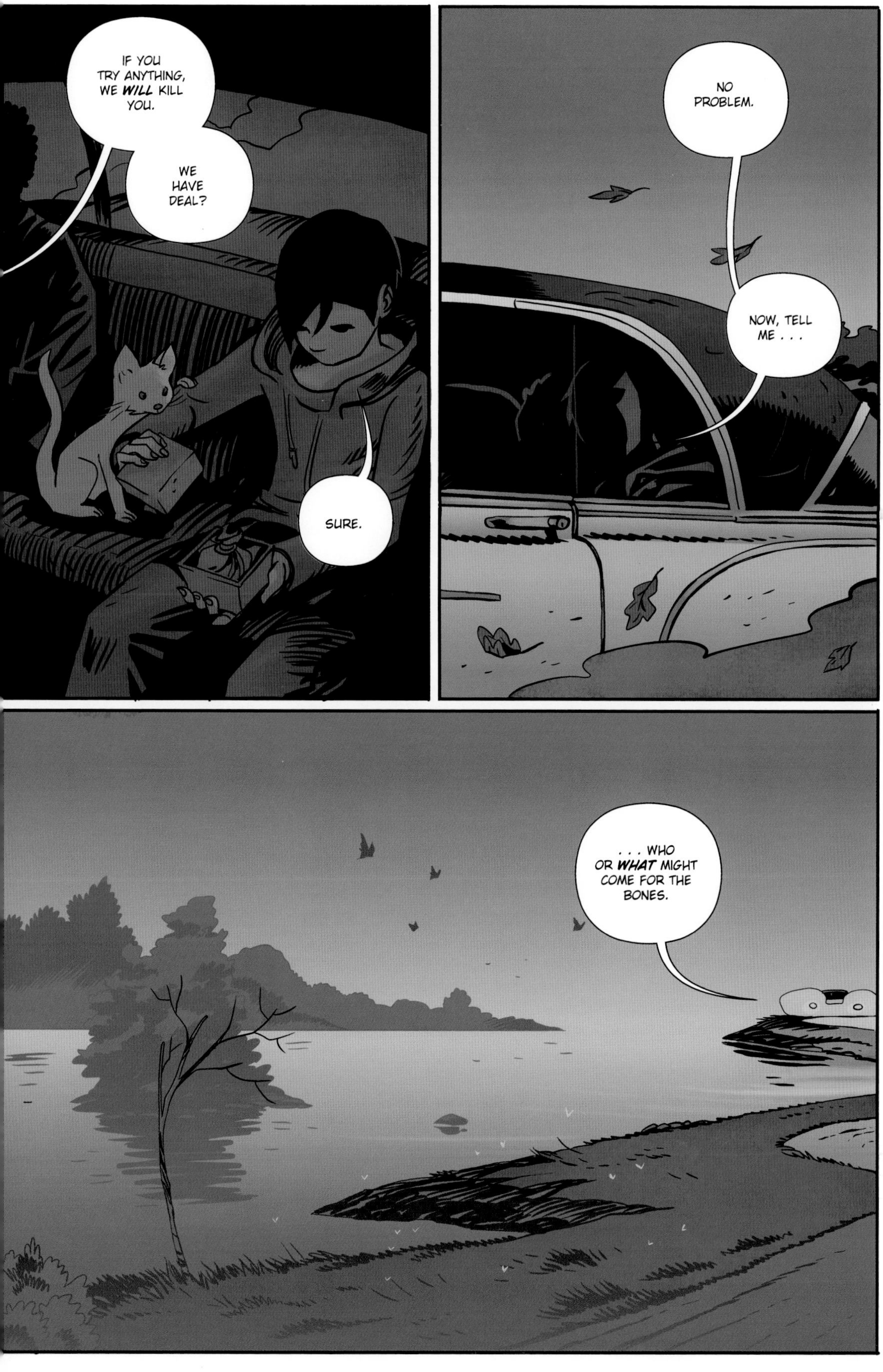
IF YOU TRY ANYTHING, WE **WILL** KILL YOU.
WE HAVE DEAL?
SURE.
NO PROBLEM.
NOW, TELL ME . . .
. . . WHO OR **WHAT** MIGHT COME FOR THE BONES.

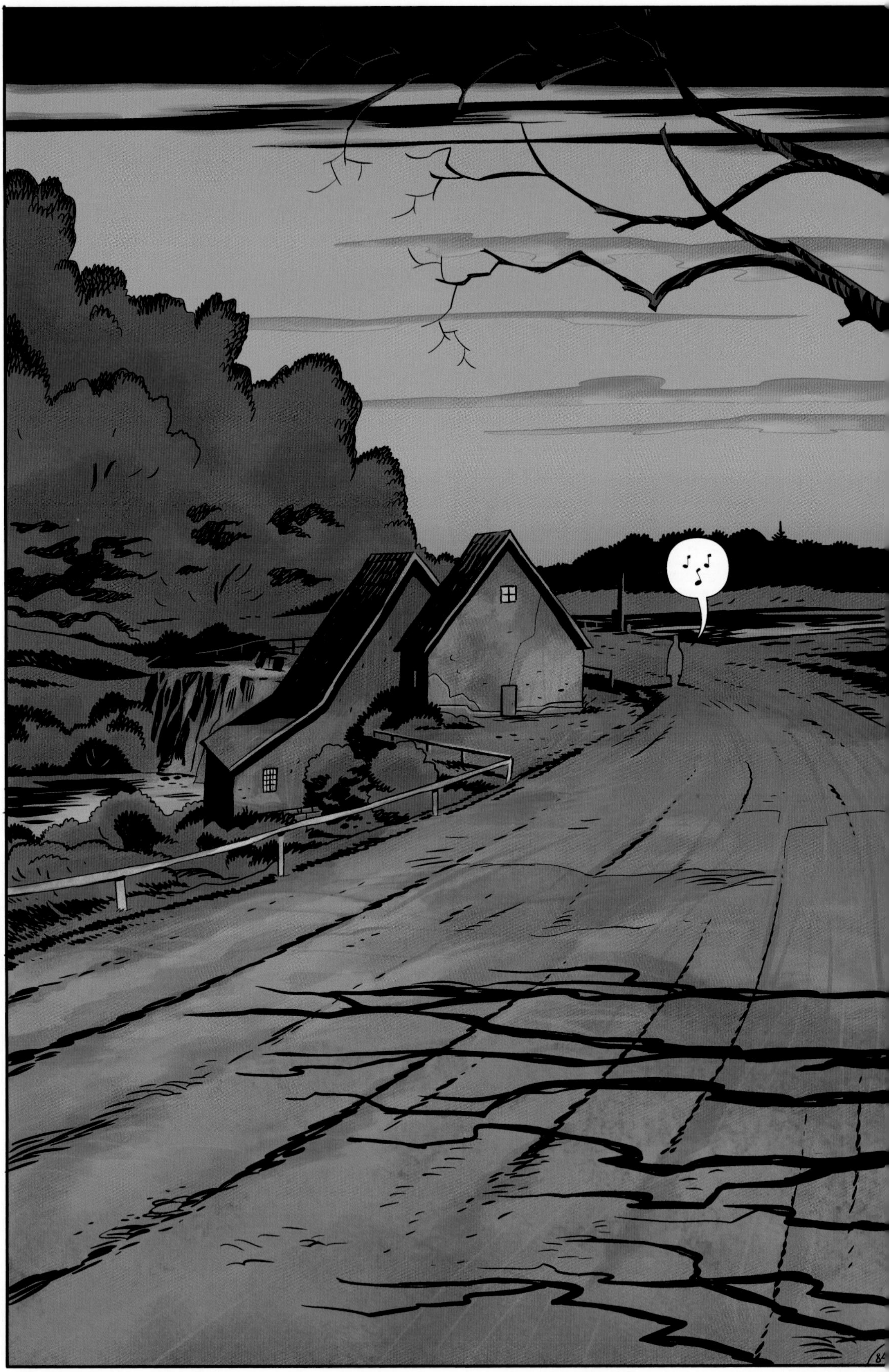

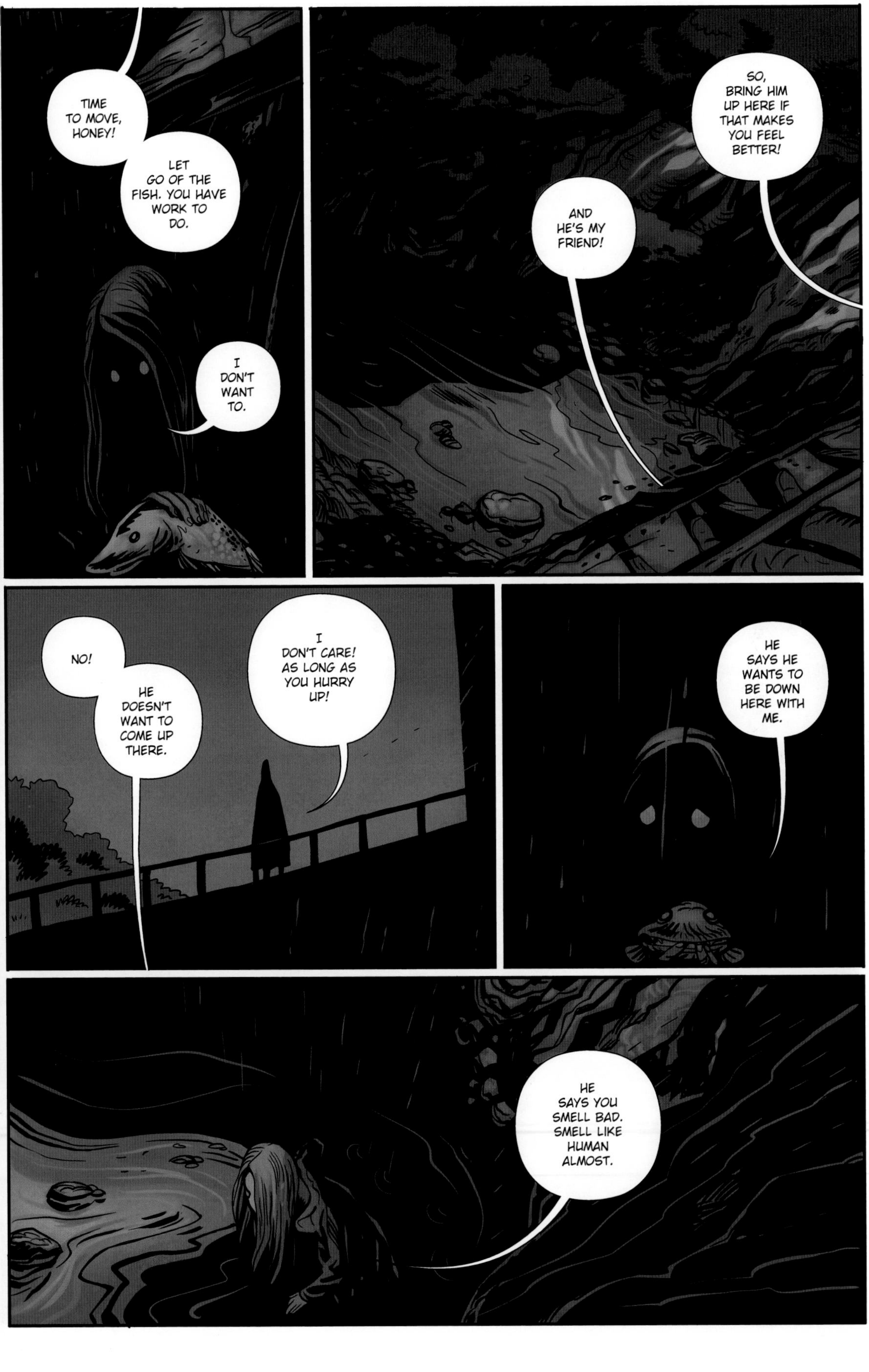
TIME TO MOVE, HONEY!
LET GO OF THE FISH. YOU HAVE WORK TO DO.
I DON'T WANT TO.
SO, BRING HIM UP HERE IF THAT MAKES YOU FEEL BETTER!
AND HE'S MY FRIEND!
NO!
HE DOESN'T WANT TO COME UP THERE.
I DON'T CARE! AS LONG AS YOU HURRY UP!
HE SAYS HE WANTS TO BE DOWN HERE WITH ME.
HE SAYS YOU SMELL BAD. SMELL LIKE HUMAN ALMOST.

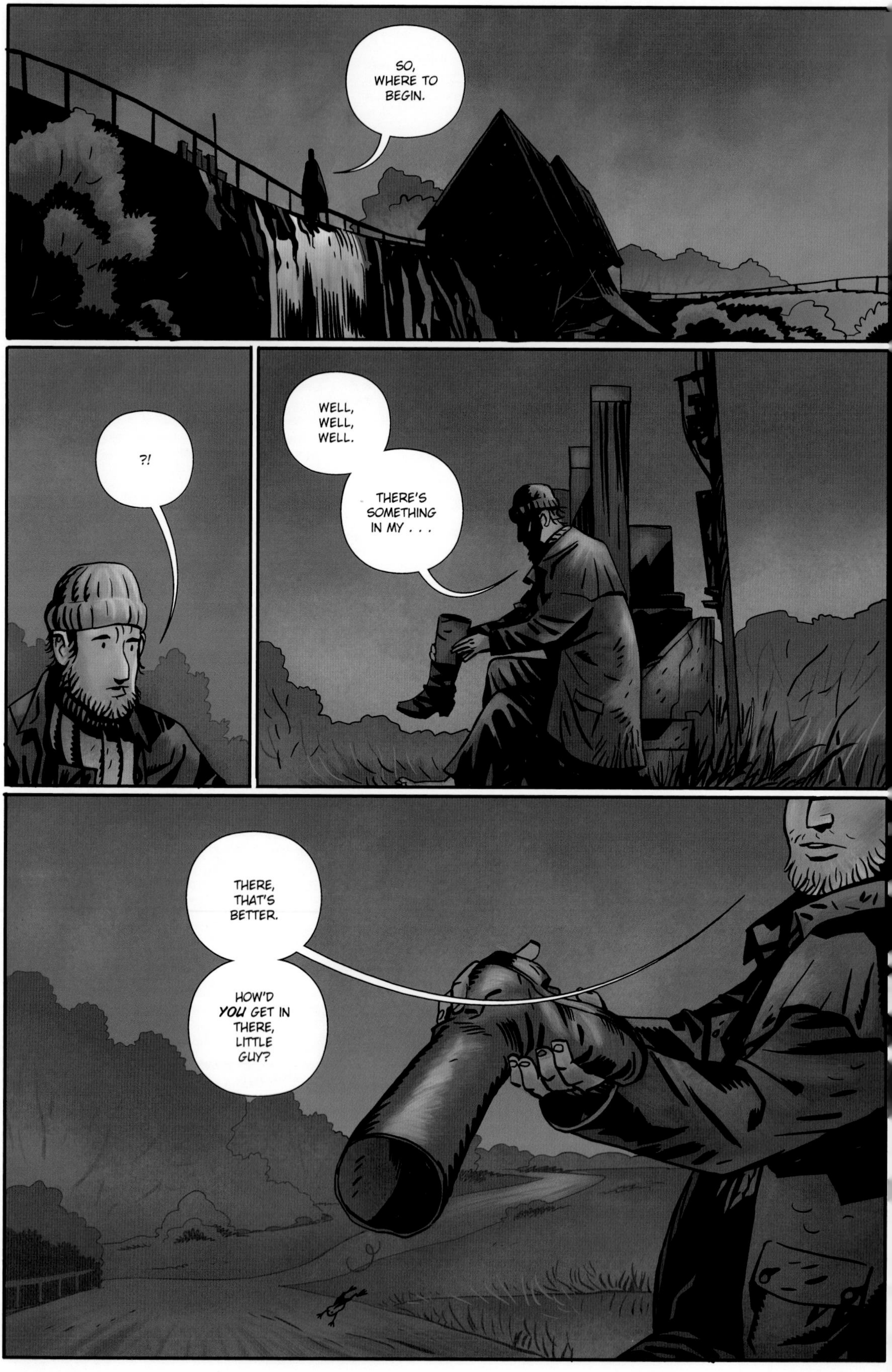
SO, WHERE TO BEGIN.
?!
WELL, WELL, WELL.
THERE'S SOMETHING IN MY . . .
THERE, THAT'S BETTER.
HOW'D *YOU* GET IN THERE, LITTLE GUY?

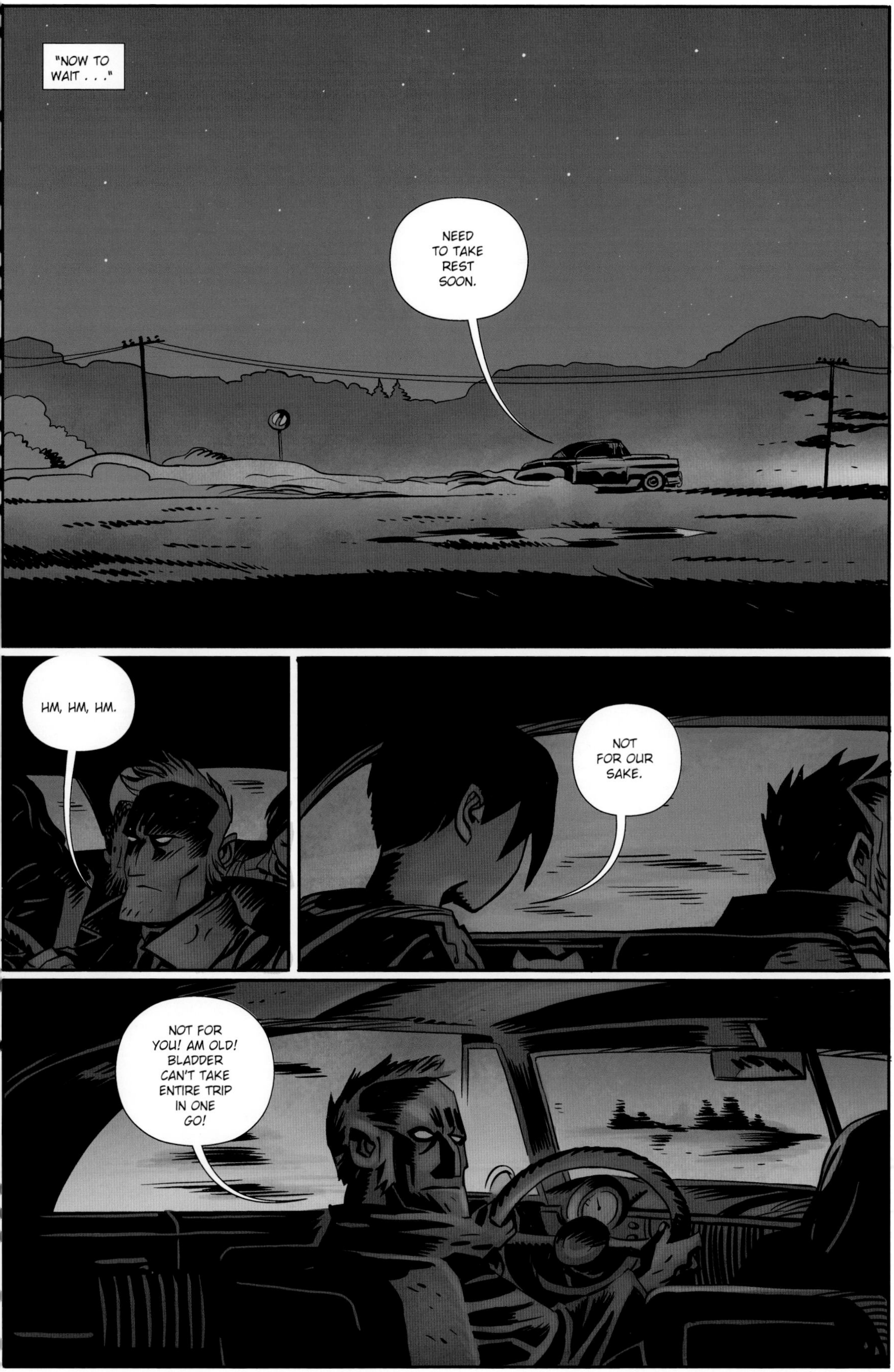

"NOW TO WAIT . . ."
NEED TO TAKE REST SOON.
HM, HM, HM.
NOT FOR OUR SAKE.
NOT FOR YOU! AM OLD! BLADDER CAN'T TAKE ENTIRE TRIP IN ONE GO!

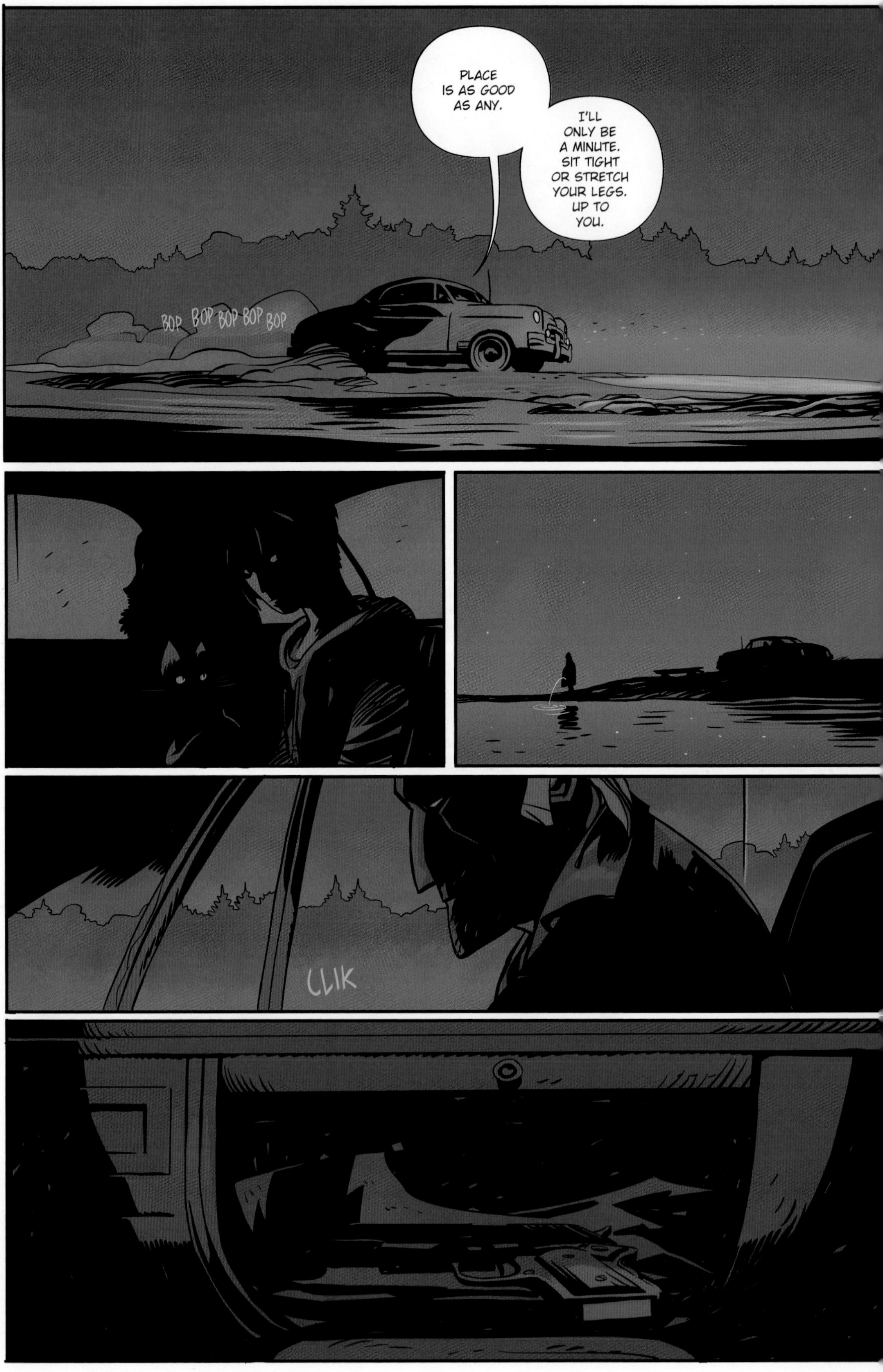
PLACE IS AS GOOD AS ANY.
I'LL ONLY BE A MINUTE. SIT TIGHT OR STRETCH YOUR LEGS. UP TO YOU.
BOP BOP BOP BOP BOP
CLIK

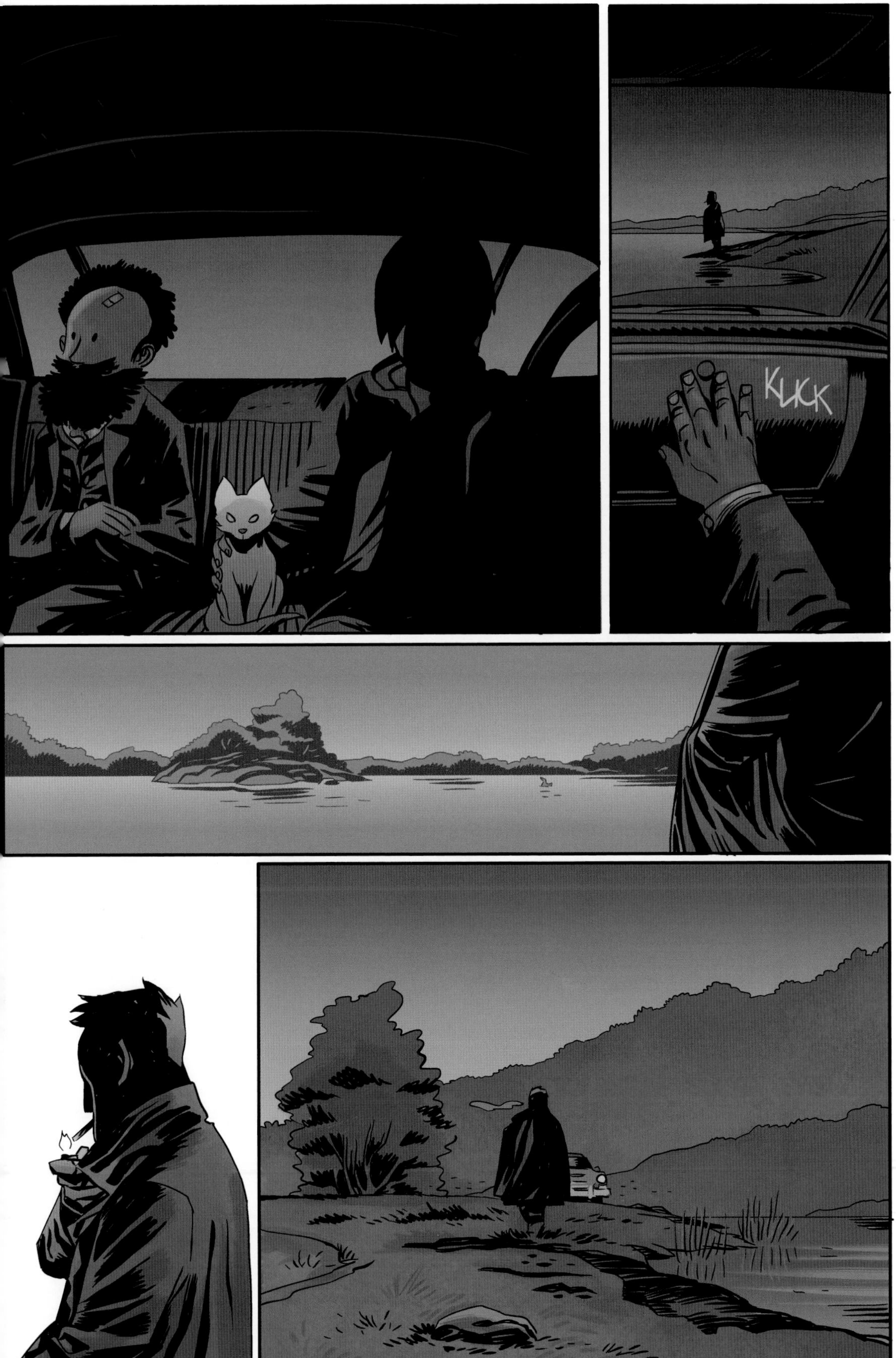
KLICK

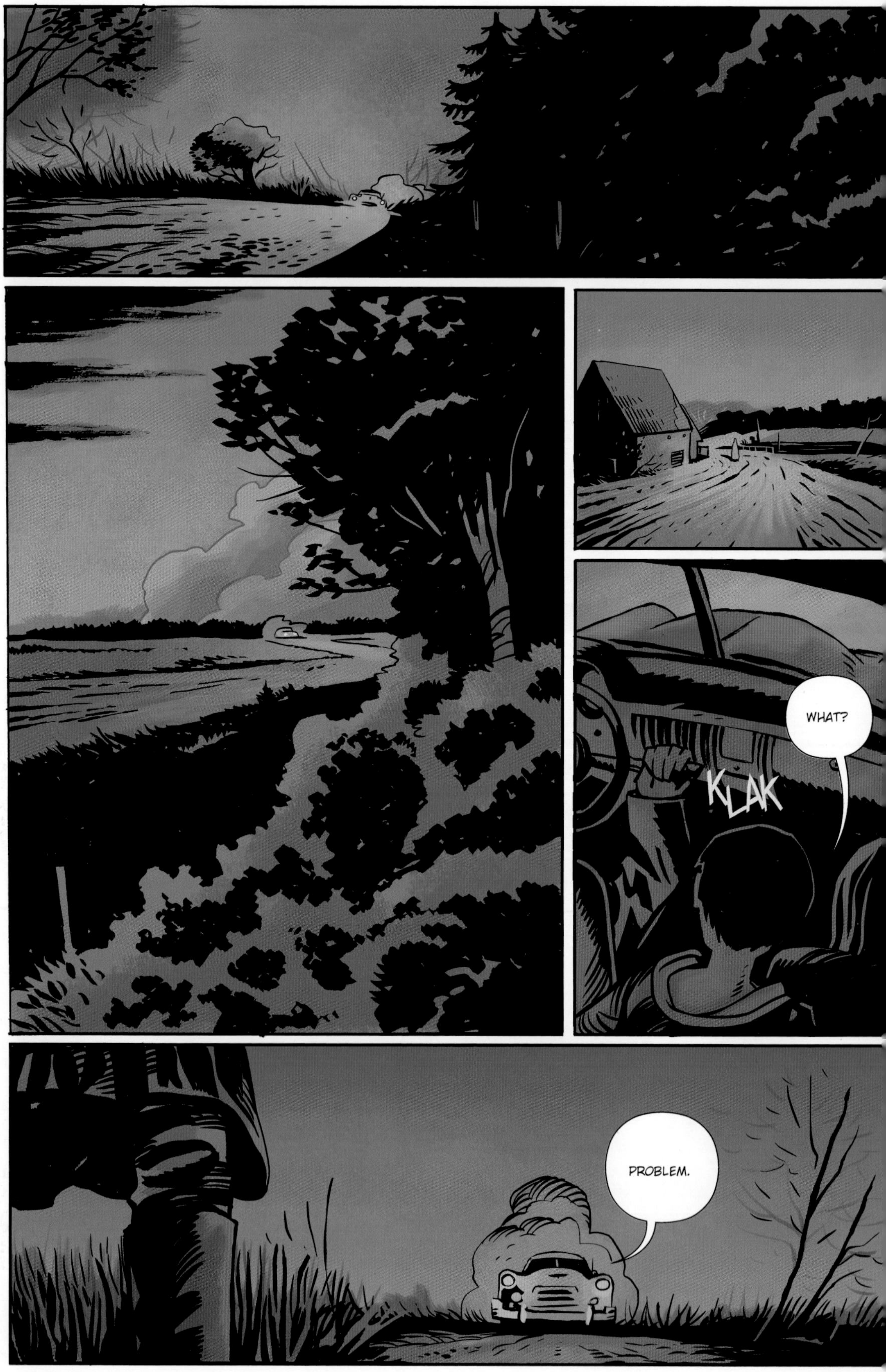
WHAT?
KLAK
PROBLEM.

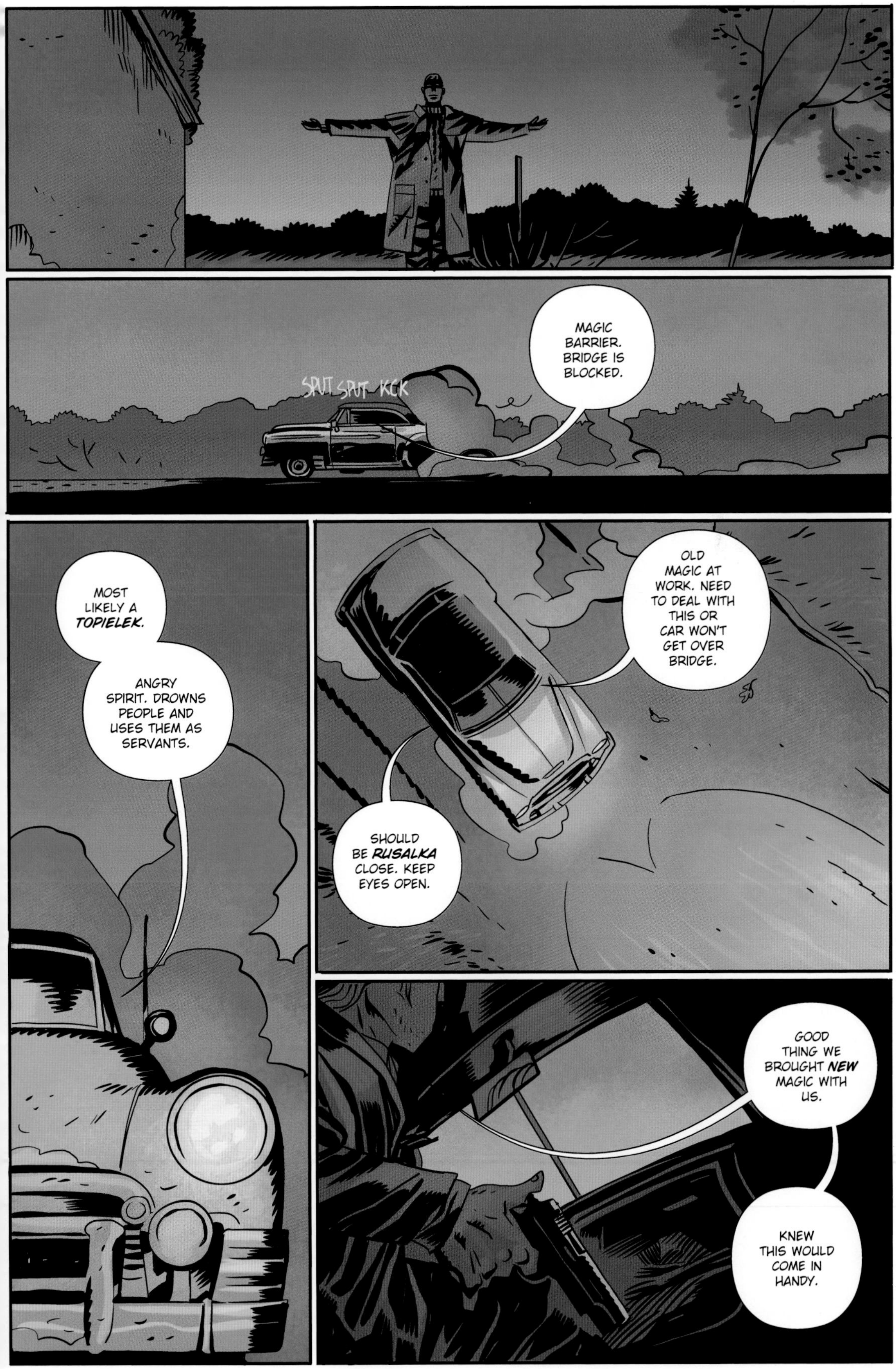

SPUT SPUT KCK
MAGIC BARRIER. BRIDGE IS BLOCKED.
MOST LIKELY A TOPIELEK.
ANGRY SPIRIT. DROWNS PEOPLE AND USES THEM AS SERVANTS.
OLD MAGIC AT WORK. NEED TO DEAL WITH THIS OR CAR WON'T GET OVER BRIDGE.
SHOULD BE RUSALKA CLOSE. KEEP EYES OPEN.
GOOD THING WE BROUGHT NEW MAGIC WITH US.
KNEW THIS WOULD COME IN HANDY.

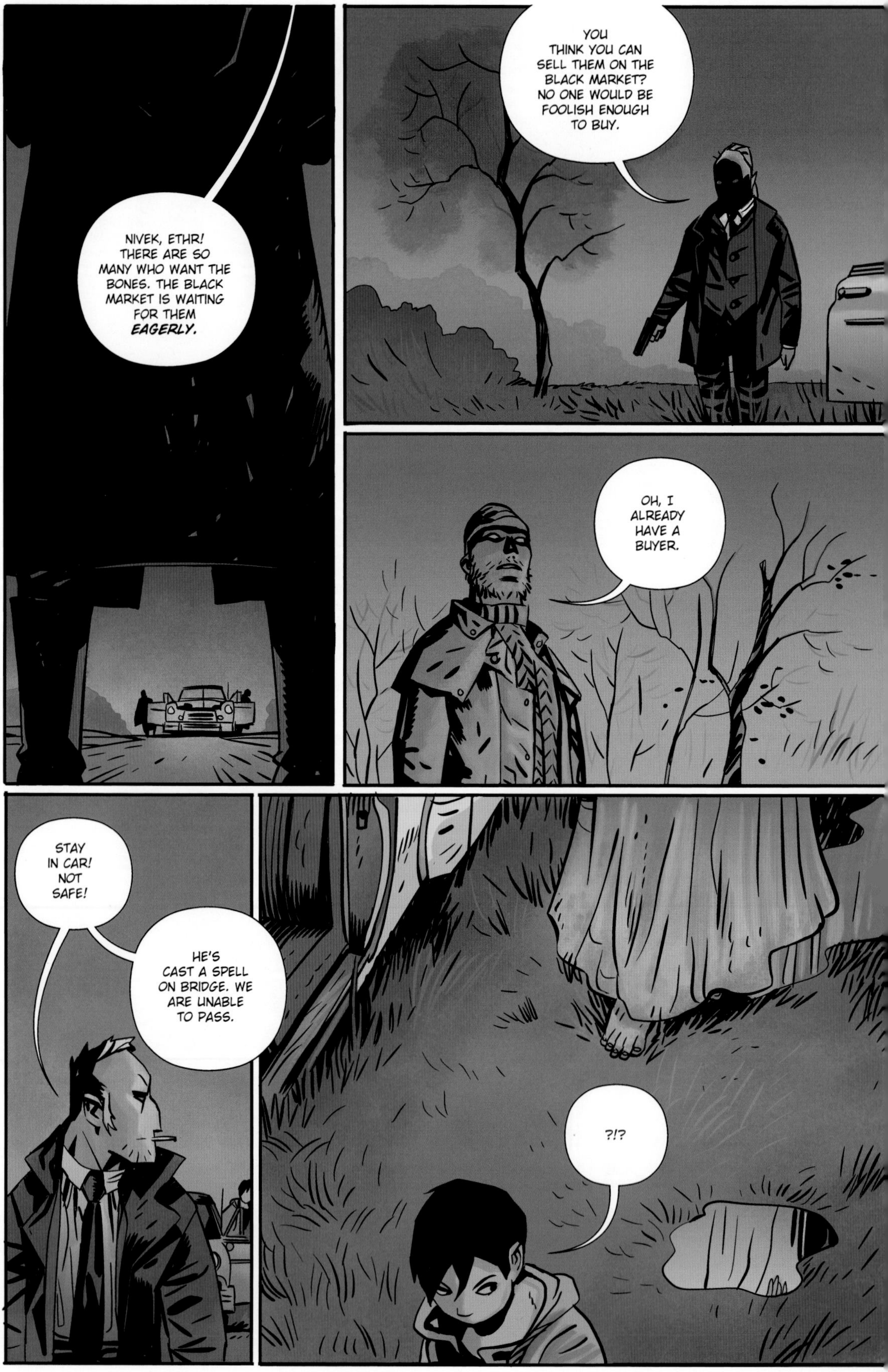
NIVEK, ETHR! THERE ARE SO MANY WHO WANT THE BONES. THE BLACK MARKET IS WAITING FOR THEM EAGERLY.
YOU THINK YOU CAN SELL THEM ON THE BLACK MARKET? NO ONE WOULD BE FOOLISH ENOUGH TO BUY.
OH, I ALREADY HAVE A BUYER.
STAY IN CAR! NOT SAFE!
HE'S CAST A SPELL ON BRIDGE. WE ARE UNABLE TO PASS.
?!?

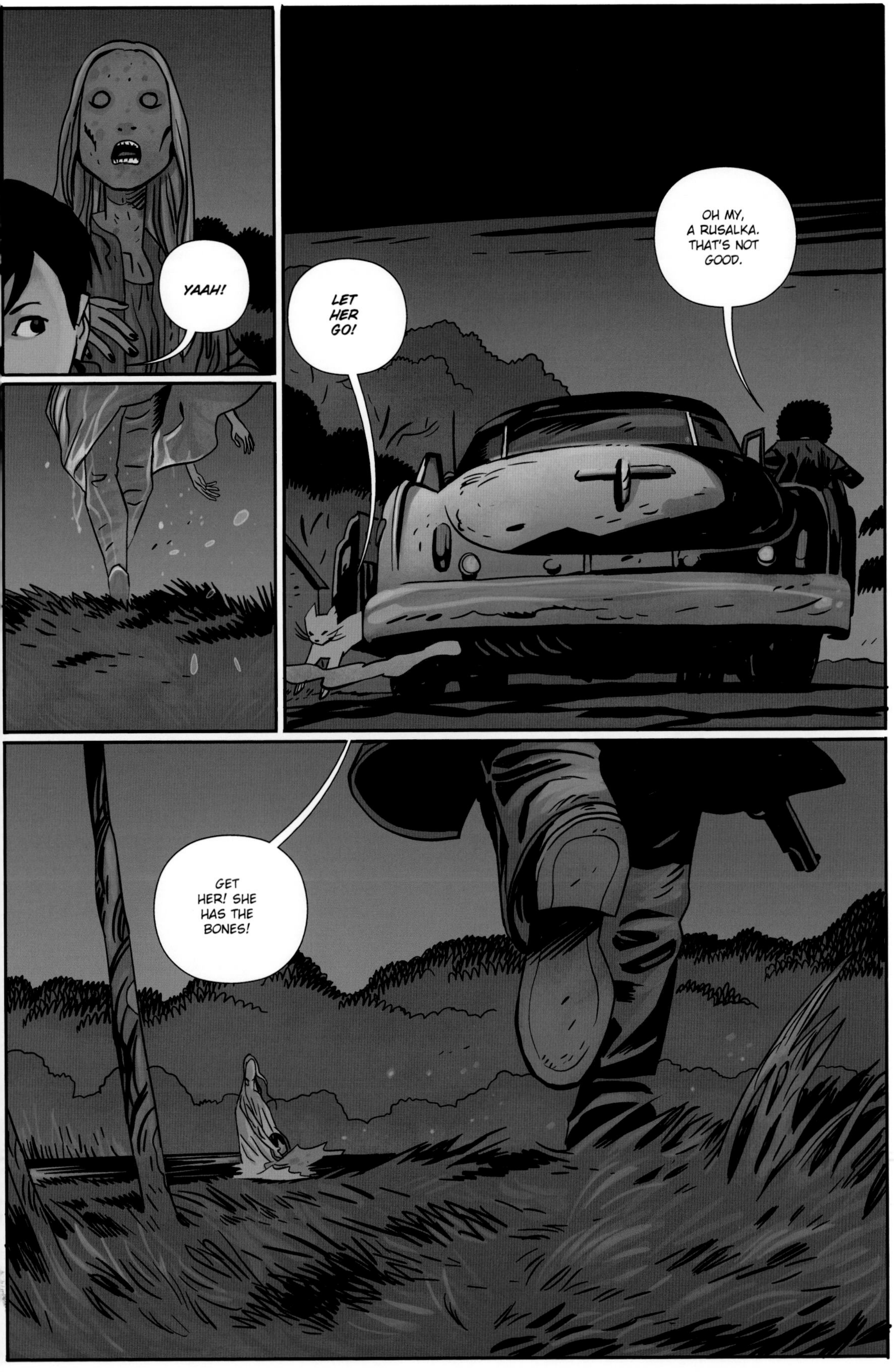
YAAH!
LET HER GO!
OH MY, A RUSALKA. THAT'S NOT GOOD.
GET HER! SHE HAS THE BONES!

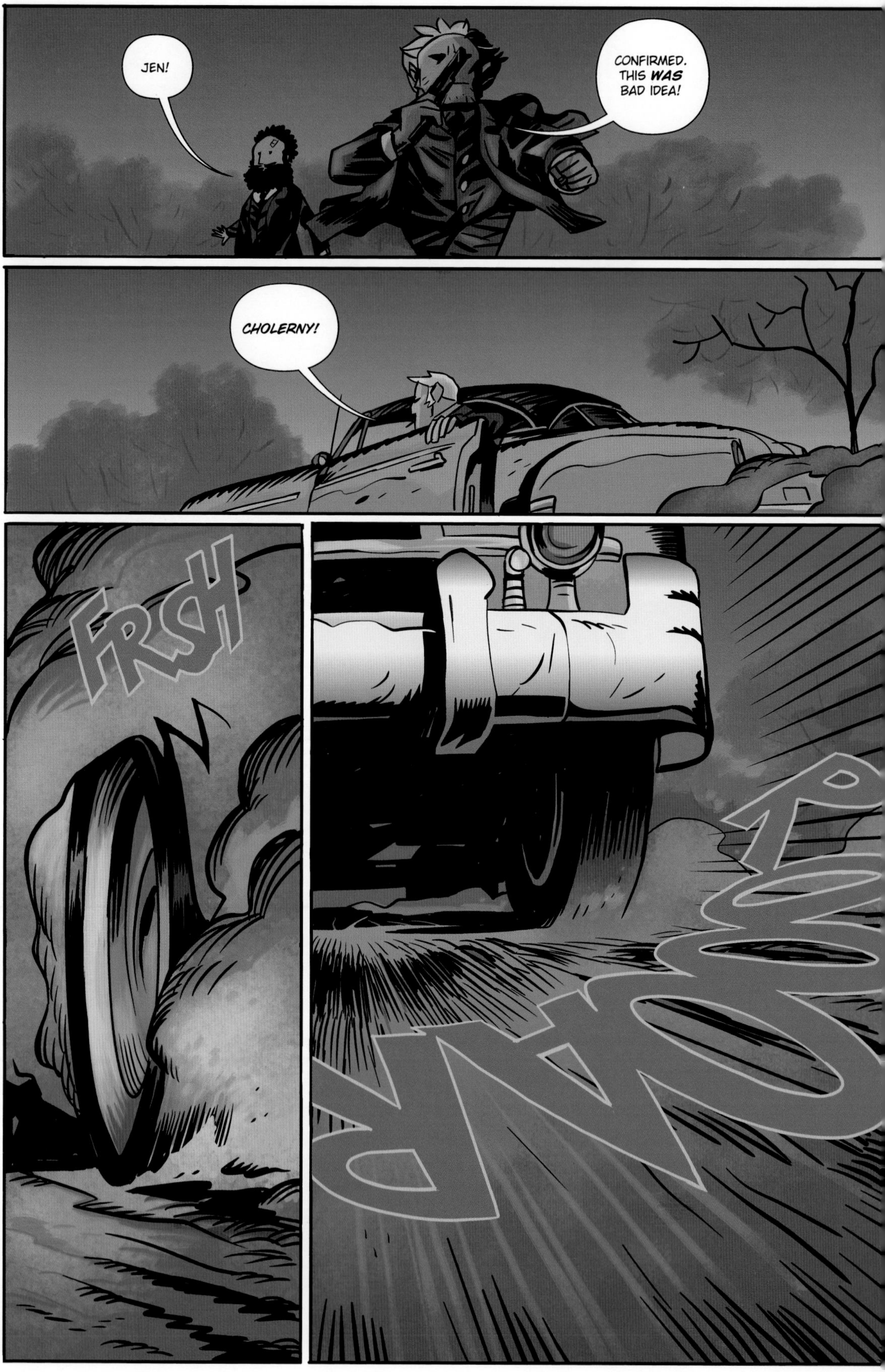
JEN!
CONFIRMED. THIS **WAS** BAD IDEA!
CHOLERNY!
FRSH

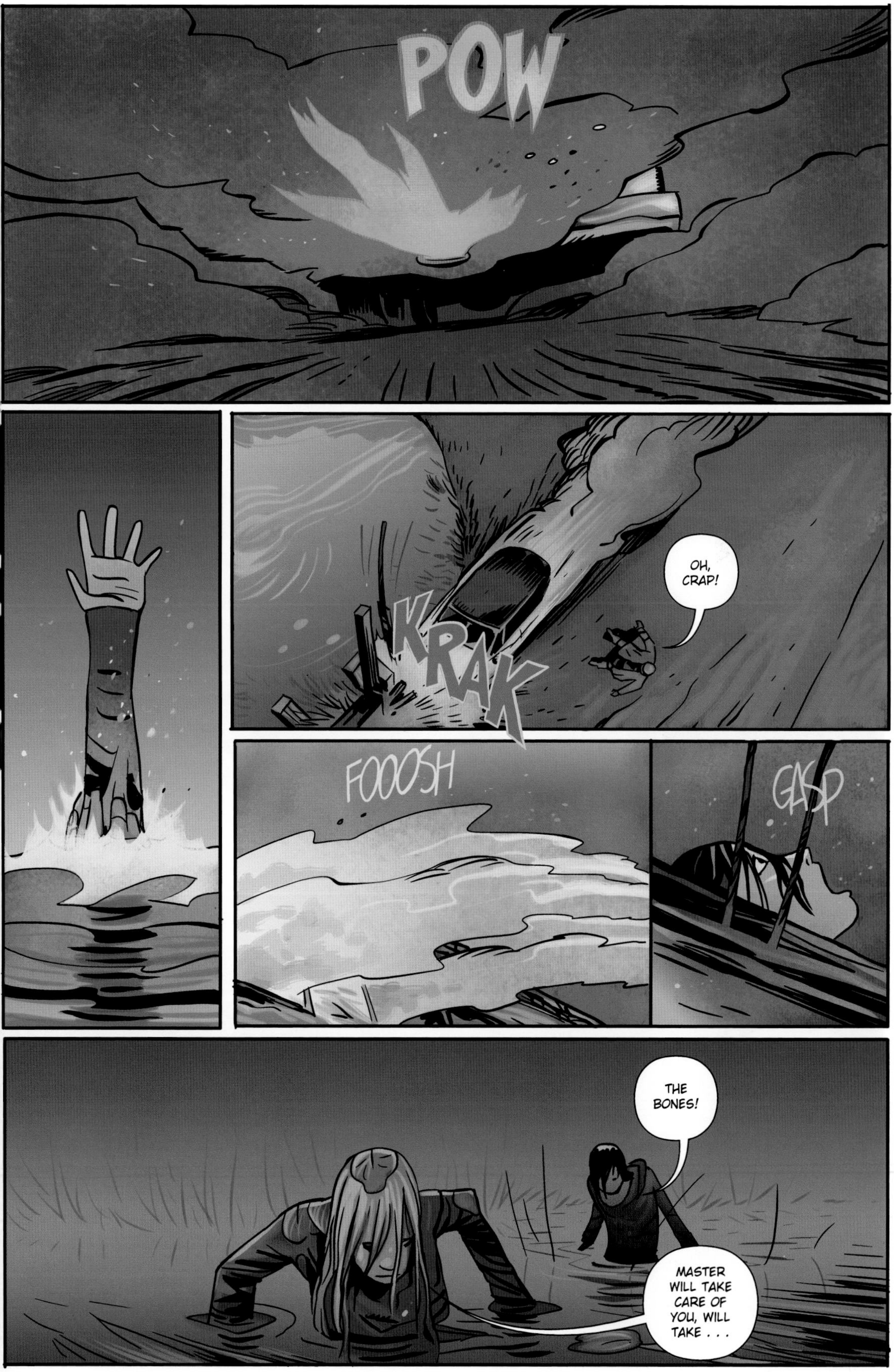
POW
KRAK
OH, CRAP!
FOOOSH
GASP
THE BONES!
MASTER WILL TAKE CARE OF YOU, WILL TAKE . . .

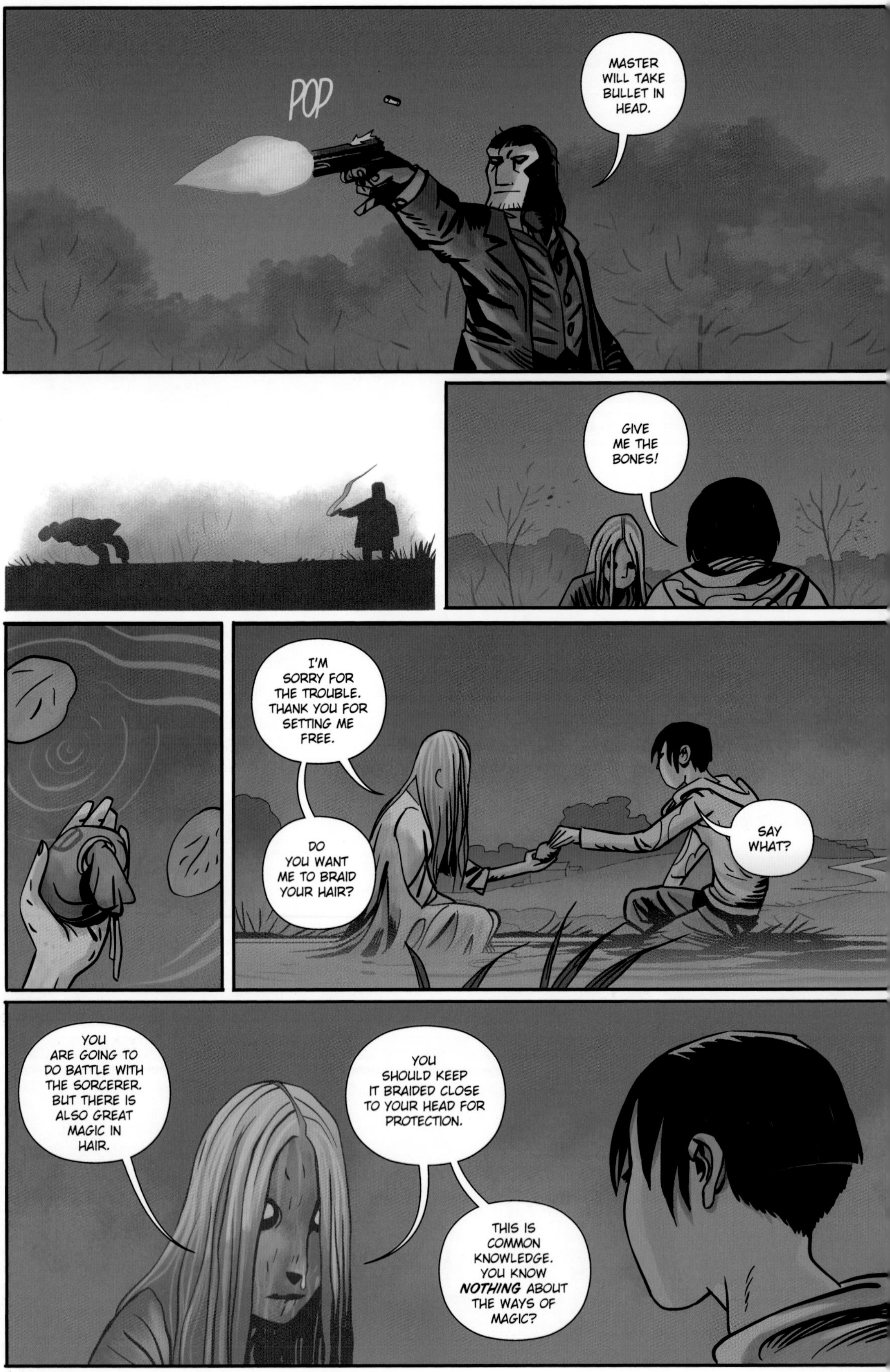
POP
MASTER WILL TAKE BULLET IN HEAD.
GIVE ME THE BONES!
I'M SORRY FOR THE TROUBLE. THANK YOU FOR SETTING ME FREE.
DO YOU WANT ME TO BRAID YOUR HAIR?
SAY WHAT?
YOU ARE GOING TO DO BATTLE WITH THE SORCERER. BUT THERE IS ALSO GREAT MAGIC IN HAIR.
YOU SHOULD KEEP IT BRAIDED CLOSE TO YOUR HEAD FOR PROTECTION.
THIS IS COMMON KNOWLEDGE. YOU KNOW NOTHING ABOUT THE WAYS OF MAGIC?

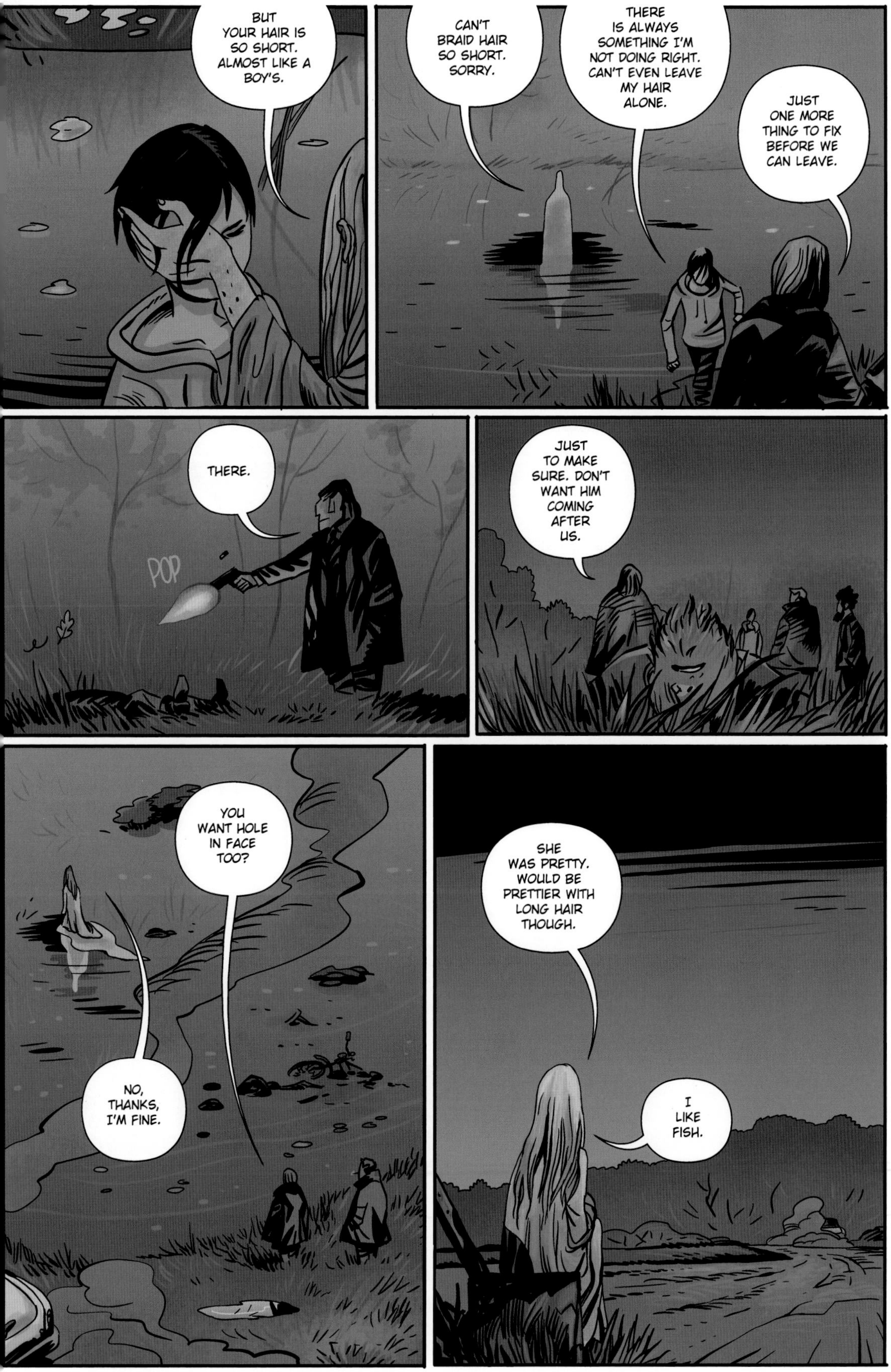
BUT YOUR HAIR IS SO SHORT. ALMOST LIKE A BOY'S.
CAN'T BRAID HAIR SO SHORT. SORRY.
THERE IS ALWAYS SOMETHING I'M NOT DOING RIGHT. CAN'T EVEN LEAVE MY HAIR ALONE.
JUST ONE MORE THING TO FIX BEFORE WE CAN LEAVE.
THERE.
POP
JUST TO MAKE SURE. DON'T WANT HIM COMING AFTER US.
YOU WANT HOLE IN FACE TOO?
NO, THANKS, I'M FINE.
SHE WAS PRETTY. WOULD BE PRETTIER WITH LONG HAIR THOUGH.
I LIKE FISH.

THIS IS IT -- FINAL STOP OF JOURNEY!

I WANT TO VISIT GRANDMA'S GRAVE. IT'S HERE, ISN'T IT?

THERE'S A CHURCH JUST BEHIND THE TREES. YOU CAN WALK UP THERE IN FIVE MINUTES.

YOU LIKE ME TO POINT OUT GRAVE? NO PROBLEM.

NO, THANKS. I'D RATHER BE ALONE.

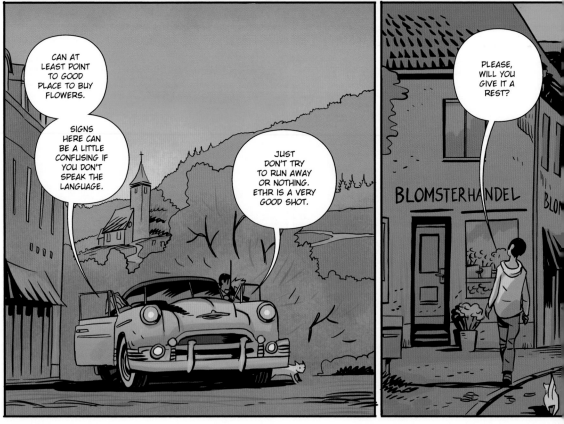

CAN AT LEAST POINT TO GOOD PLACE TO BUY FLOWERS.

SIGNS HERE CAN BE A LITTLE CONFUSING IF YOU DON'T SPEAK THE LANGUAGE.

JUST DON'T TRY TO RUN AWAY OR NOTHING. ETHR IS A VERY GOOD SHOT.

PLEASE, WILL YOU GIVE IT A REST?

BLOMSTERHANDEL

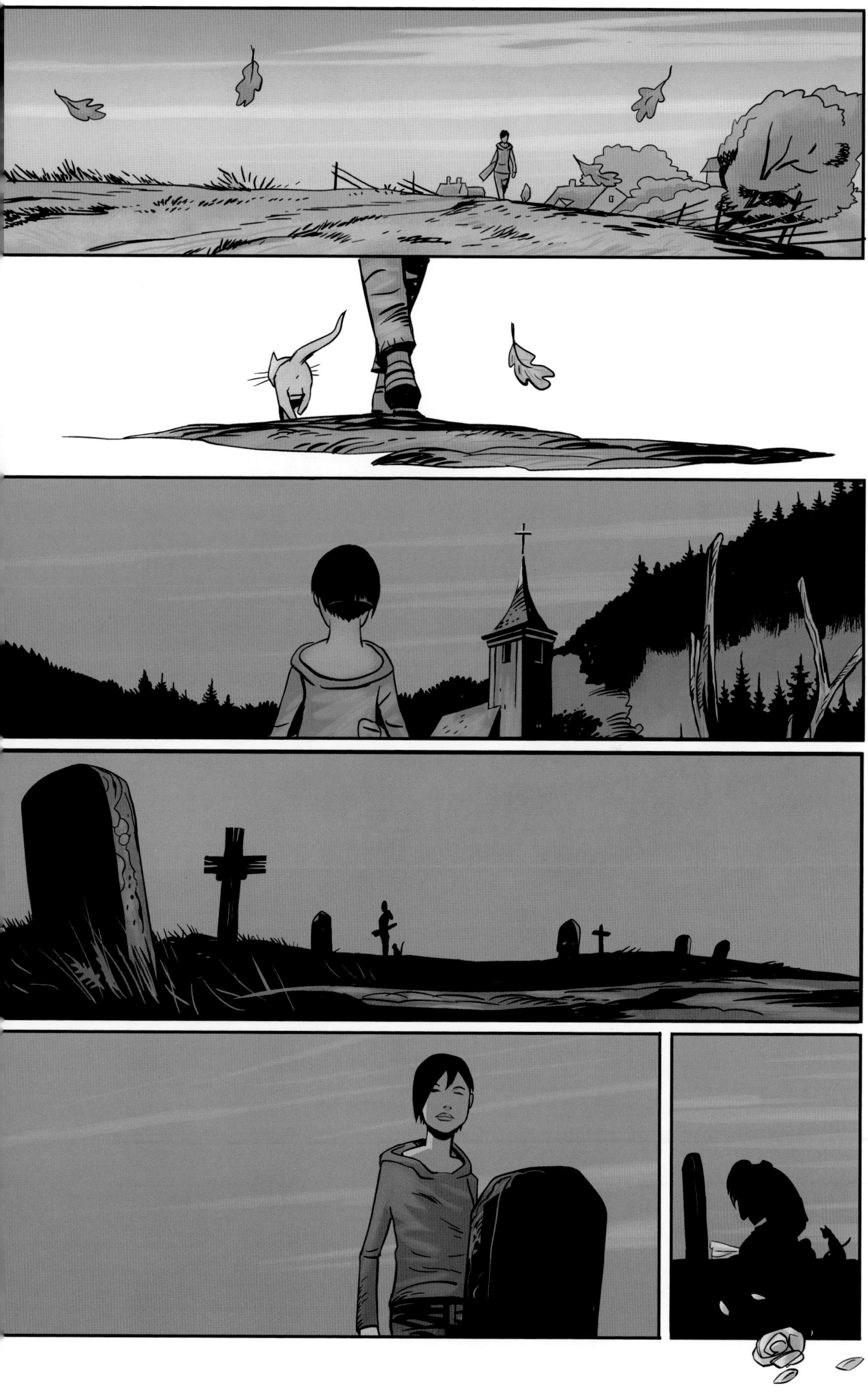

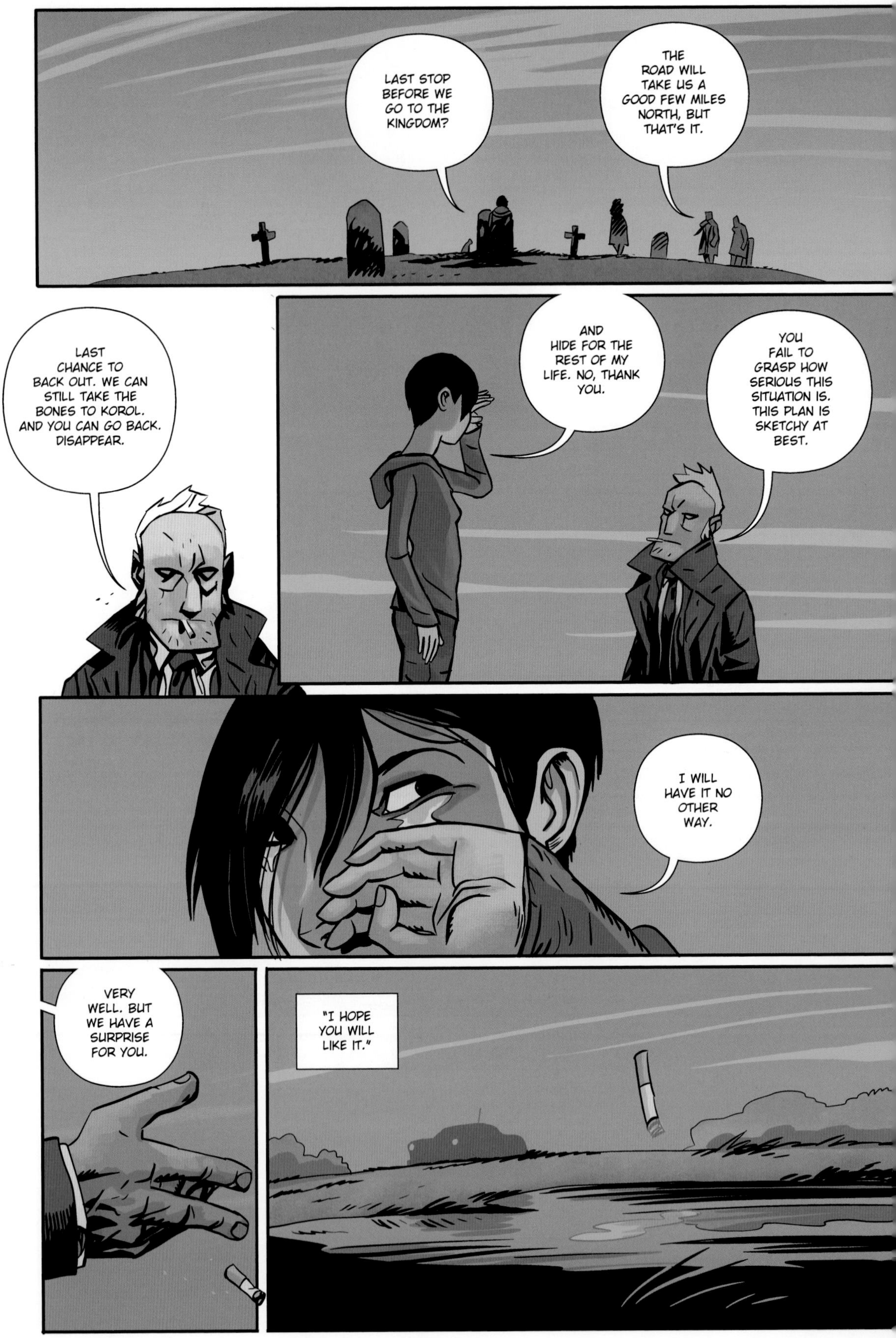

LAST STOP BEFORE WE GO TO THE KINGDOM?
THE ROAD WILL TAKE US A GOOD FEW MILES NORTH, BUT THAT'S IT.
LAST CHANCE TO BACK OUT. WE CAN STILL TAKE THE BONES TO KOROL. AND YOU CAN GO BACK. DISAPPEAR.
AND HIDE FOR THE REST OF MY LIFE. NO, THANK YOU.
YOU FAIL TO GRASP HOW SERIOUS THIS SITUATION IS. THIS PLAN IS SKETCHY AT BEST.
I WILL HAVE IT NO OTHER WAY.
VERY WELL. BUT WE HAVE A SURPRISE FOR YOU.
"I HOPE YOU WILL LIKE IT."

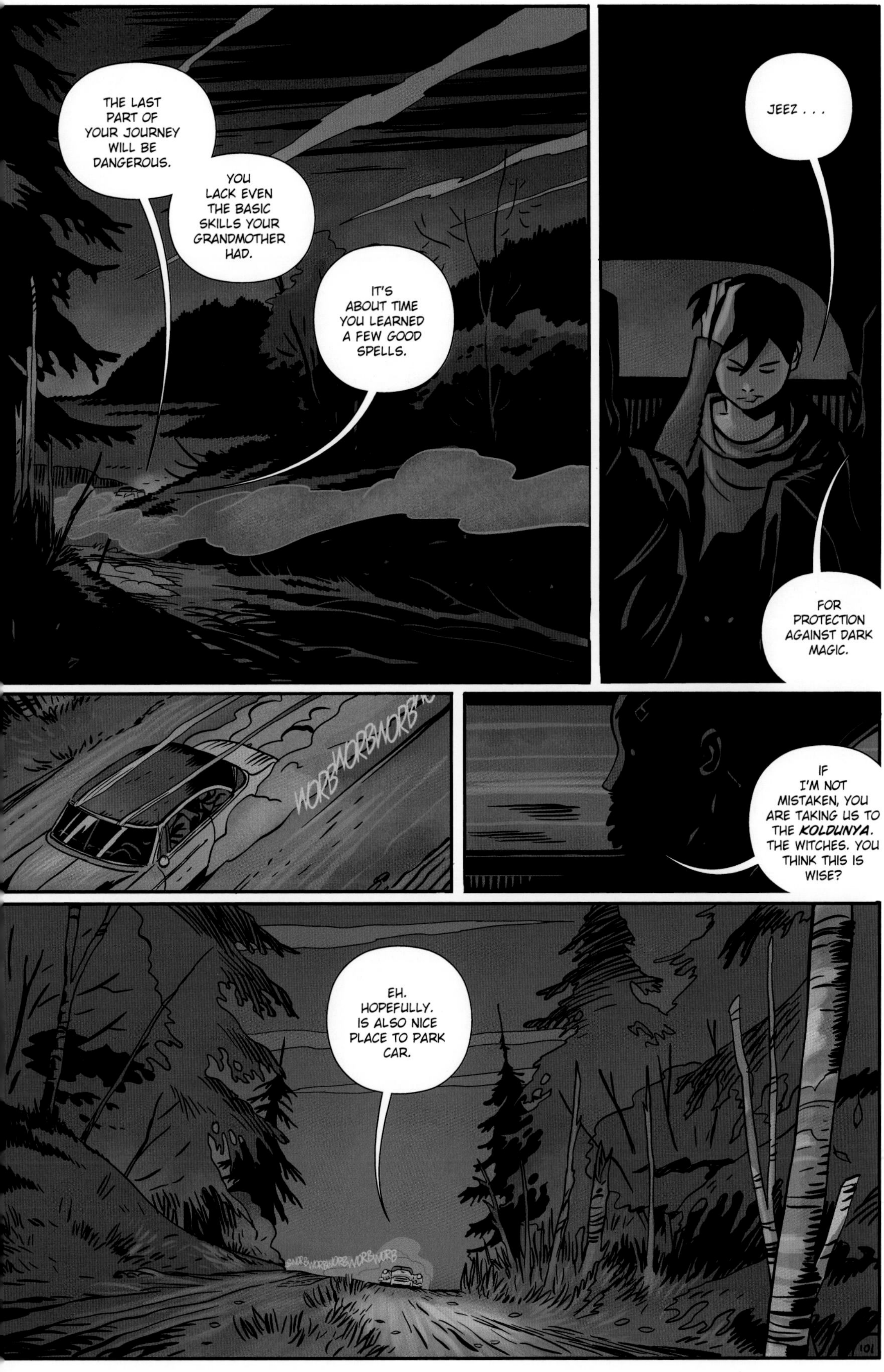
THE LAST PART OF YOUR JOURNEY WILL BE DANGEROUS.
YOU LACK EVEN THE BASIC SKILLS YOUR GRANDMOTHER HAD.
IT'S ABOUT TIME YOU LEARNED A FEW GOOD SPELLS.
JEEZ . . .
FOR PROTECTION AGAINST DARK MAGIC.
WORBWORBWORB
IF I'M NOT MISTAKEN, YOU ARE TAKING US TO THE *KOLDUNYA*. THE WITCHES. YOU THINK THIS IS WISE?
EH. HOPEFULLY. IS ALSO NICE PLACE TO PARK CAR.
WORBWORBWORBWORBWORB

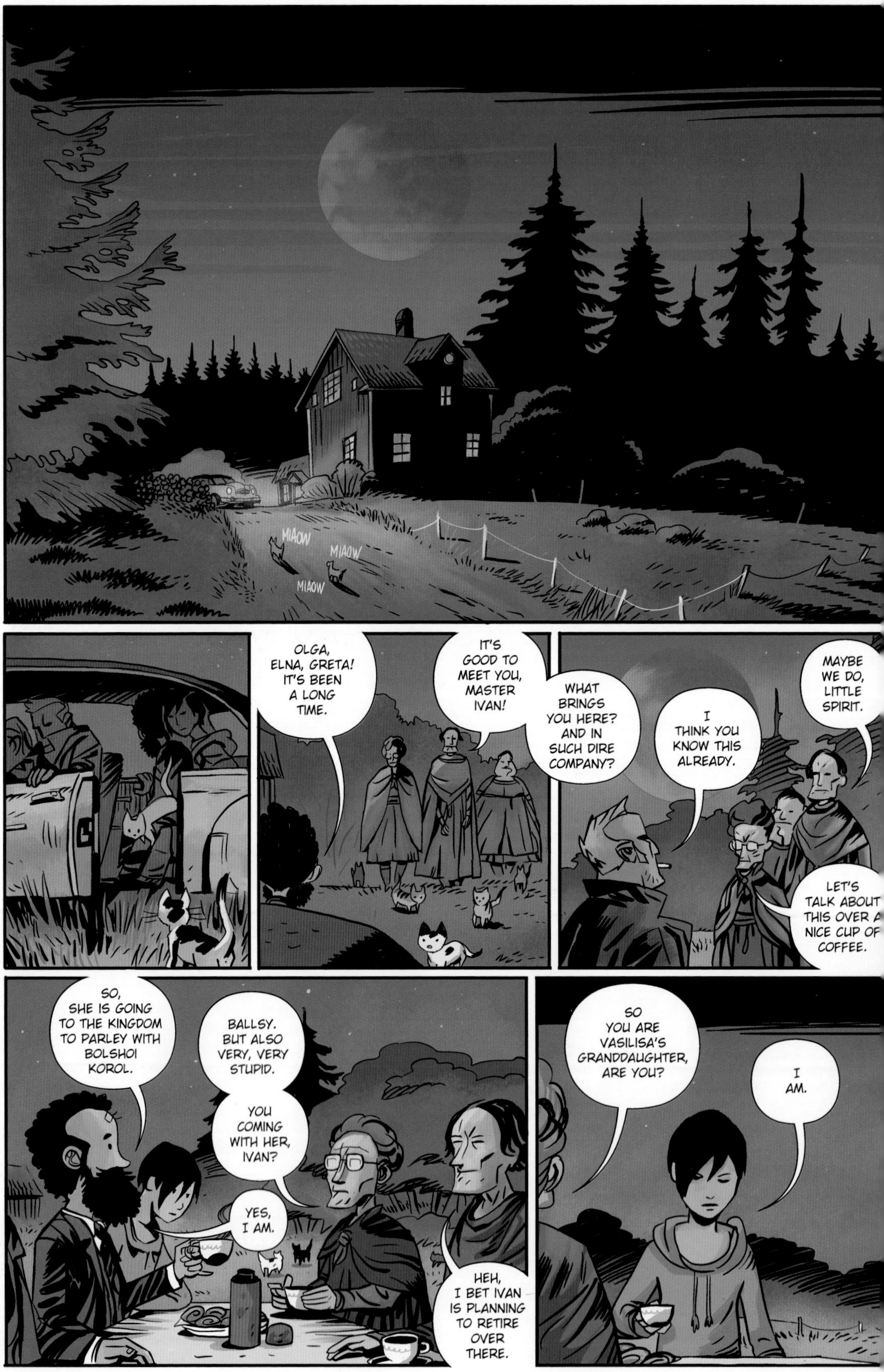
MIAOW
MIAOW
MIAOW
OLGA, ELNA, GRETA! IT'S BEEN A LONG TIME.
IT'S GOOD TO MEET YOU, MASTER IVAN!
WHAT BRINGS YOU HERE? AND IN SUCH DIRE COMPANY?
I THINK YOU KNOW THIS ALREADY.
MAYBE WE DO, LITTLE SPIRIT.
LET'S TALK ABOUT THIS OVER A NICE CUP OF COFFEE.
SO, SHE IS GOING TO THE KINGDOM TO PARLEY WITH BOLSHOI KOROL.
BALLSY. BUT ALSO VERY, VERY STUPID.
YOU COMING WITH HER, IVAN?
YES, I AM.
HEH, I BET IVAN IS PLANNING TO RETIRE OVER THERE.
SO YOU ARE VASILISA'S GRANDDAUGHTER, ARE YOU?
I AM.

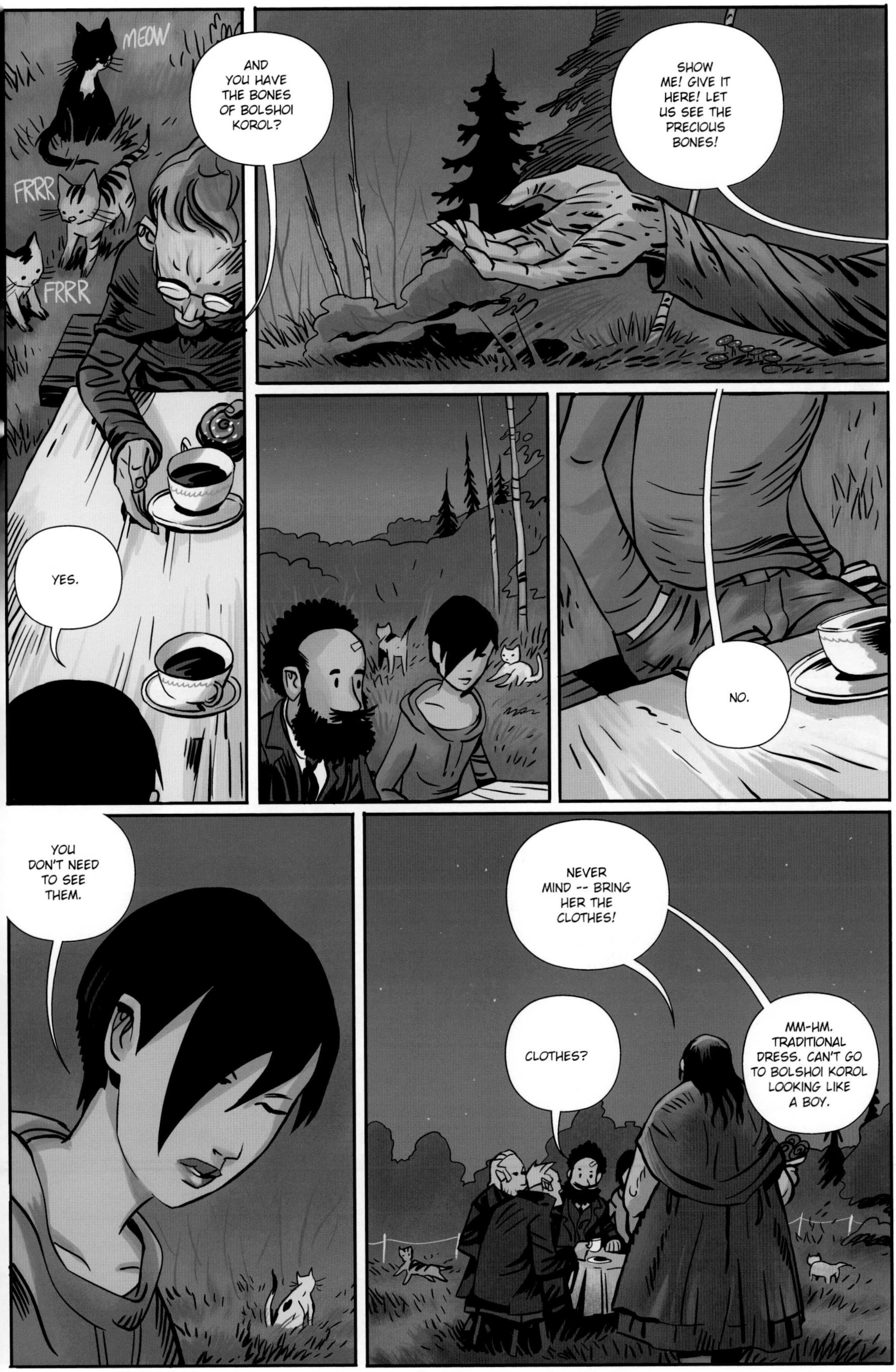
MEOW
FRRR
FRRR
AND YOU HAVE THE BONES OF BOLSHOI KOROL?
SHOW ME! GIVE IT HERE! LET US SEE THE PRECIOUS BONES!
YES.
NO.
YOU DON'T NEED TO SEE THEM.
NEVER MIND -- BRING HER THE CLOTHES!
CLOTHES?
MM-HM. TRADITIONAL DRESS. CAN'T GO TO BOLSHOI KOROL LOOKING LIKE A BOY.

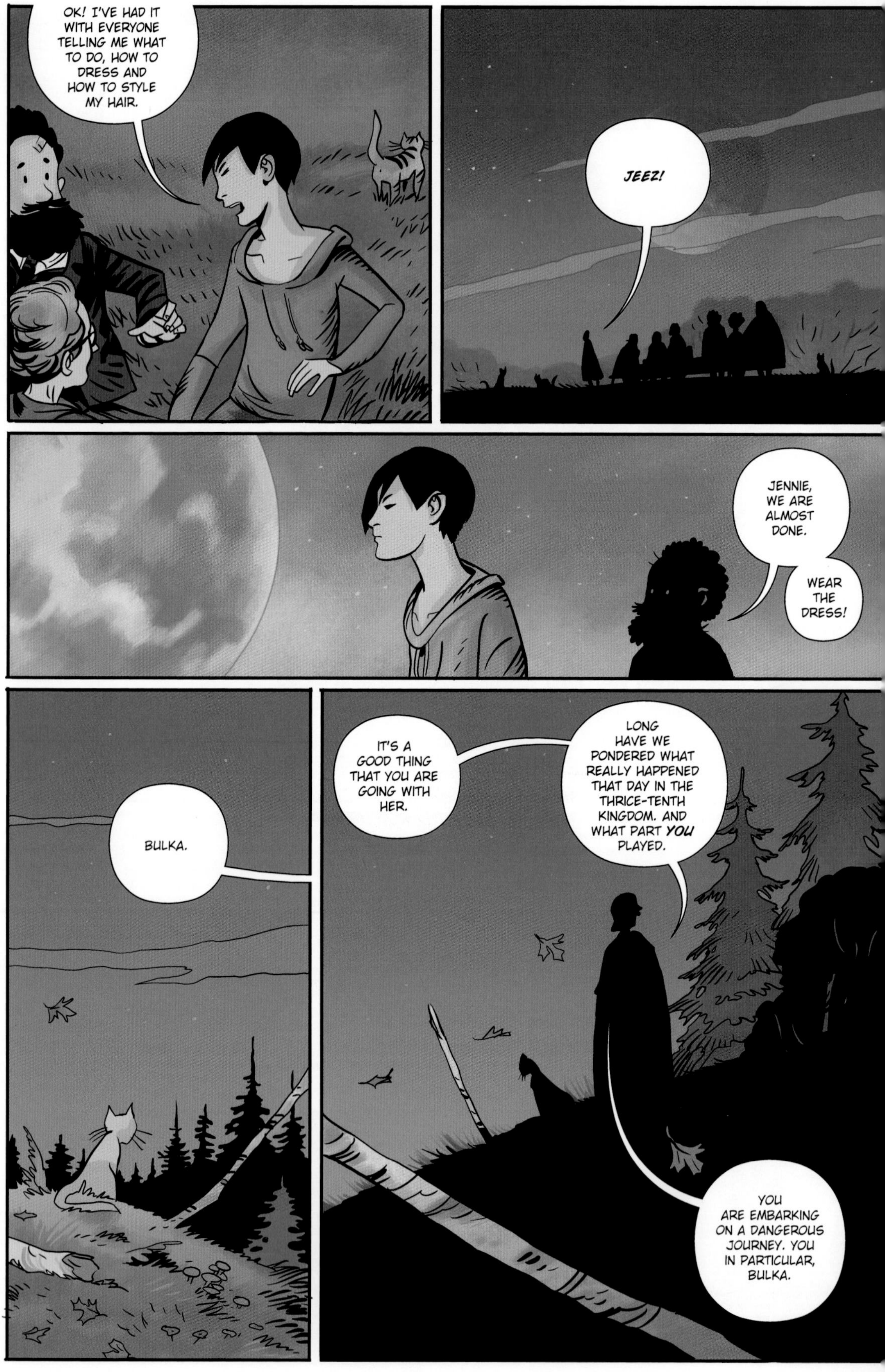
OK! I'VE HAD IT WITH EVERYONE TELLING ME WHAT TO DO, HOW TO DRESS AND HOW TO STYLE MY HAIR.
JEEZ!
JENNIE, WE ARE ALMOST DONE.
WEAR THE DRESS!
BULKA.
IT'S A GOOD THING THAT YOU ARE GOING WITH HER.
LONG HAVE WE PONDERED WHAT REALLY HAPPENED THAT DAY IN THE THRICE-TENTH KINGDOM. AND WHAT PART YOU PLAYED.
YOU ARE EMBARKING ON A DANGEROUS JOURNEY. YOU IN PARTICULAR, BULKA.

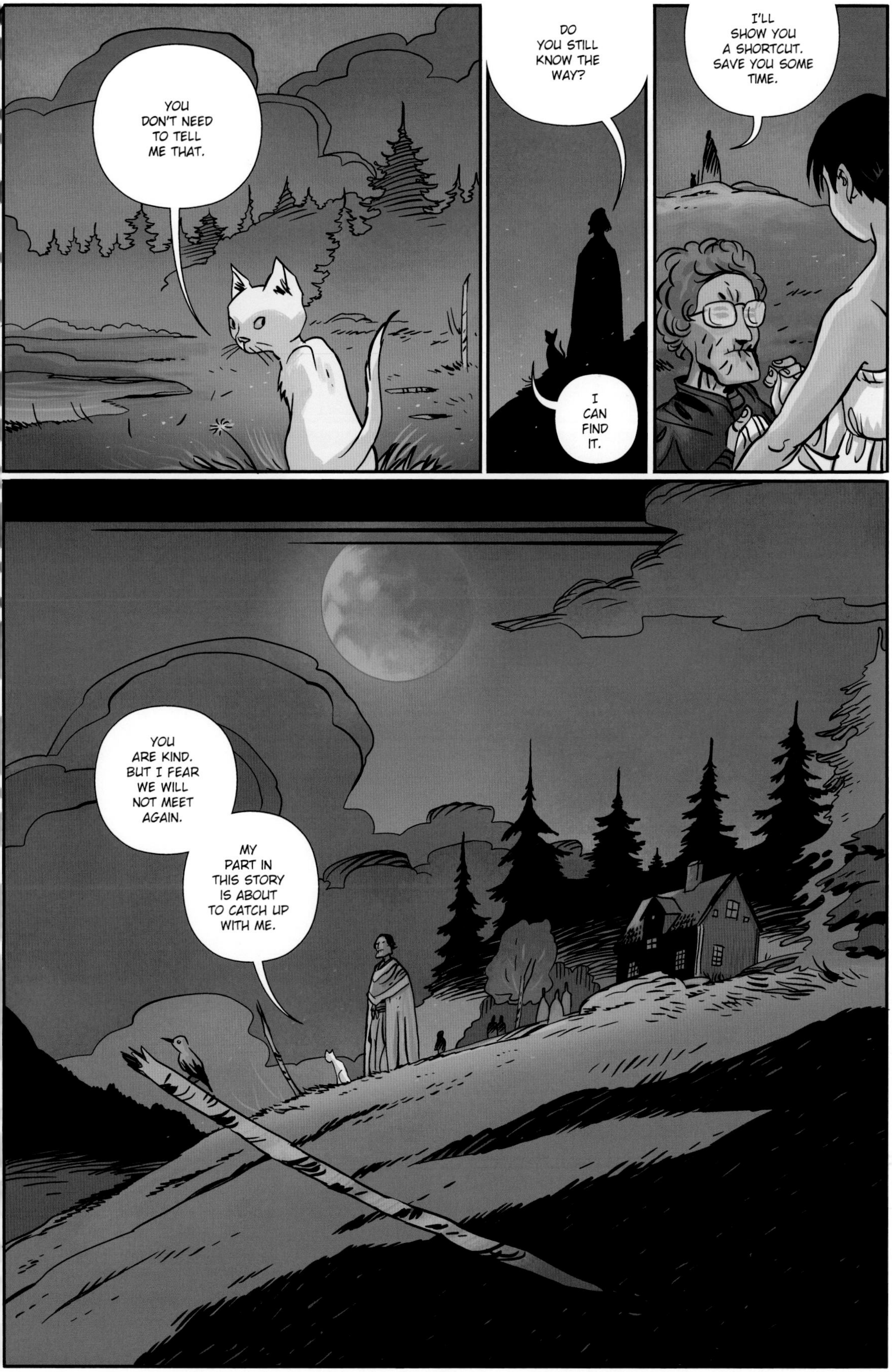
YOU DON'T NEED TO TELL ME THAT.
DO YOU STILL KNOW THE WAY?
I CAN FIND IT.
I'LL SHOW YOU A SHORTCUT. SAVE YOU SOME TIME.
YOU ARE KIND. BUT I FEAR WE WILL NOT MEET AGAIN.
MY PART IN THIS STORY IS ABOUT TO CATCH UP WITH ME.

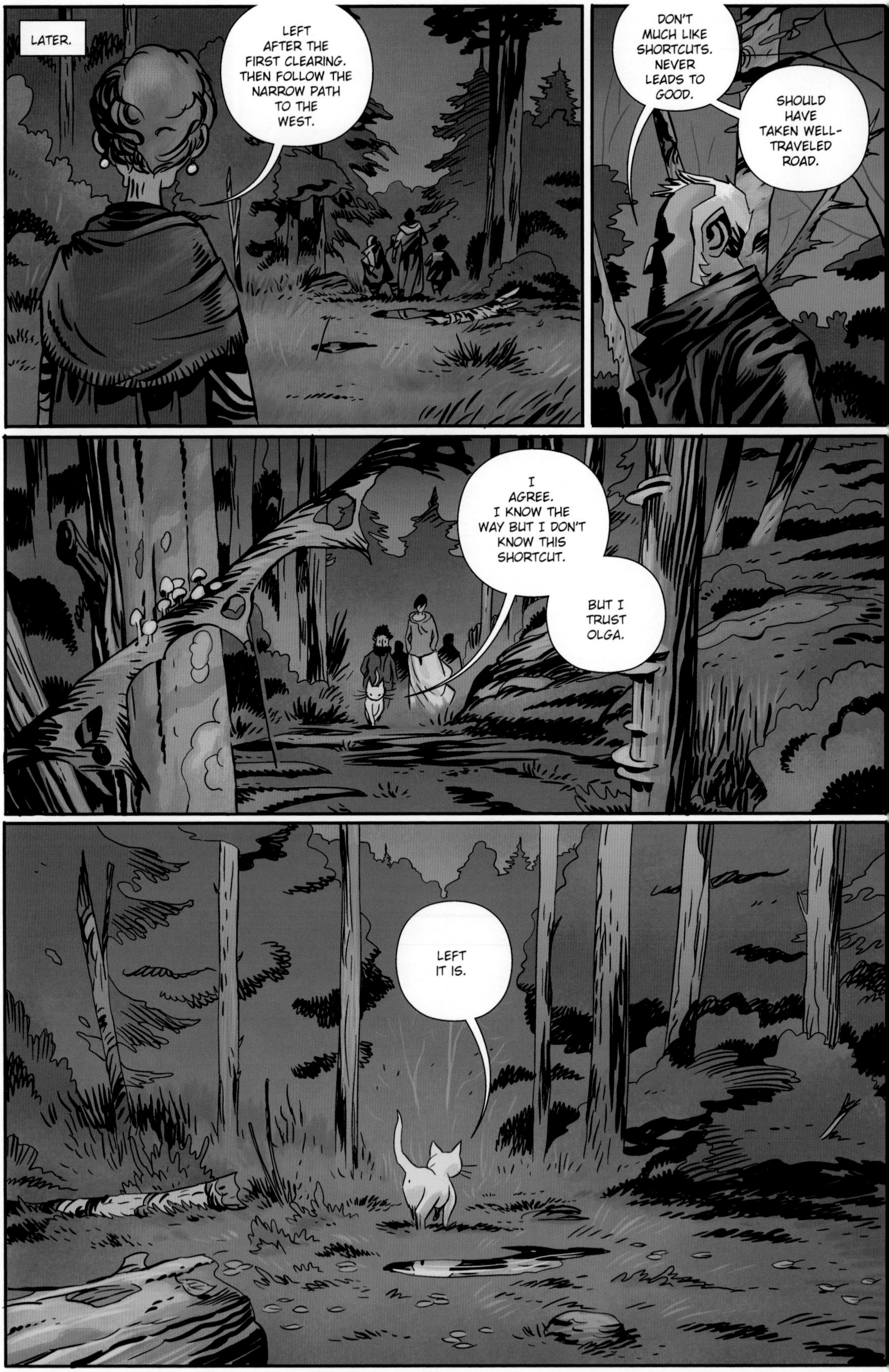
LATER.
LEFT AFTER THE FIRST CLEARING. THEN FOLLOW THE NARROW PATH TO THE WEST.
DON'T MUCH LIKE SHORTCUTS. NEVER LEADS TO GOOD.
SHOULD HAVE TAKEN WELL-TRAVELED ROAD.
I AGREE. I KNOW THE WAY BUT I DON'T KNOW THIS SHORTCUT.
BUT I TRUST OLGA.
LEFT IT IS.

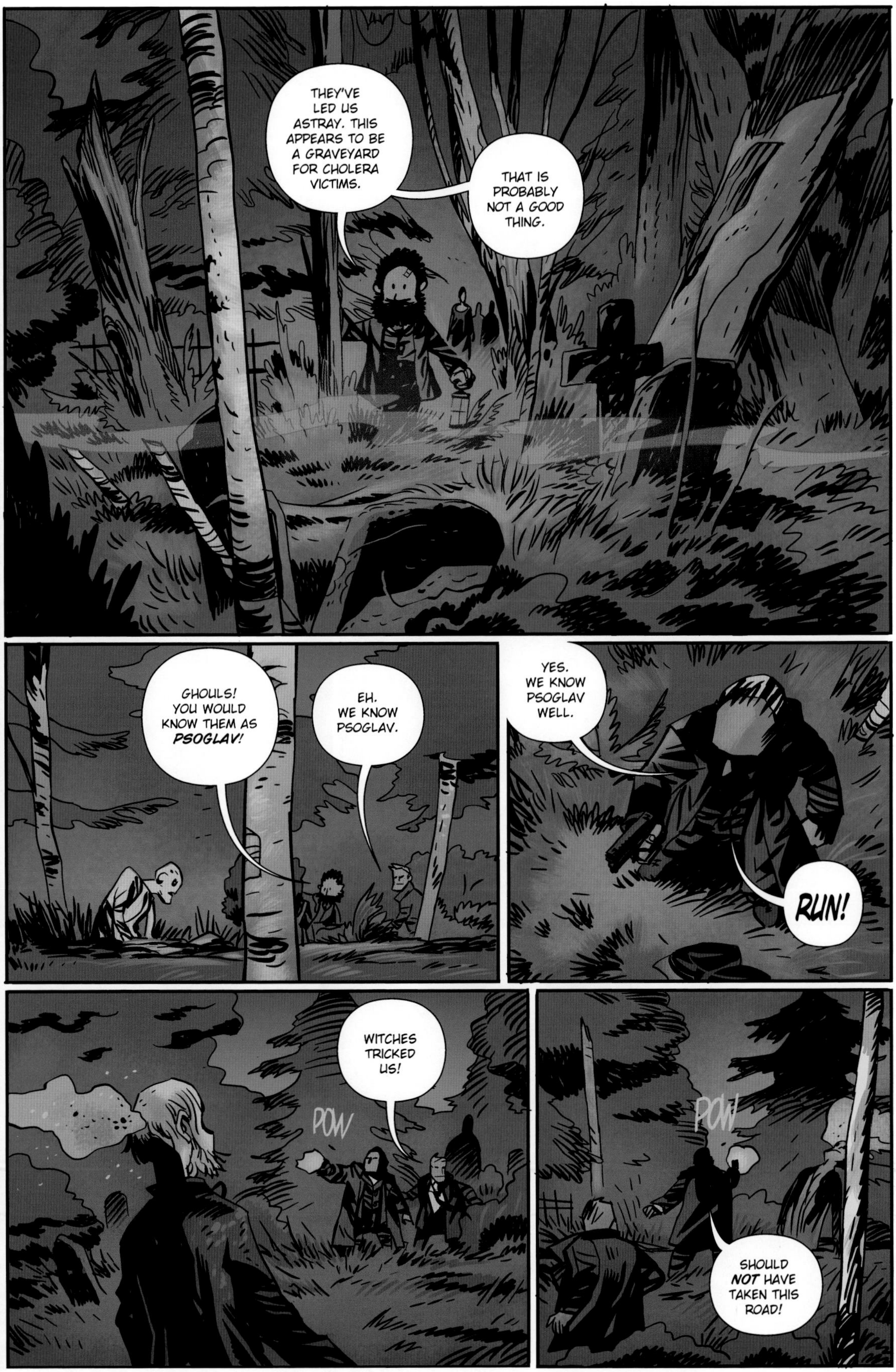

THEY'VE LED US ASTRAY. THIS APPEARS TO BE A GRAVEYARD FOR CHOLERA VICTIMS.
THAT IS PROBABLY NOT A GOOD THING.
GHOULS! YOU WOULD KNOW THEM AS *PSOGLAV*!
EH. WE KNOW PSOGLAV.
YES. WE KNOW PSOGLAV WELL.
RUN!
WITCHES TRICKED US!
POW
POW
SHOULD *NOT* HAVE TAKEN THIS ROAD!

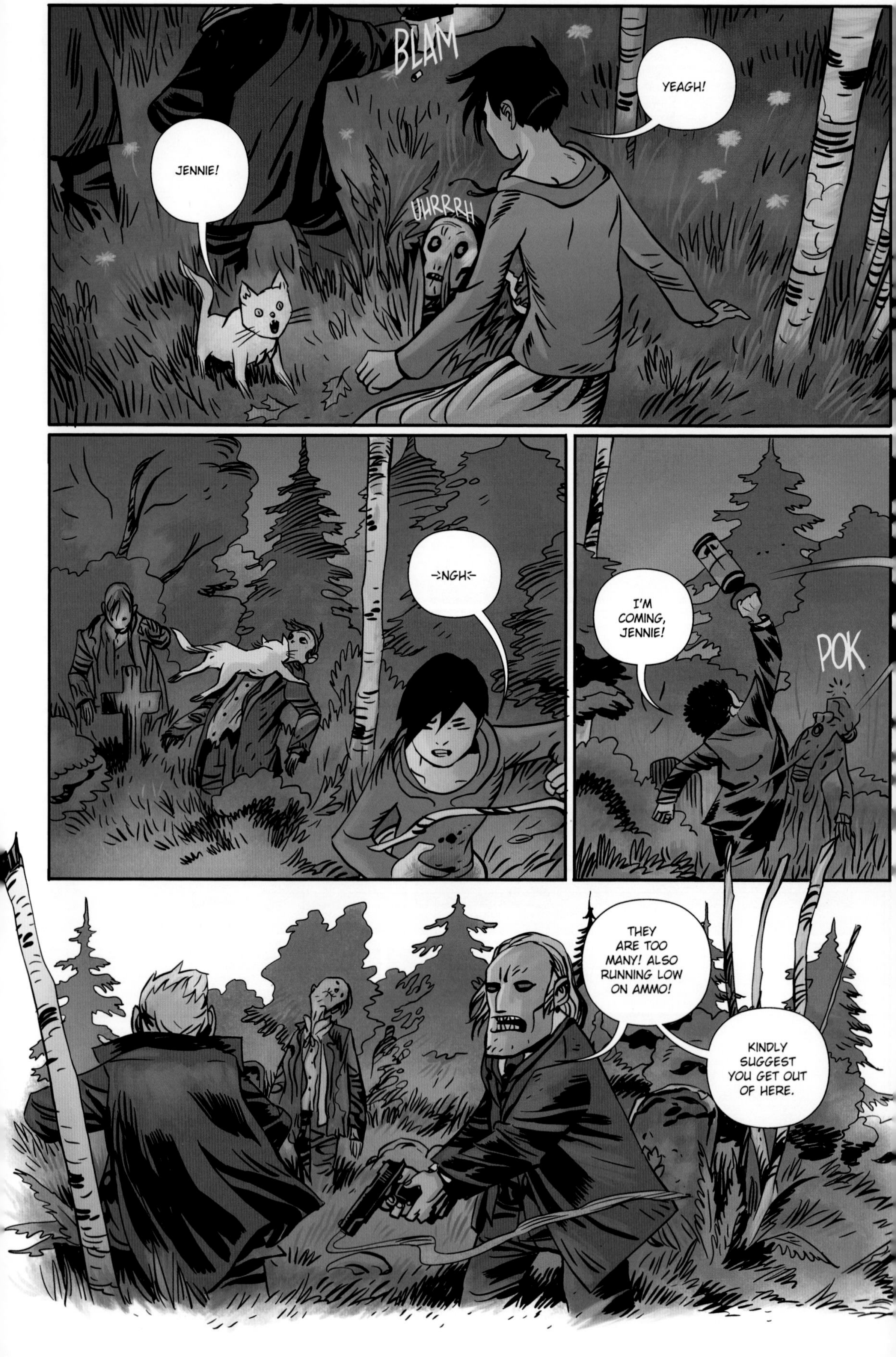
BLAM
YEAGH!
JENNIE!
UHRRRH
NGH
I'M COMING, JENNIE!
POK
THEY ARE TOO MANY! ALSO RUNNING LOW ON AMMO!
KINDLY SUGGEST YOU GET OUT OF HERE.

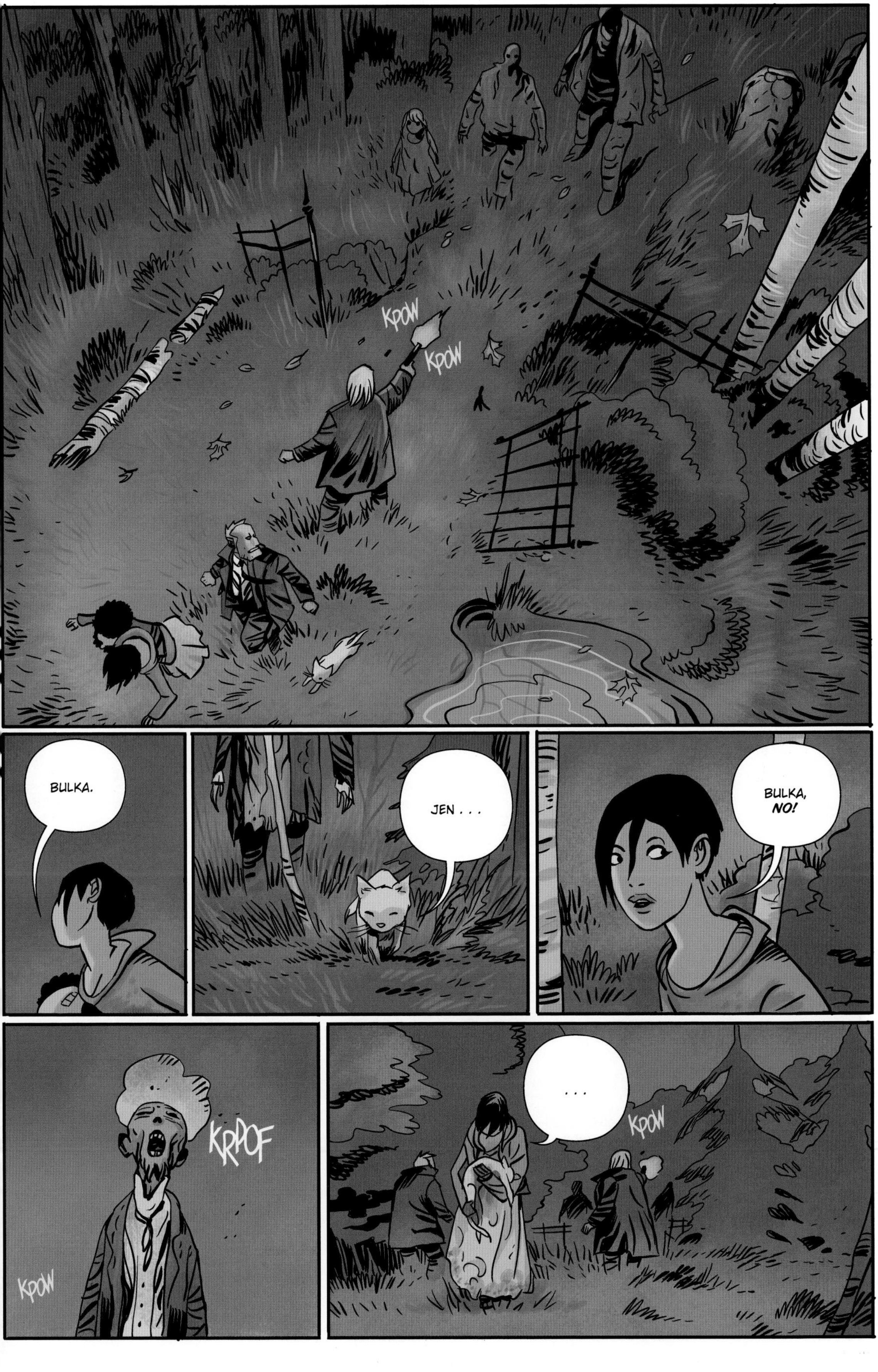
KPOW
KPOW
BULKA.
JEN . . .
BULKA,
NO!
KRPOF
KPOW
. . .
KPOW

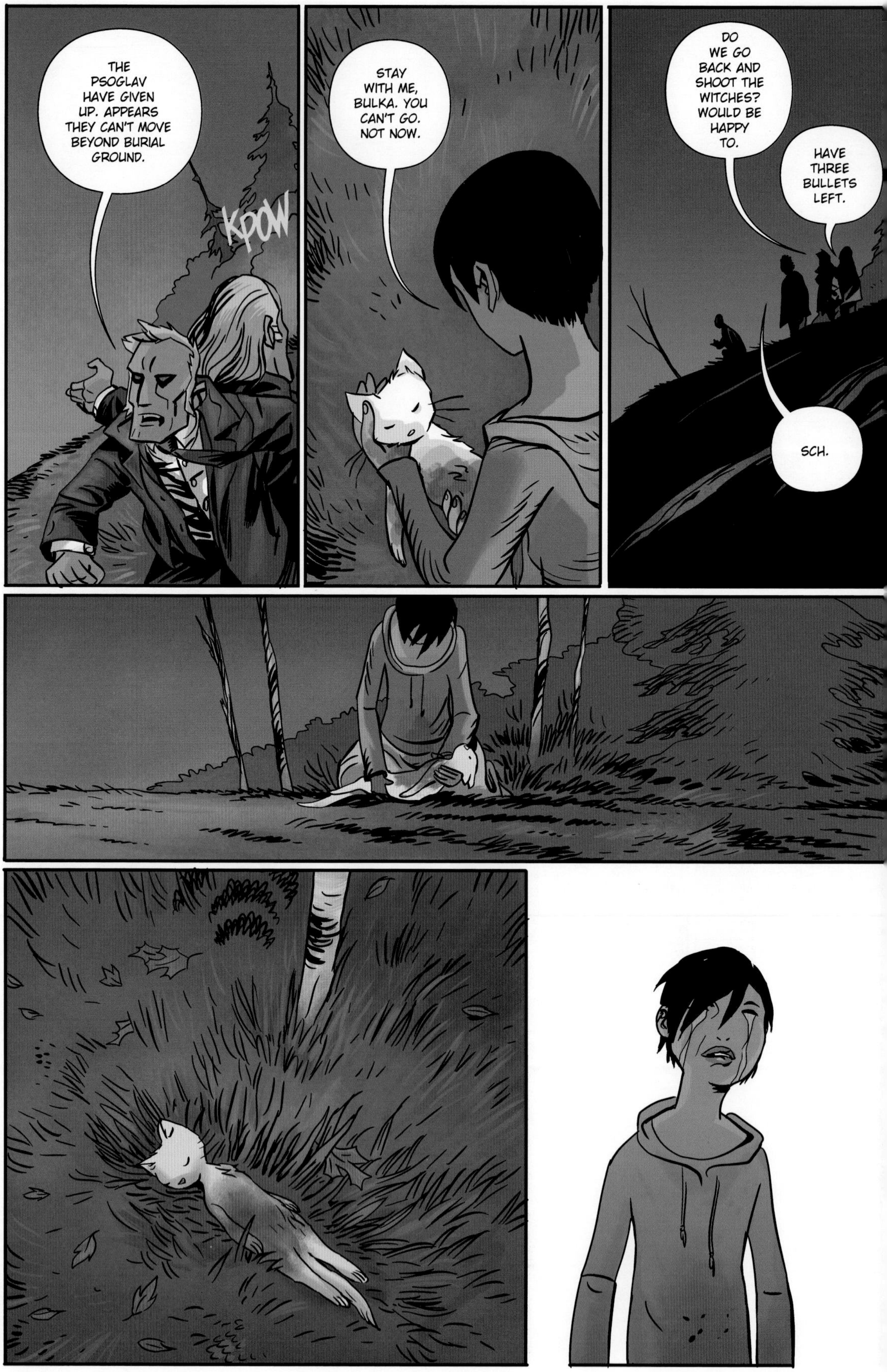
THE PSOGLAV HAVE GIVEN UP. APPEARS THEY CAN'T MOVE BEYOND BURIAL GROUND.
KPOW
STAY WITH ME, BULKA. YOU CAN'T GO. NOT NOW.
DO WE GO BACK AND SHOOT THE WITCHES? WOULD BE HAPPY TO.
HAVE THREE BULLETS LEFT.
SCH.

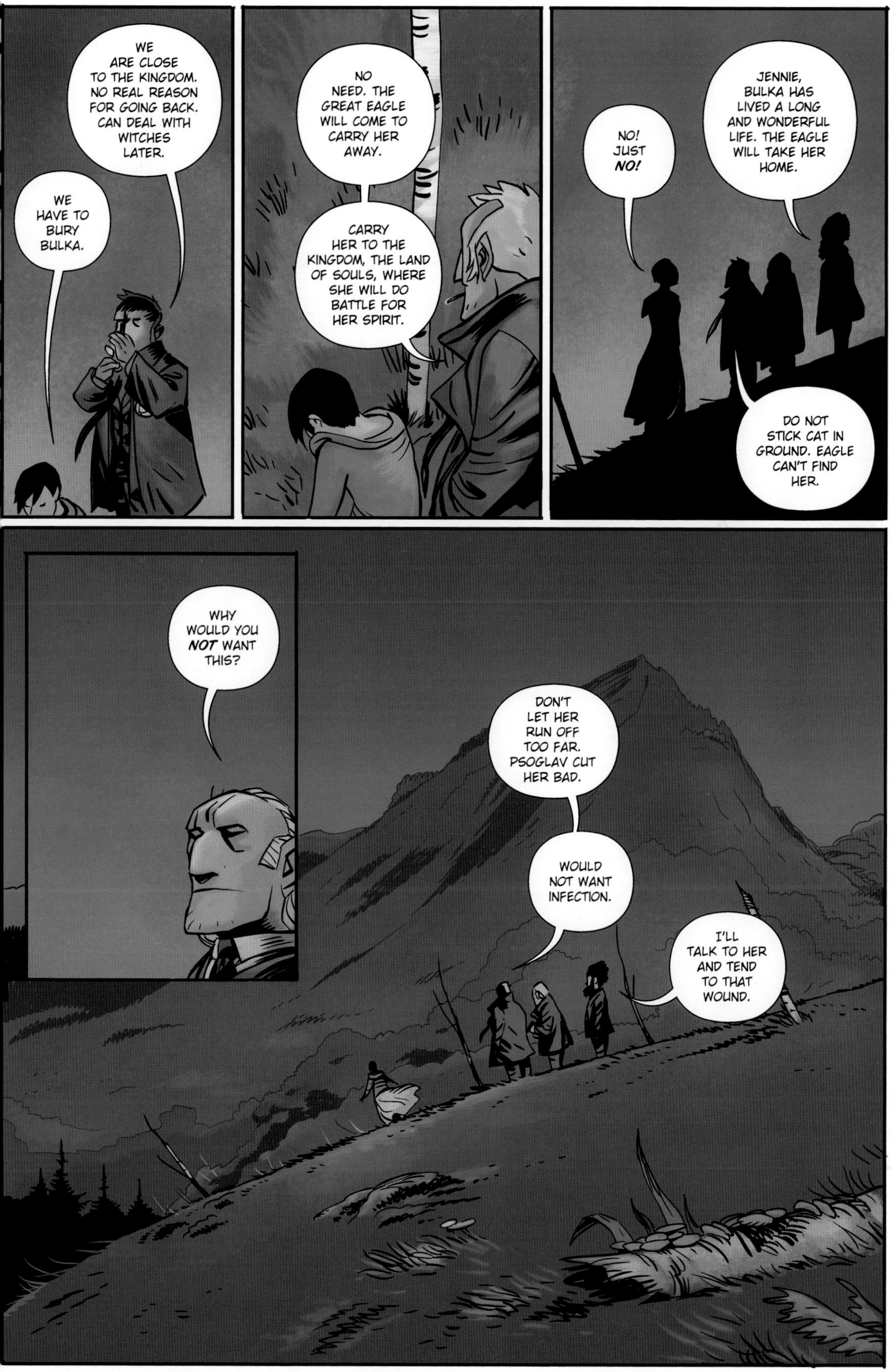
WE ARE CLOSE TO THE KINGDOM. NO REAL REASON FOR GOING BACK. CAN DEAL WITH WITCHES LATER.
WE HAVE TO BURY BULKA.
NO NEED. THE GREAT EAGLE WILL COME TO CARRY HER AWAY.
CARRY HER TO THE KINGDOM, THE LAND OF SOULS, WHERE SHE WILL DO BATTLE FOR HER SPIRIT.
NO! JUST NO!
JENNIE, BULKA HAS LIVED A LONG AND WONDERFUL LIFE. THE EAGLE WILL TAKE HER HOME.
DO NOT STICK CAT IN GROUND. EAGLE CAN'T FIND HER.
WHY WOULD YOU NOT WANT THIS?
DON'T LET HER RUN OFF TOO FAR. PSOGLAV CUT HER BAD.
WOULD NOT WANT INFECTION.
I'LL TALK TO HER AND TEND TO THAT WOUND.

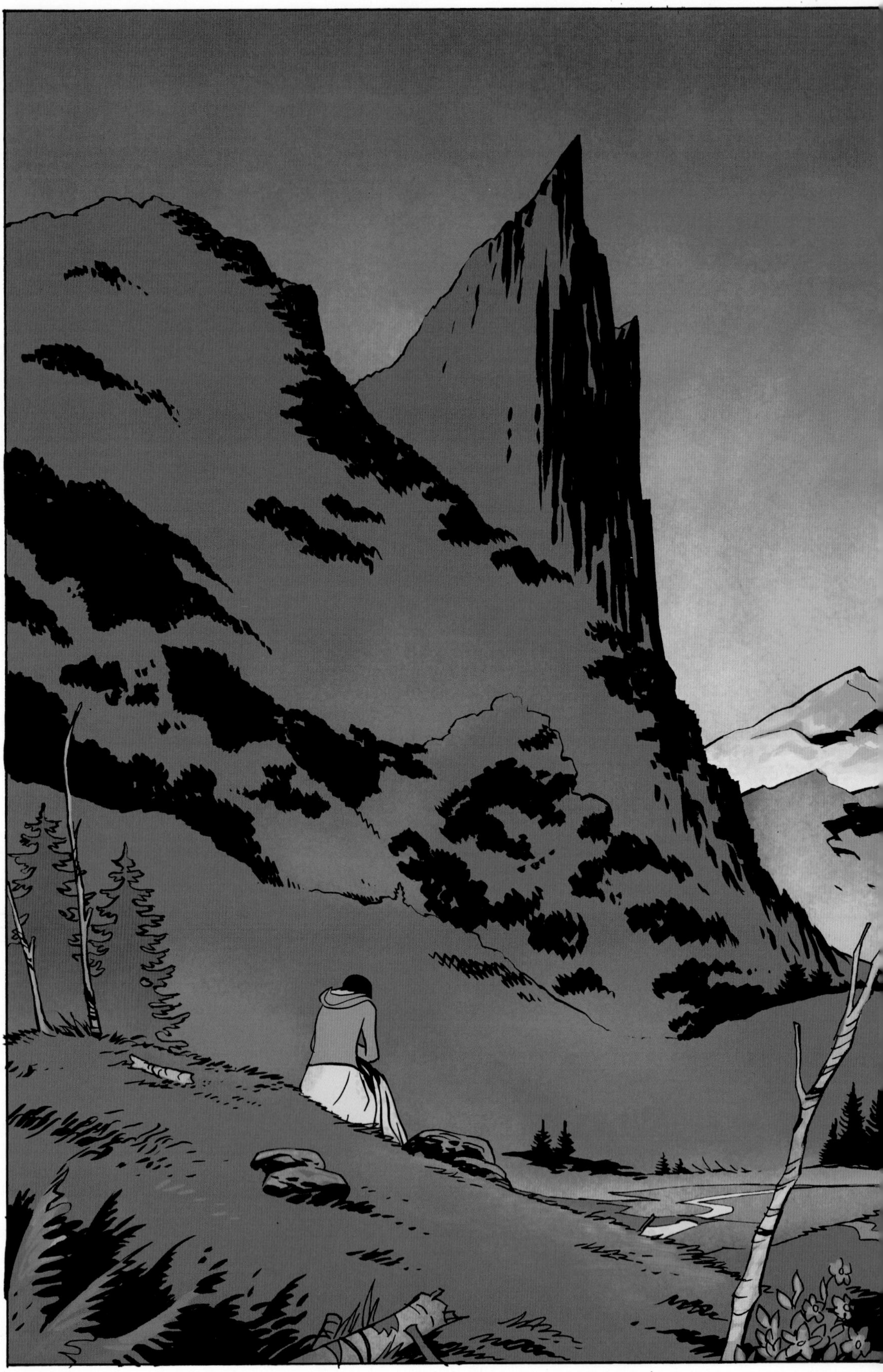

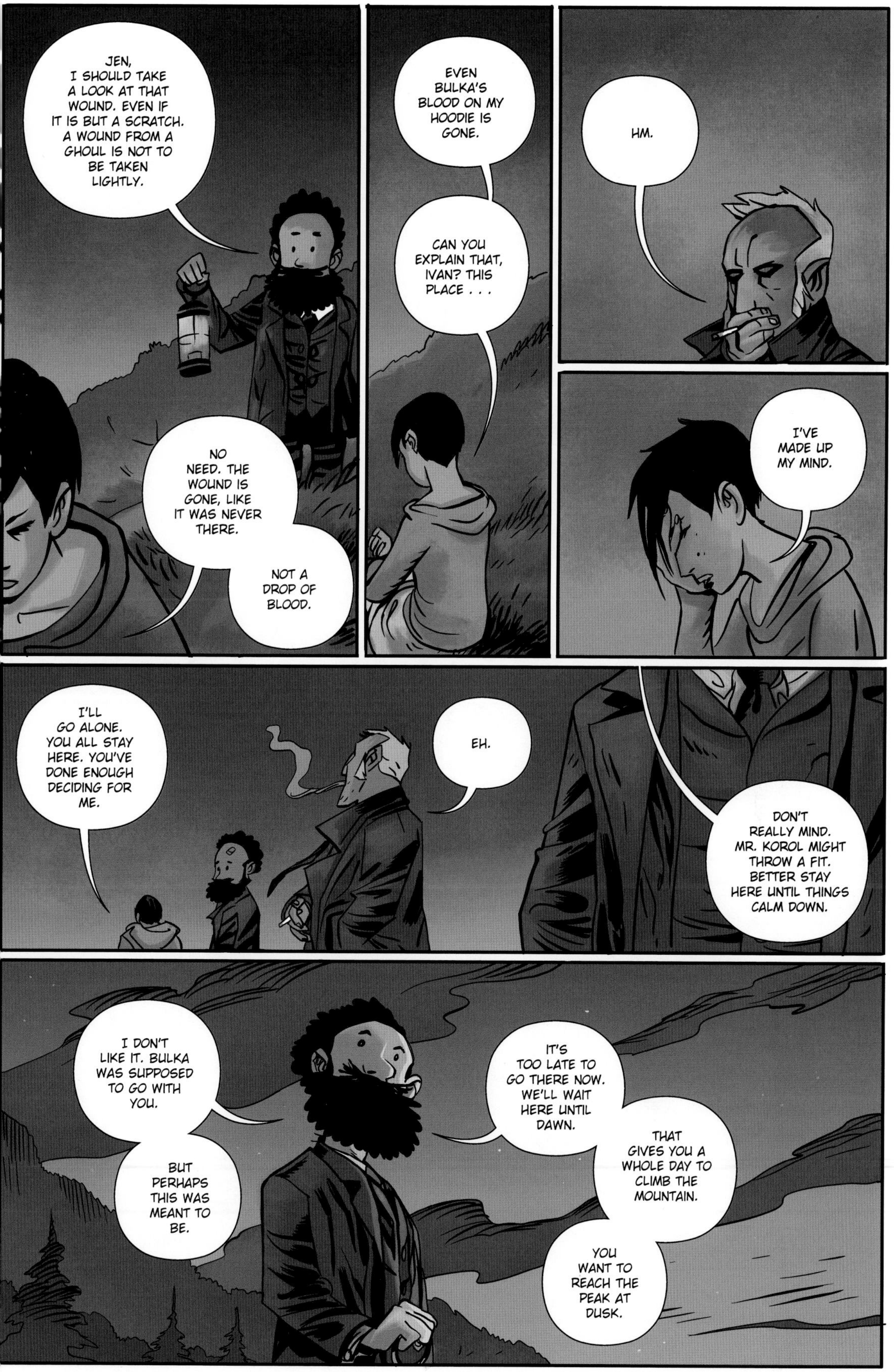

JEN, I SHOULD TAKE A LOOK AT THAT WOUND. EVEN IF IT IS BUT A SCRATCH. A WOUND FROM A GHOUL IS NOT TO BE TAKEN LIGHTLY.
NO NEED. THE WOUND IS GONE, LIKE IT WAS NEVER THERE.
NOT A DROP OF BLOOD.
EVEN BULKA'S BLOOD ON MY HOODIE IS GONE.
CAN YOU EXPLAIN THAT, IVAN? THIS PLACE . . .
HM.
I'VE MADE UP MY MIND.
I'LL GO ALONE. YOU ALL STAY HERE. YOU'VE DONE ENOUGH DECIDING FOR ME.
EH.
DON'T REALLY MIND. MR. KOROL MIGHT THROW A FIT. BETTER STAY HERE UNTIL THINGS CALM DOWN.
I DON'T LIKE IT. BULKA WAS SUPPOSED TO GO WITH YOU.
BUT PERHAPS THIS WAS MEANT TO BE.
IT'S TOO LATE TO GO THERE NOW. WE'LL WAIT HERE UNTIL DAWN.
THAT GIVES YOU A WHOLE DAY TO CLIMB THE MOUNTAIN.
YOU WANT TO REACH THE PEAK AT DUSK.

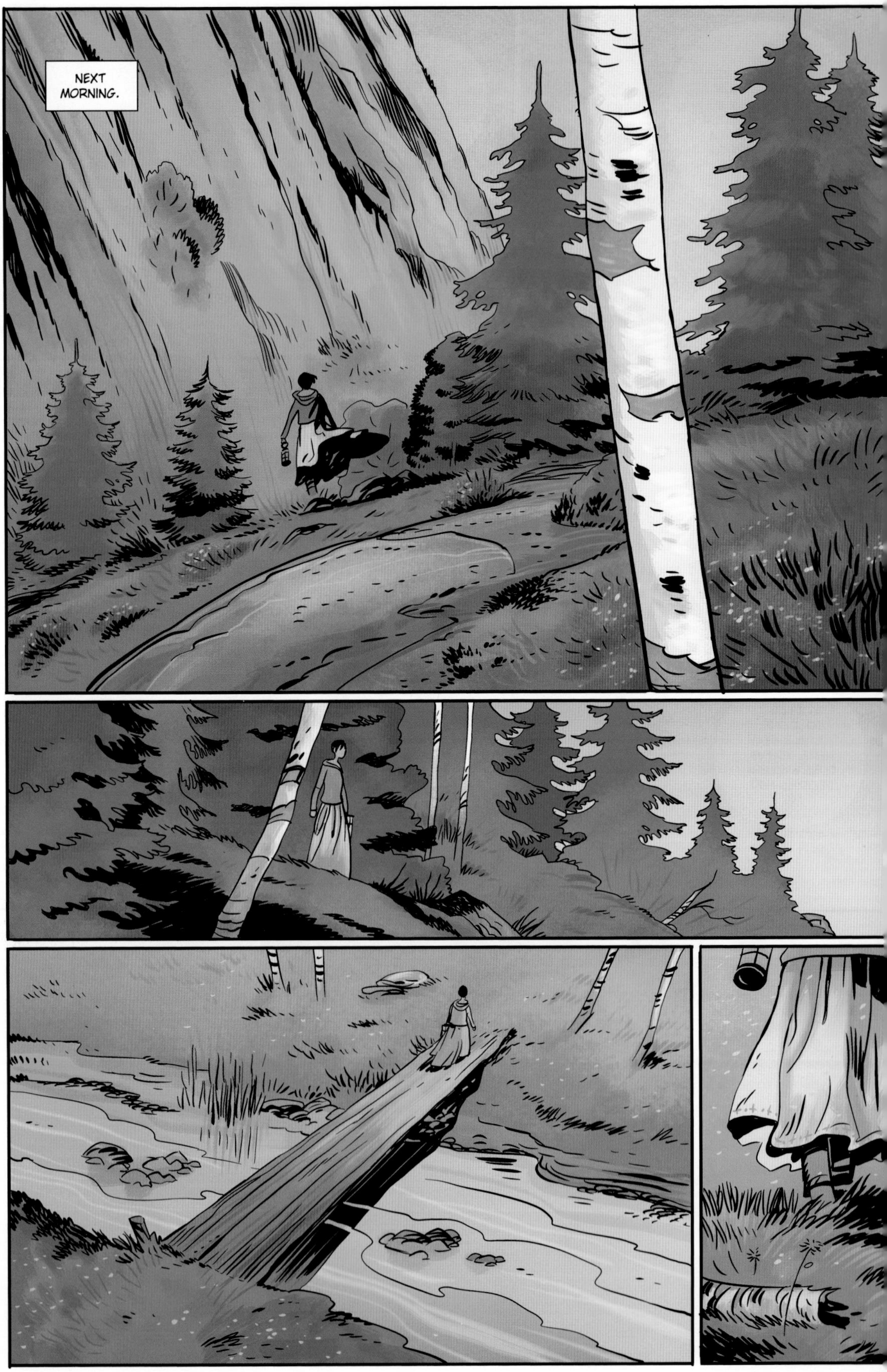
NEXT
MORNING.

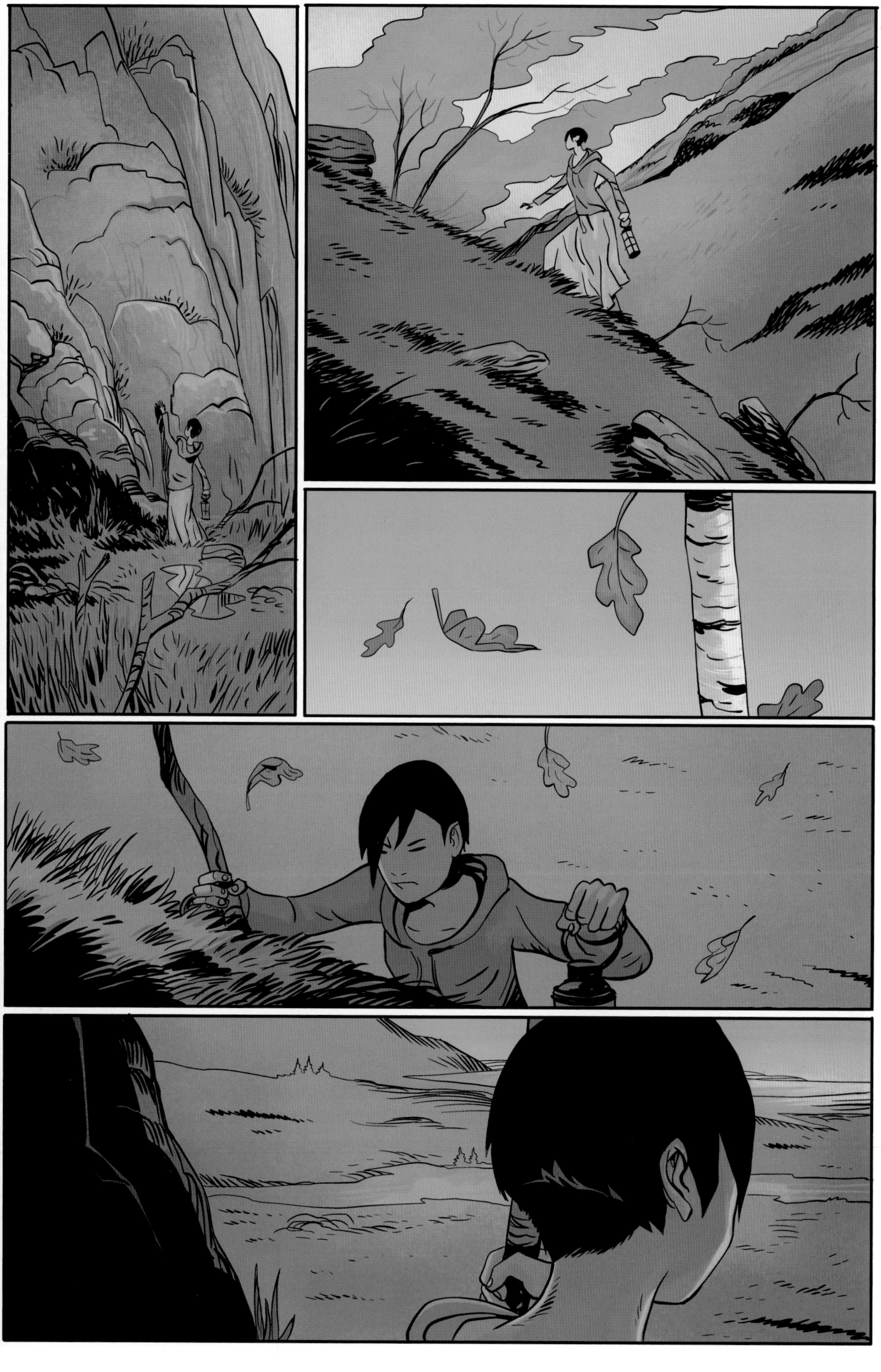

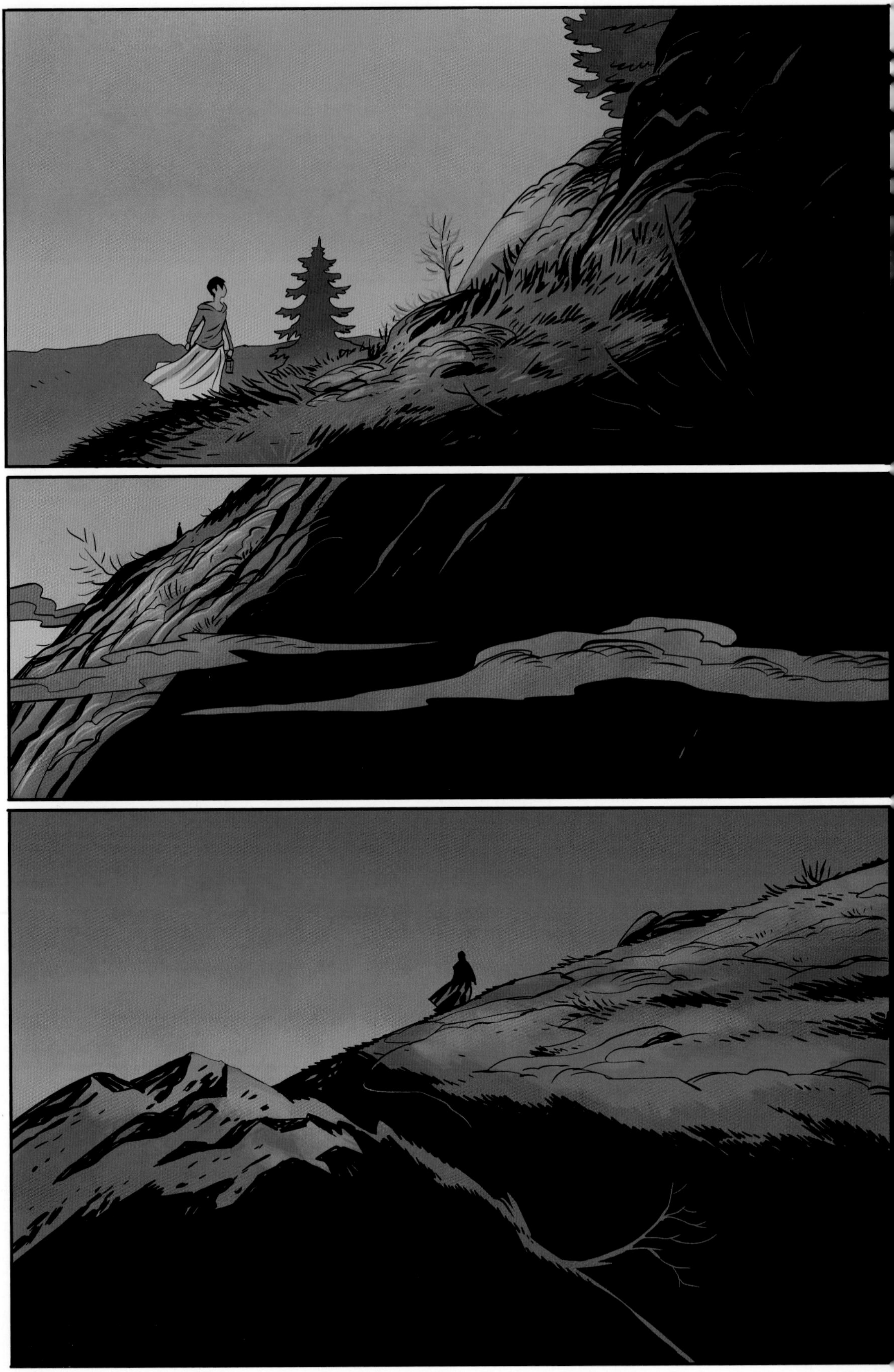

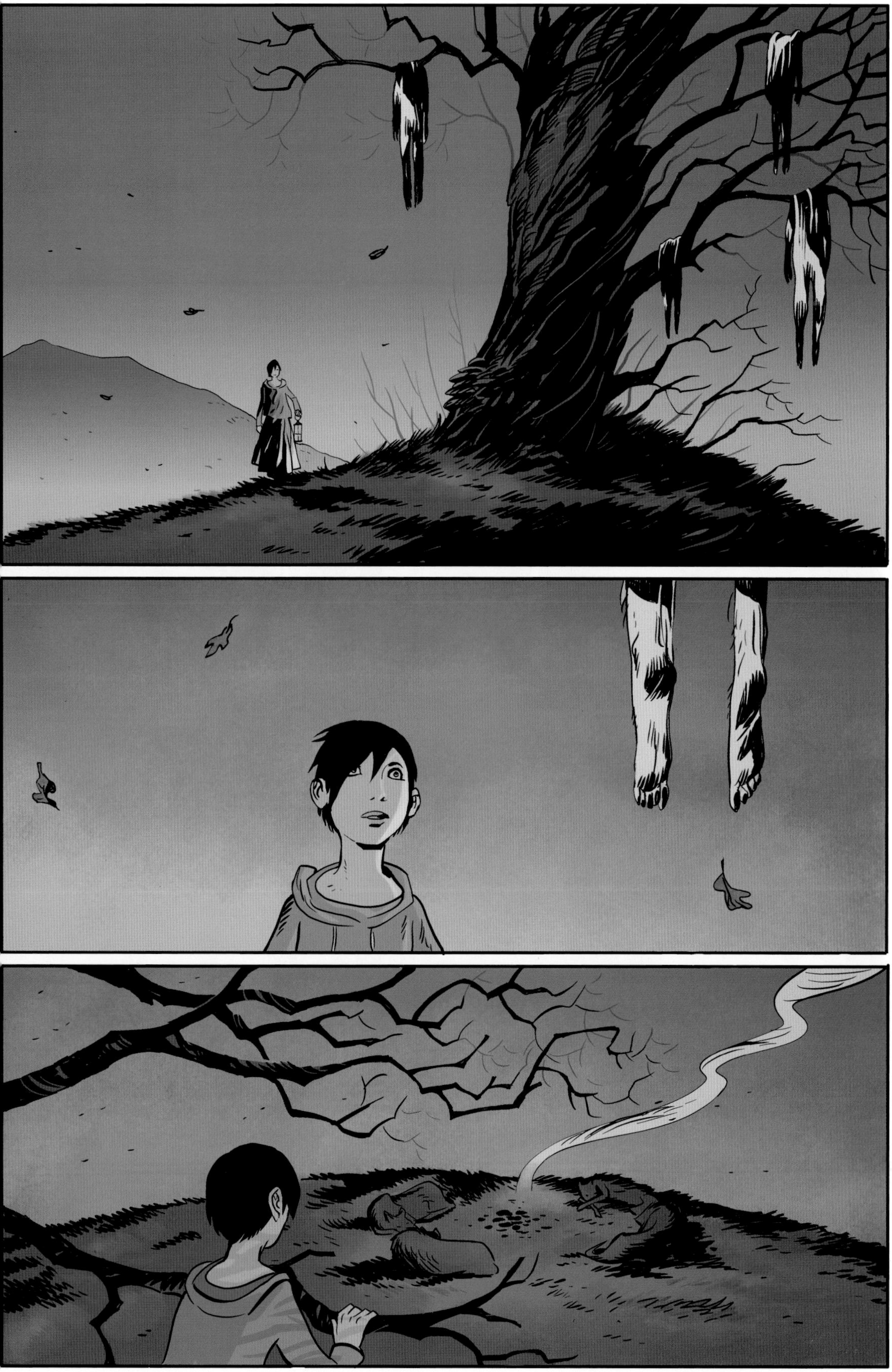

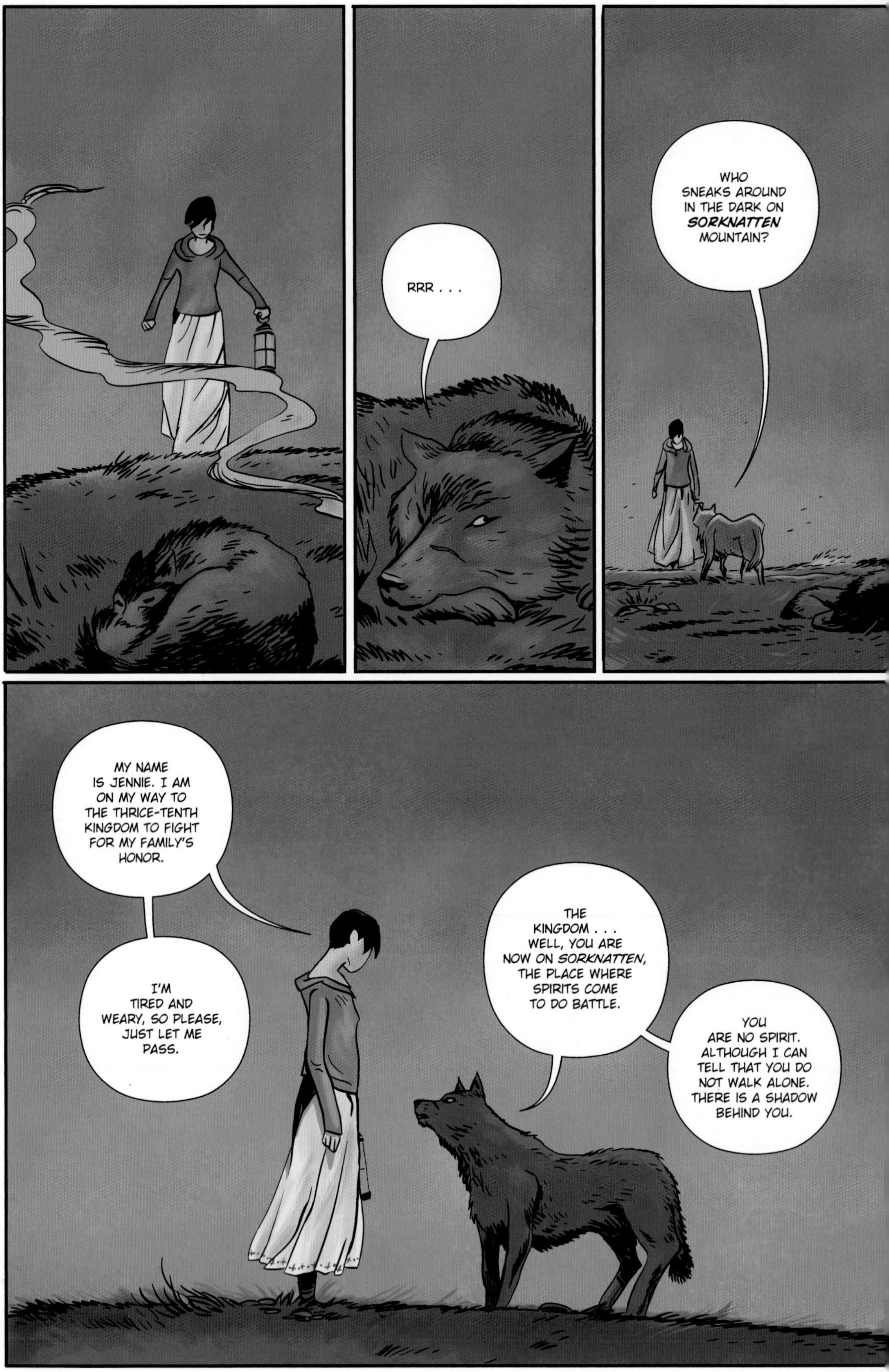
RRR . . .
WHO SNEAKS AROUND IN THE DARK ON *SORKNATTEN* MOUNTAIN?
MY NAME IS JENNIE. I AM ON MY WAY TO THE THRICE-TENTH KINGDOM TO FIGHT FOR MY FAMILY'S HONOR.
I'M TIRED AND WEARY, SO PLEASE, JUST LET ME PASS.
THE KINGDOM . . . WELL, YOU ARE NOW ON *SORKNATTEN*, THE PLACE WHERE SPIRITS COME TO DO BATTLE.
YOU ARE NO SPIRIT. ALTHOUGH I CAN TELL THAT YOU DO NOT WALK ALONE. THERE IS A SHADOW BEHIND YOU.

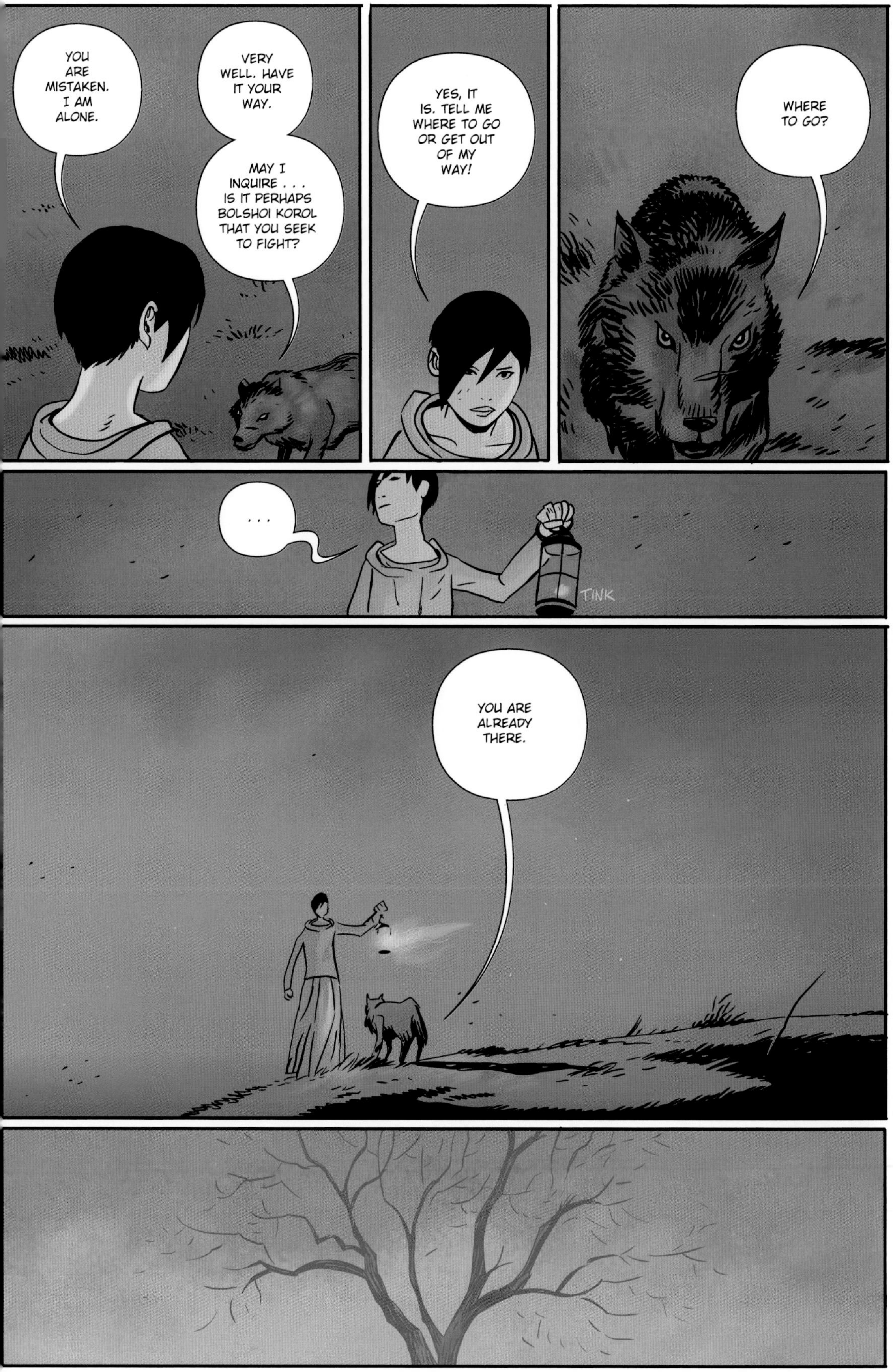
YOU ARE MISTAKEN. I AM ALONE.
VERY WELL. HAVE IT YOUR WAY.
MAY I INQUIRE . . . IS IT PERHAPS BOLSHOI KOROL THAT YOU SEEK TO FIGHT?
YES, IT IS. TELL ME WHERE TO GO OR GET OUT OF MY WAY!
WHERE TO GO?
. . .
TINK
YOU ARE ALREADY THERE.

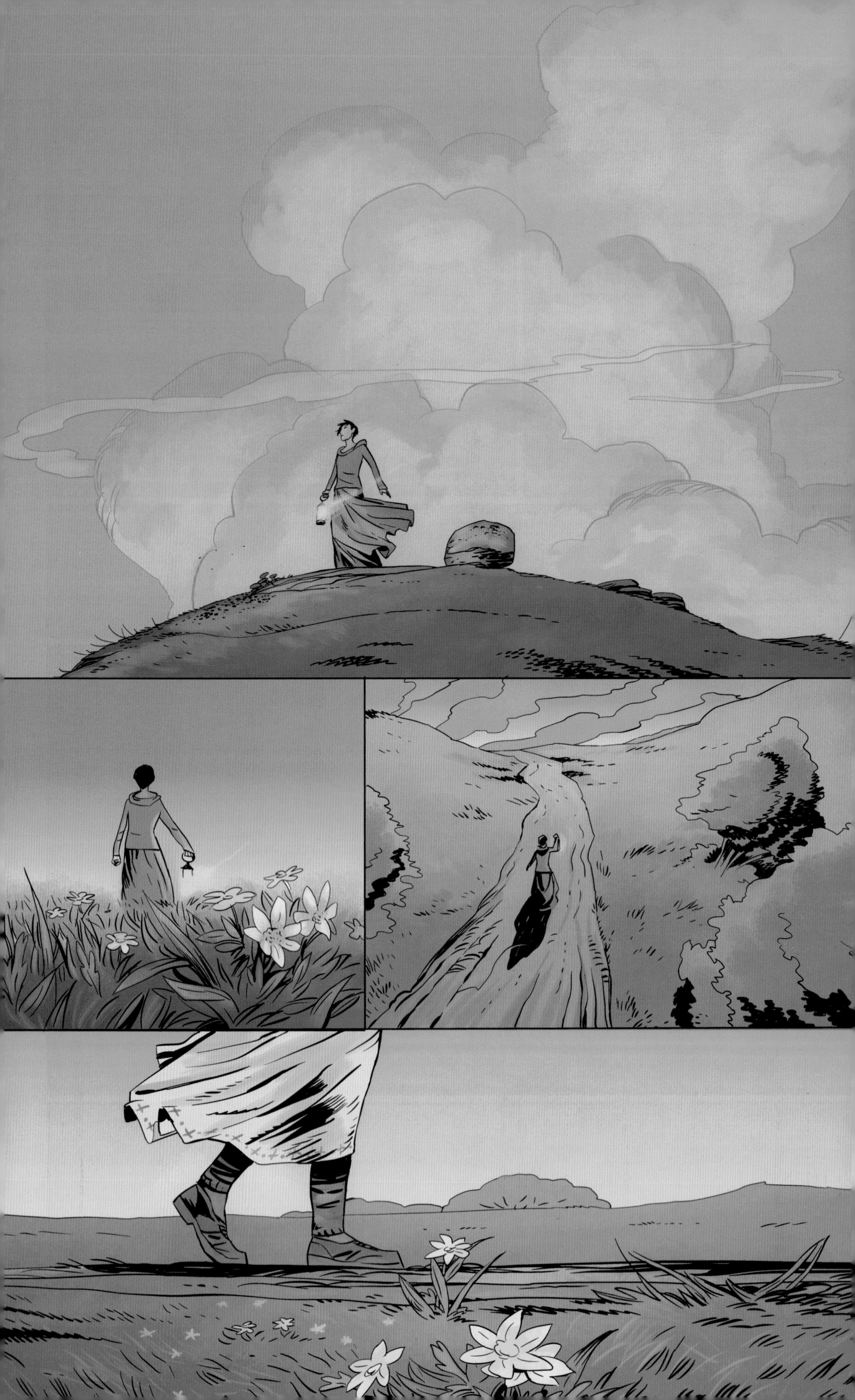

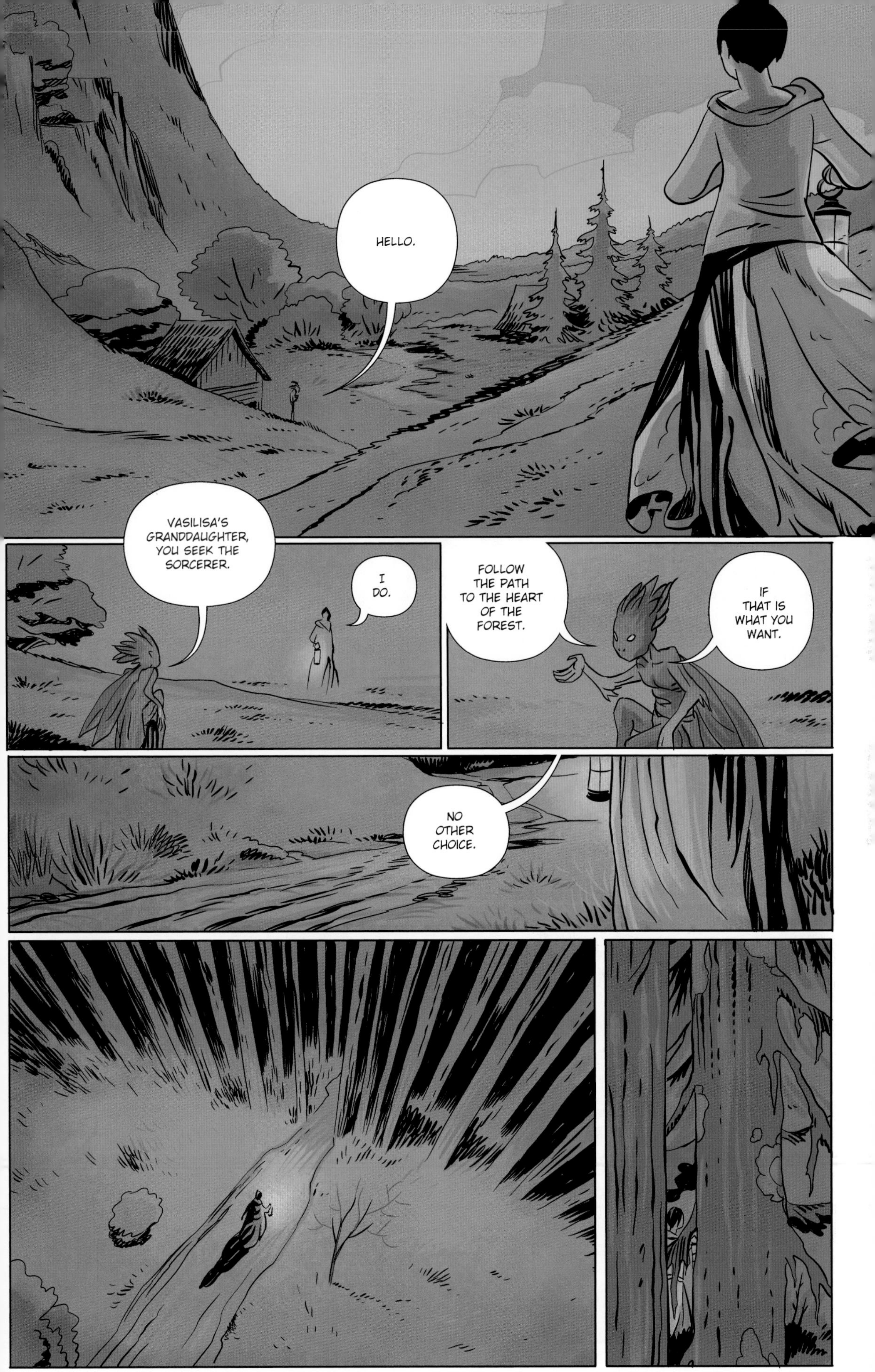
HELLO.
VASILISA'S GRANDDAUGHTER, YOU SEEK THE SORCERER.
I DO.
FOLLOW THE PATH TO THE HEART OF THE FOREST.
IF THAT IS WHAT YOU WANT.
NO OTHER CHOICE.

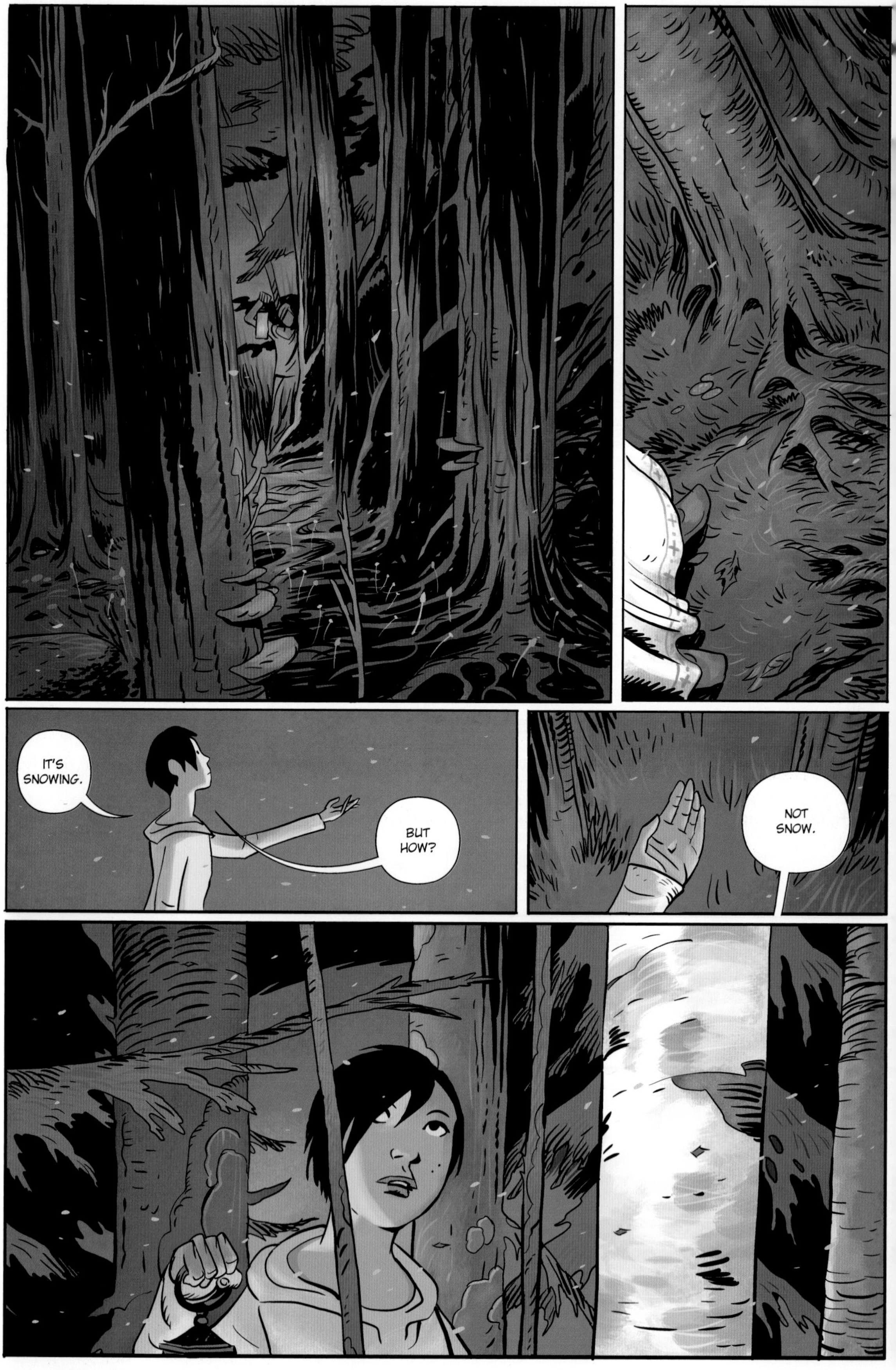
IT'S SNOWING.
BUT HOW?
NOT SNOW.

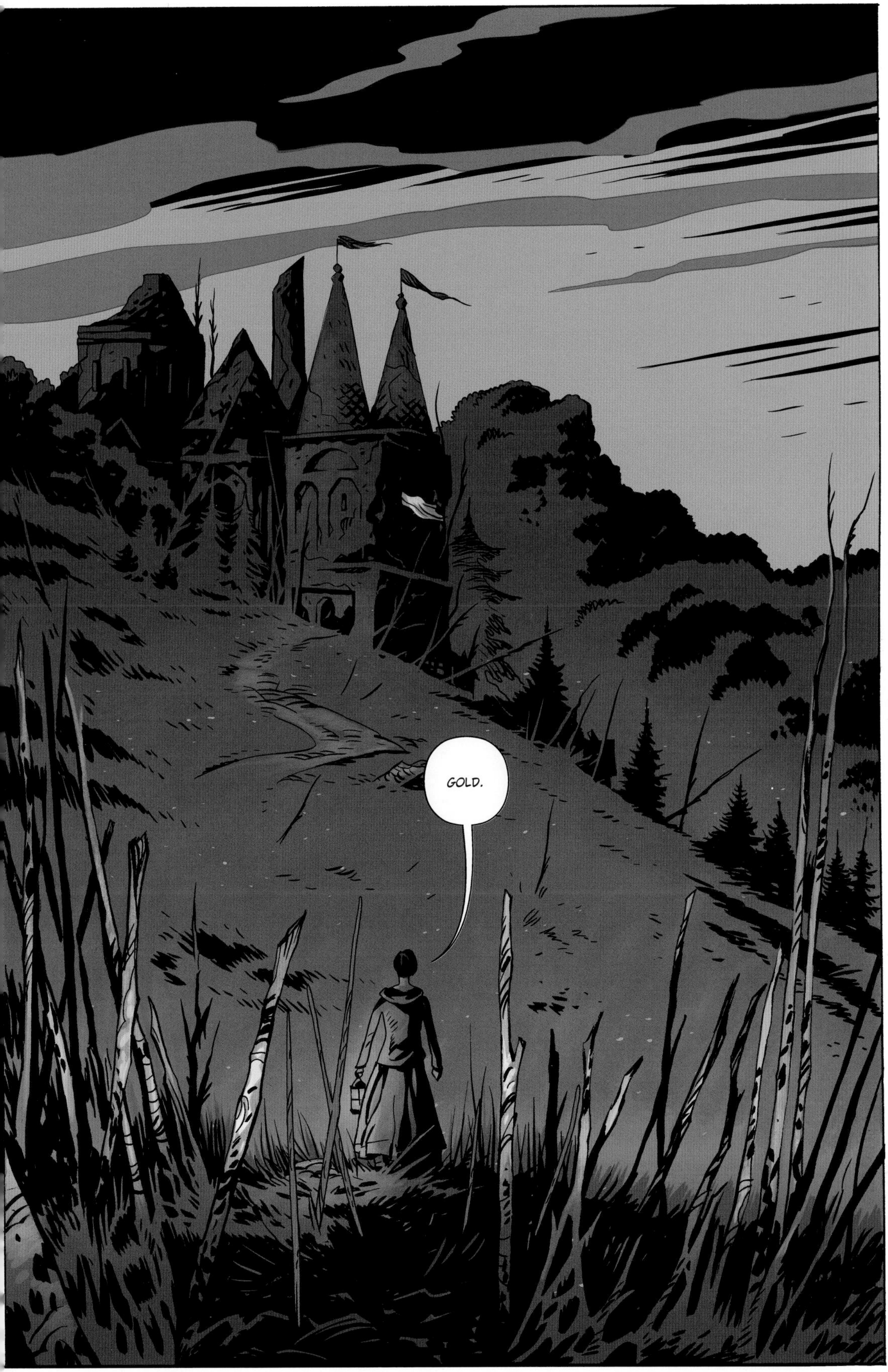
GOLD.

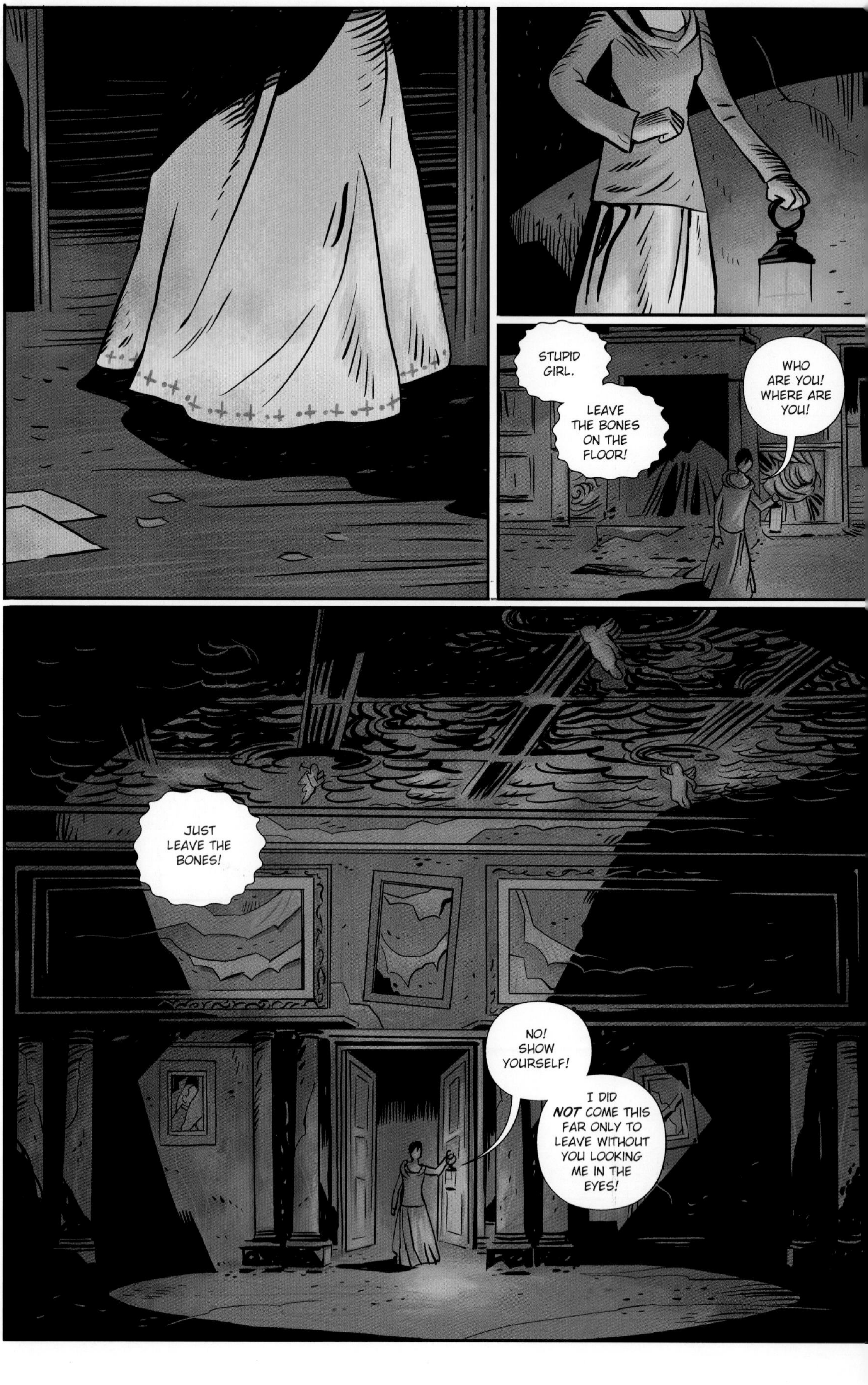
STUPID GIRL.
LEAVE THE BONES ON THE FLOOR!
WHO ARE YOU! WHERE ARE YOU!
JUST LEAVE THE BONES!
NO! SHOW YOURSELF!
I DID **NOT** COME THIS FAR ONLY TO LEAVE WITHOUT YOU LOOKING ME IN THE EYES!

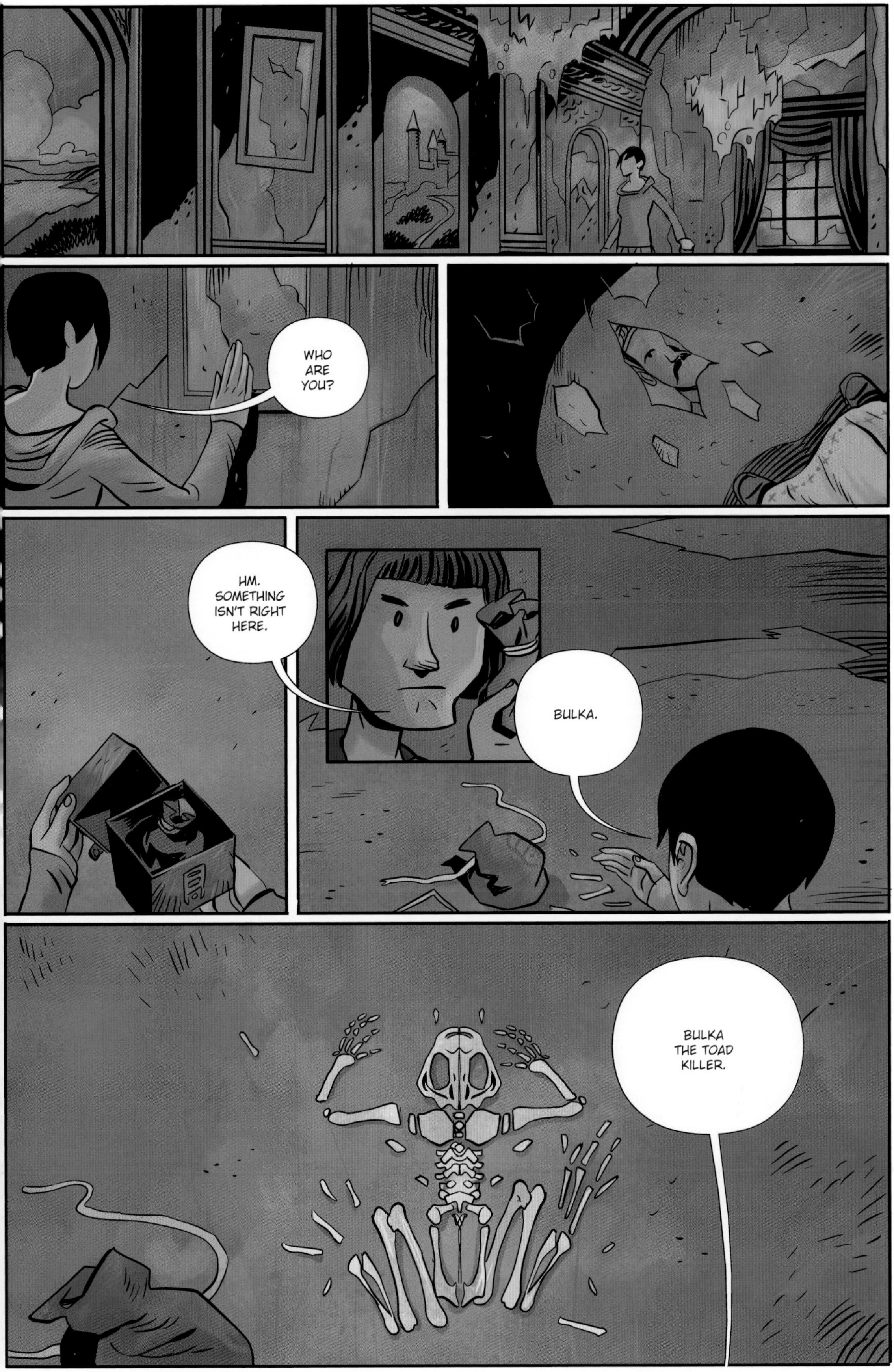
WHO ARE YOU?
HM. SOMETHING ISN'T RIGHT HERE.
BULKA.
BULKA THE TOAD KILLER.

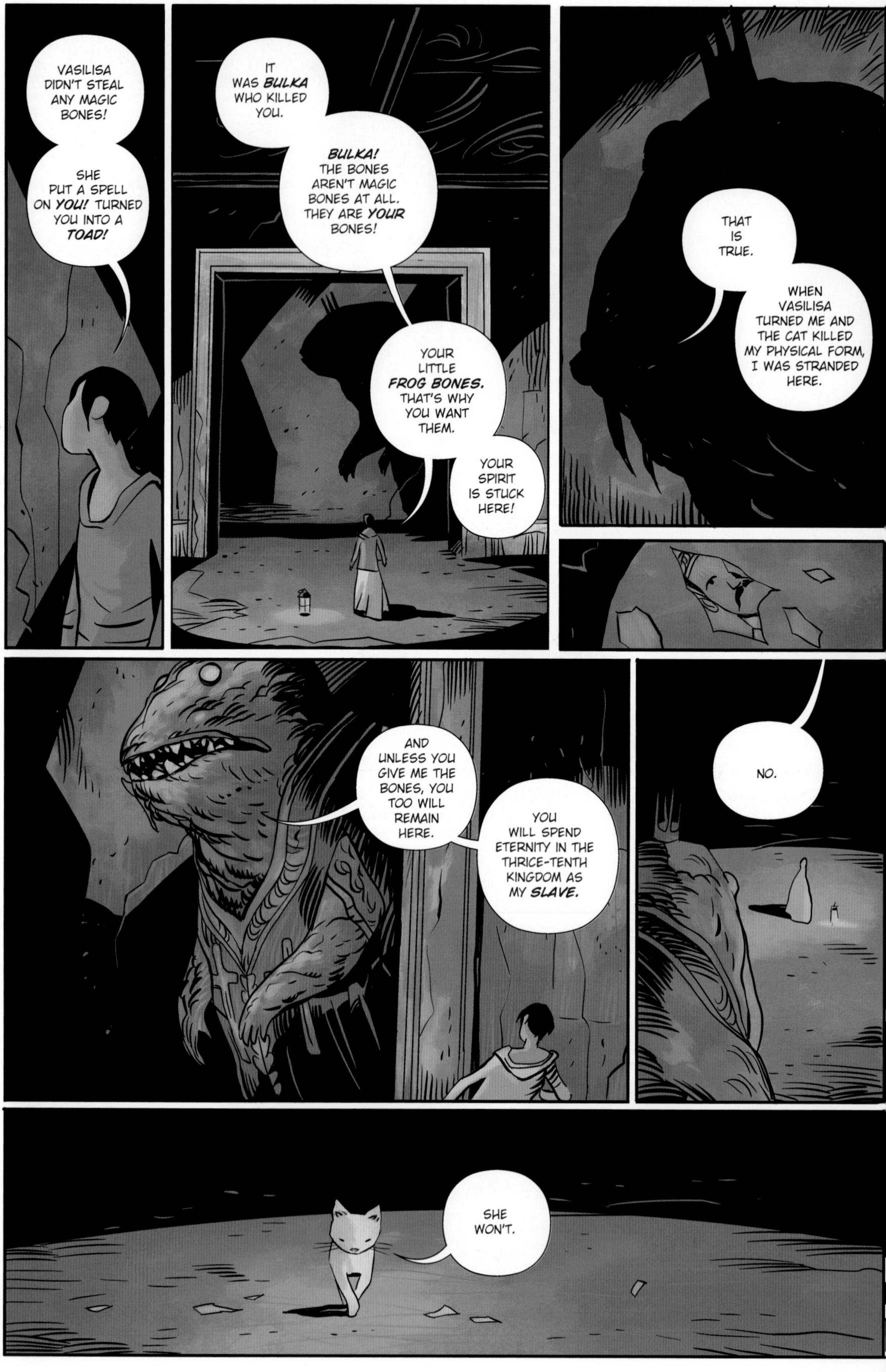
VASILISA DIDN'T STEAL ANY MAGIC BONES!
SHE PUT A SPELL ON YOU! TURNED YOU INTO A TOAD!
IT WAS BULKA WHO KILLED YOU.
BULKA! THE BONES AREN'T MAGIC BONES AT ALL. THEY ARE YOUR BONES!
YOUR LITTLE FROG BONES. THAT'S WHY YOU WANT THEM.
YOUR SPIRIT IS STUCK HERE!
THAT IS TRUE.
WHEN VASILISA TURNED ME AND THE CAT KILLED MY PHYSICAL FORM, I WAS STRANDED HERE.
AND UNLESS YOU GIVE ME THE BONES, YOU TOO WILL REMAIN HERE.
YOU WILL SPEND ETERNITY IN THE THRICE-TENTH KINGDOM AS MY SLAVE.
NO.
SHE WON'T.

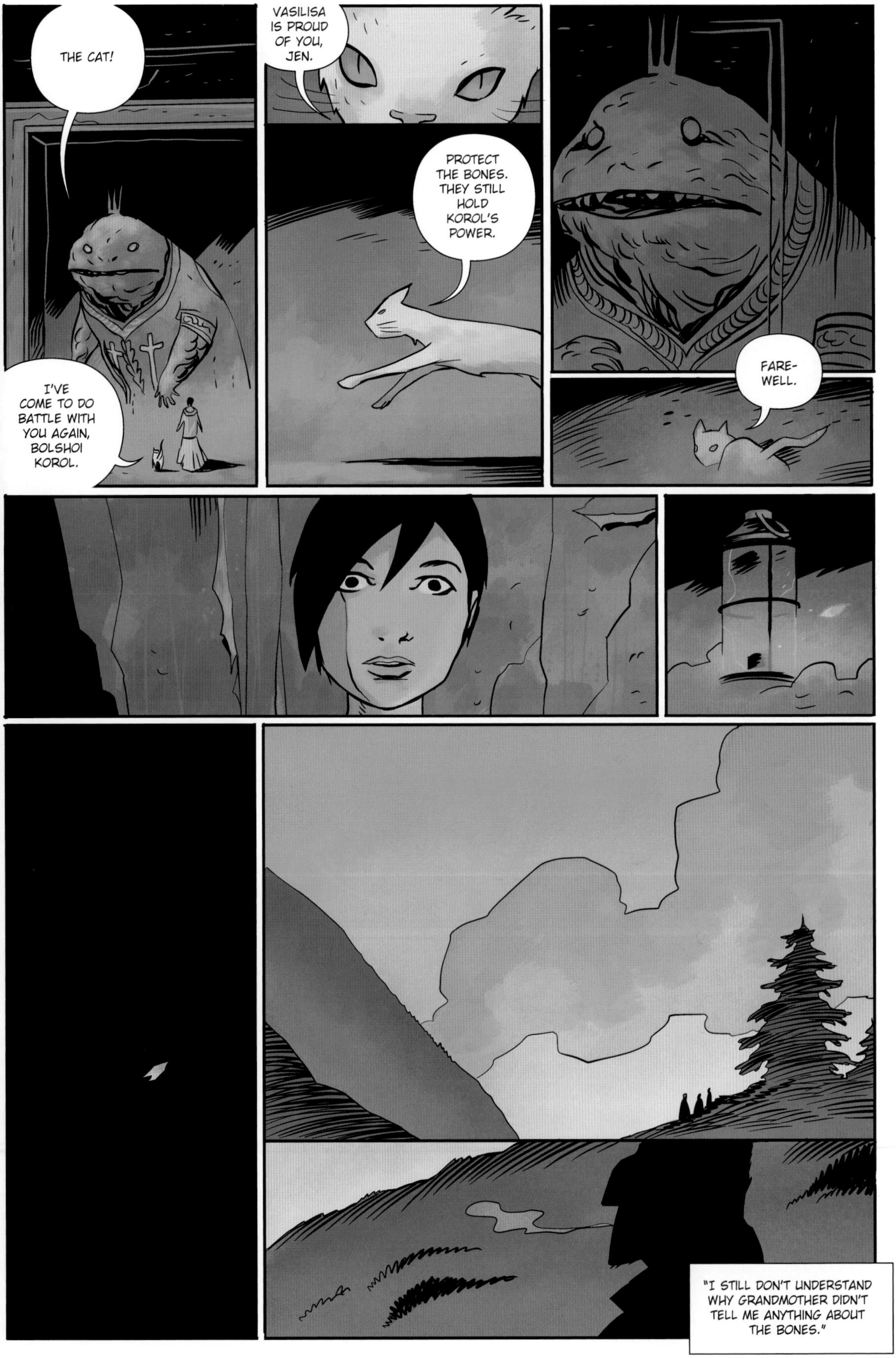
THE CAT!
I'VE COME TO DO BATTLE WITH YOU AGAIN, BOLSHOI KOROL.
VASILISA IS PROUD OF YOU, JEN.
PROTECT THE BONES. THEY STILL HOLD KOROL'S POWER.
FARE-WELL.
"I STILL DON'T UNDERSTAND WHY GRANDMOTHER DIDN'T TELL ME ANYTHING ABOUT THE BONES."

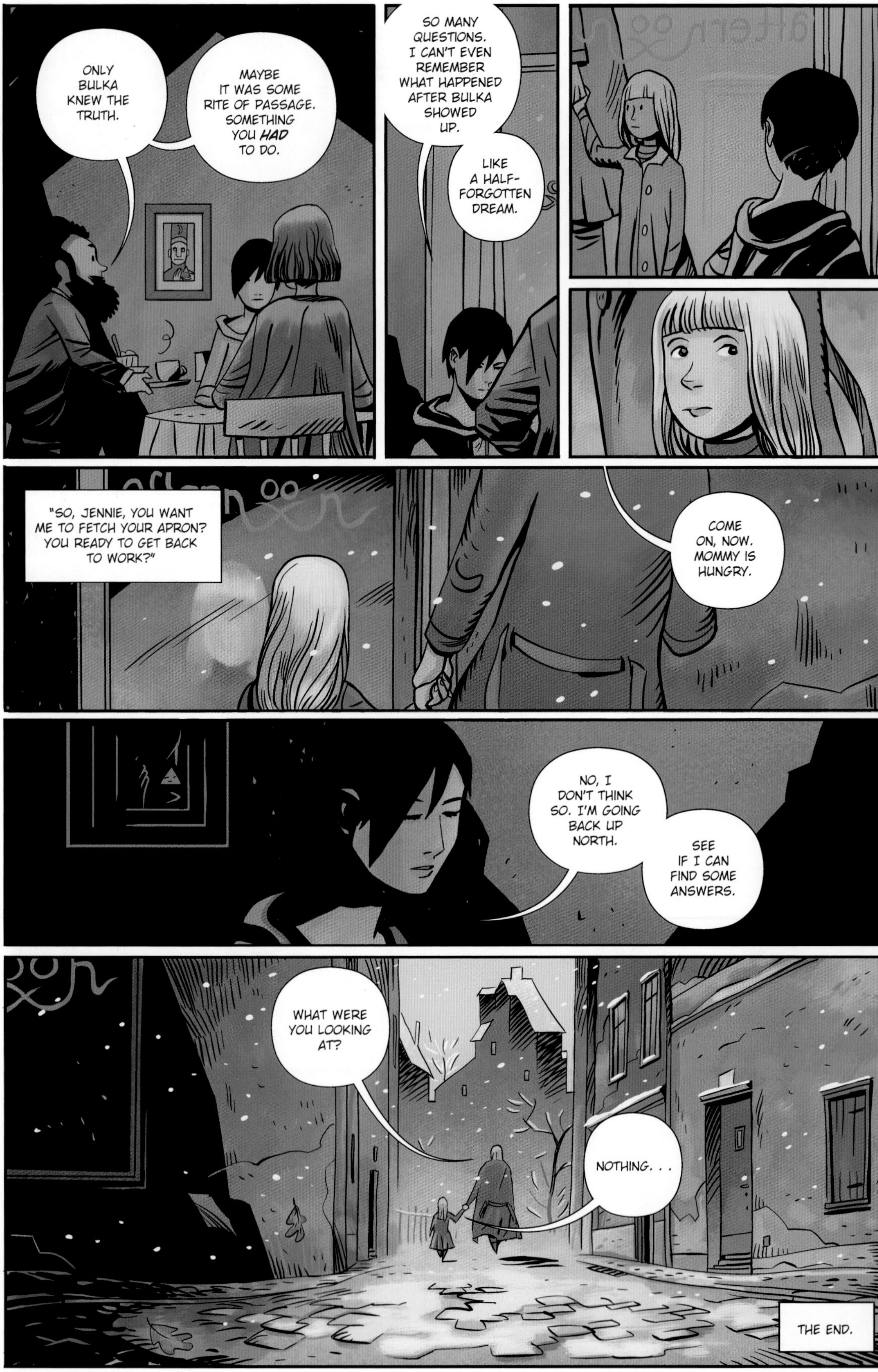
ONLY BULKA KNEW THE TRUTH.
MAYBE IT WAS SOME RITE OF PASSAGE. SOMETHING YOU HAD TO DO.
SO MANY QUESTIONS. I CAN'T EVEN REMEMBER WHAT HAPPENED AFTER BULKA SHOWED UP.
LIKE A HALF-FORGOTTEN DREAM.
"SO, JENNIE, YOU WANT ME TO FETCH YOUR APRON? YOU READY TO GET BACK TO WORK?"
COME ON, NOW. MOMMY IS HUNGRY.
NO, I DON'T THINK SO. I'M GOING BACK UP NORTH.
SEE IF I CAN FIND SOME ANSWERS.
WHAT WERE YOU LOOKING AT?
NOTHING. . .
THE END.

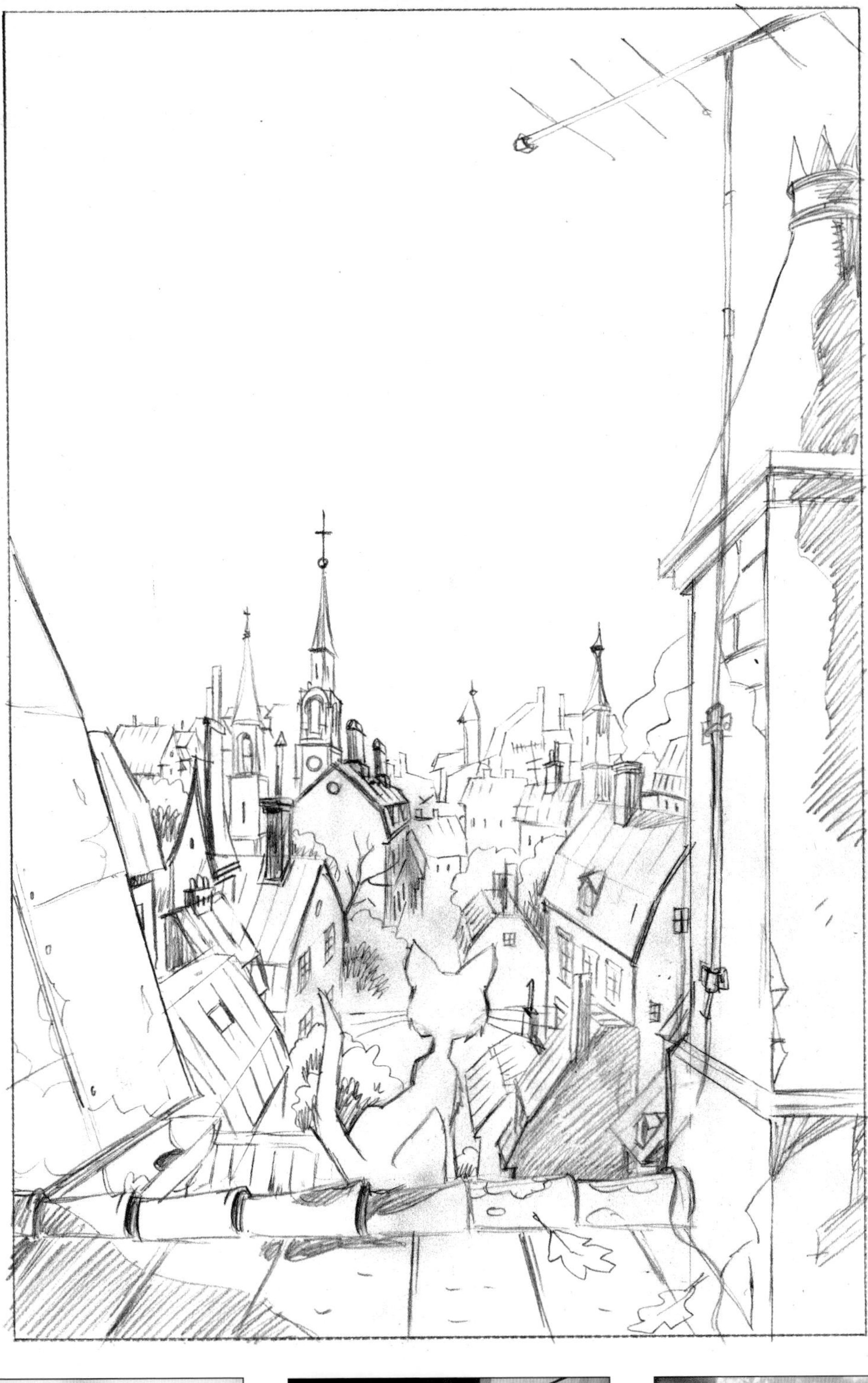

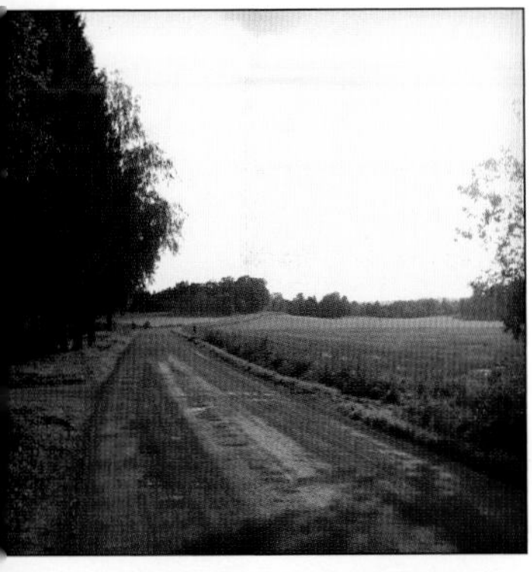

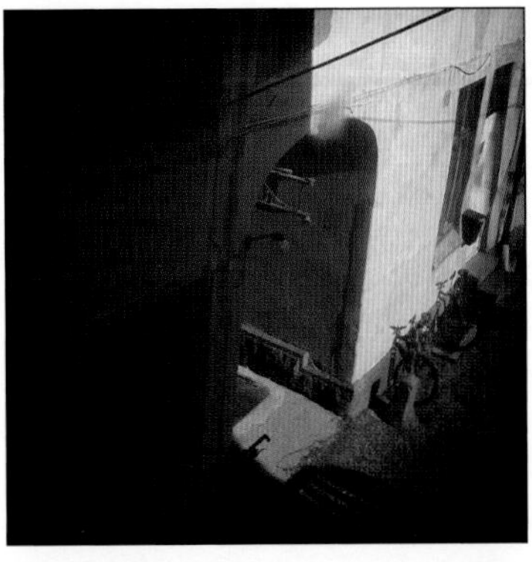

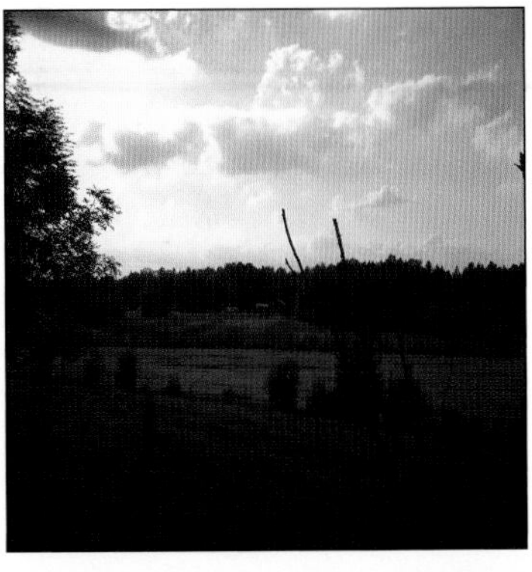

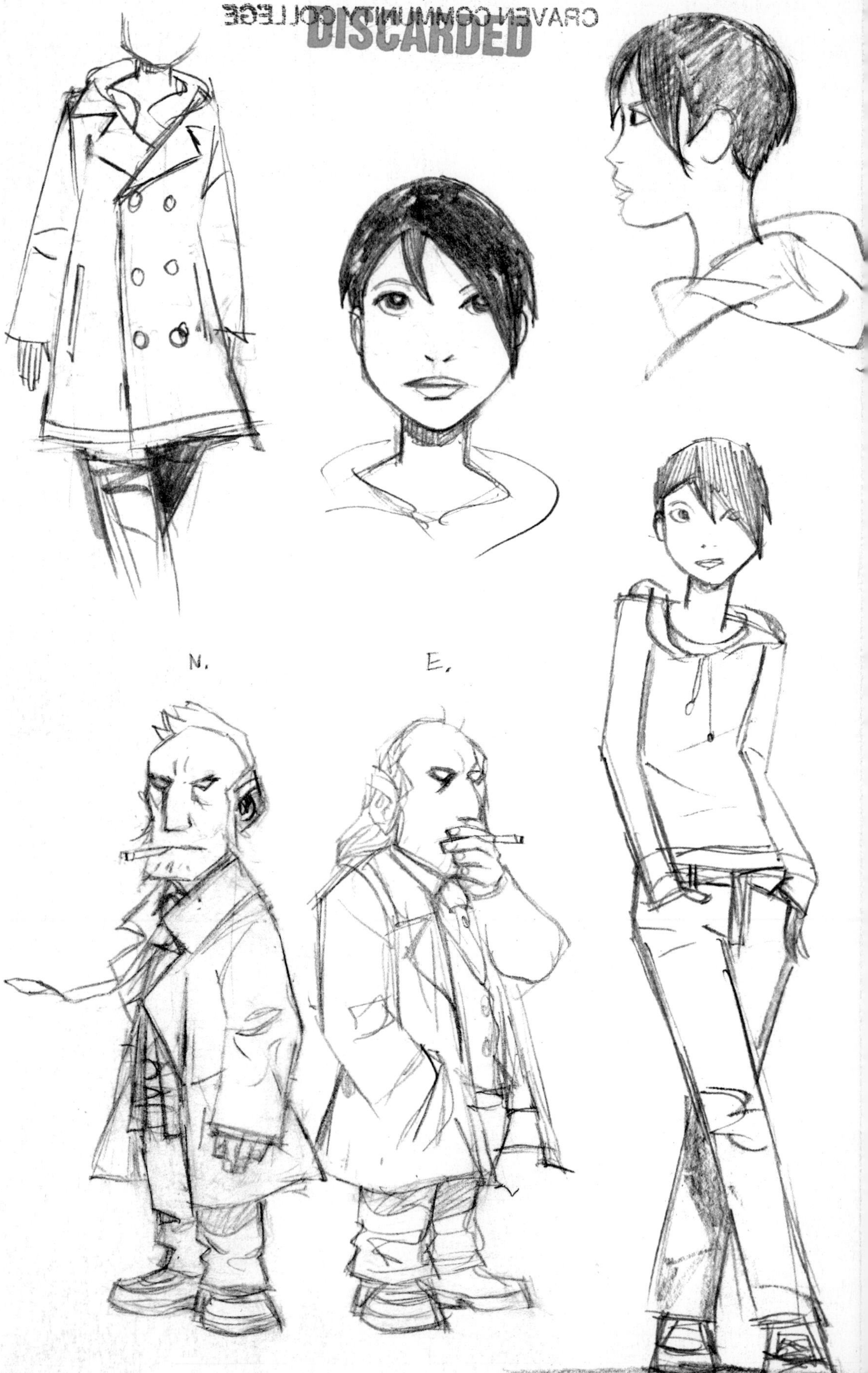
N.
E.